POLITICS AND GOVERNMENT
IN TURKEY

Politics and Government in Turkey

by

C. H. DODD

UNIVERSITY OF CALIFORNIA PRESS

Berkeley and Los Angeles · 1969

University of California Press
Berkeley and Los Angeles, California
© 1969 C. H. Dodd

Library of Congress Catalog Card Number: 78-85453

Printed in Great Britain

Contents

v

98177

List of Tables

Preface

This study has to rely on reading that has been restricted for the most part by the availability of material outside Turkey. This is not so much a problem for governmental and other publications, which can often be obtained, but it is so for the quite copious newspaper and magazine material that is available in Turkey. This material has not been thoroughly exhausted for this study and a great deal more information could no doubt also be obtained by extensive interviewing of politicians who have played significant roles during the period from 1961. The political history of the period covered by this book awaits a thorough historical investigation when passions have cooled, and a longer view may be taken.

As to the method of approach employed in this book, the relatively straightforward scheme that is used will perhaps seem unsophisticated to those who are committed to the sometimes revealing but in practice often inhibiting and sometimes stultifying functional approach to the study of politics. To emphasize institutions seems to me more important in more complex societies; and in Turkey by virtue of the functions they are acknowledged to perform political institutions are not sham. However, what this book is principally concerned with is the range of Turkish political problems that seem important not only to myself, but also, and chiefly, to the Turks who think and write about them—since in addition to my own enquiries I have chiefly relied on the writings of Turkish scholars (though I have not given much prominence to legalistic discussion of political problems).

In order then to escape the bonds of a sociological or legalistic framework I have sought to lay emphasis in this study on what actually happens, in and through the political and administrative institutions, that seems significant for the making and agreeing of policy and for deciding who shall exercise political power. This involves consideration of the forces in Turkish society that help to fashion policies and advance persons to positions of political influence. My object becomes then to discuss Turkish political and administrative institutions without artificially isolating them from the society in which they operate, but also without making too many assumptions about the 'roles' they play in the Turkish political system as a whole.

*   *   *

My first acknowledgment must be to the Turkish scholars and other writers on whose work I have so much relied and of whom so many belong to, or have graduated from, the Faculty of Political Science of the University of Ankara. My grateful thanks are also due to those in public life who granted me interviews, including Turhan Feyzioğlu, Bülent Ecevit, Kemal Kurdaş and also to the many senior Turkish civil servants who kindly gave of their time. To the political parties I am also grateful for valuable help and for an invariably sympathetic reception even at the most hectic moments of Turkish politics. Other Turkish institutions to whom I acknowledge a particular debt of gratitude for advice and information are the Grand National Assembly, the Prime Minister's Office, the Ministry of Finance, the State Personnel Office, the State Statistics Institute, the State Planning Organization and, not least, the Institute of Public Administration for Turkey and the Middle East.

In the treatment of the work of the Turkish Commission on Administrative Functions I have profited from the help and advice of Mr J. Foster, Institute of Public Administration for Turkey and the Middle East. To Miss Mary Sales and Mr J. Hilal I am indebted for much laborious statistical work and to Bayan Neval Asım for valuable help with surveys in Turkey and in other ways. For guidance on the analysis of the occupations of members of the Grand National Assembly I should like to record my thanks to Professor F. W. Frey, of the Massachusetts Institute of Technology. To the editors and publishers of *Public Administration* and *Middle Eastern Studies* I am grateful for permission to reproduce in part material I have previously published in those journals.

No acknowledgment is complete without a recognition of the help of the institutions who largely make research possible at all. The University of Leeds was particularly generous in granting extended leave of absence to enable me to take up a temporary appointment in the Middle East Technical University, Ankara. Through funds provided under the Hayter scheme the University of Durham made it possible to visit Turkey in 1964 and 1965; and I am grateful for the unfailing help of the staff of the oriental section of the University Library. To the Faculty of Administrative Sciences of the Middle East Technical University I owe a particular debt for friendship (and hospitality) that derives from shared struggles in the troubled early years of the Middle East Technical University. To the staff and students of the Faculty of Administrative Sciences I would like to dedicate this book.

Two particular acknowledgments remain. The first is to Professor A. H. Hanson of the University of Leeds who kindly gave of his time to read the manuscript and made many valuable suggestions. Finally, it must be said that without the ungrudging forbearance of wives and families, married men would probably never write any books.

C. H. D.

The University,
Manchester

Transcription, Pronunciation of Turkish Words and Abbreviations

Ottoman Turkish words have been transcribed into modern Turkish orthography. For those who prefer to know how the Turkish words in the text are pronounced the following notes on the pronunciation of certain letters should remove the principal difficulties.

c is pronounced as j in judge
ç ,, ,, ,, ch in church
g ,, ,, ,, g in gate
ğ ,, ,, ,, y after e and i, but is otherwise hardly sounded except that it lengthens a preceding a or ı.
j ,, ,, ,, j in French *jour*
i ,, ,, ,, i in fit
ı ,, ,, ,, i in first
ö ,, ,, ,, eu in French *deux*
ü ,, ,, ,, u in French *lune*
ş ,, ,, ,, sh in ship.

In the text the Republican People's Party (*Cumhuriyet Halk Partisi*) is usually shortened to People's Party, the Worker's Party of Turkey (*Türkiye İşçi Partisi*) to Workers' Party and the Republican Peasant Nation Party (*Cumhuriyetçi Köylü Millet Partisi*), where confusion does not arise, to Peasants' Party.

Ankara Siyasal Bilgiler Fakültesi (Faculty of Political Science, Ankara University) is abbreviated to *Ank. Univ. S.B.F.* and *Türkiye ve Orta Doğu Âmme İdaresi Enstitüsü* (Public Administration Institute for Turkey and the Middle East) to *T.O.D.A.I.E.*

Introduction

The common image of Turkey has long ceased to be one of oriental sumptuousness. The image now seems to be of a relatively efficient, purposeful and modernizing state noted for the pride and valour of its people. Turkey is also one of the few states in the third world that can show a record of political stability. The military revolution of 1960 might seem to belie this claim, but the Turkish military actually kept their promise to restore power to the people's elected representatives.

It is a very important, but also a very difficult, task to try to postulate the economic and social prerequisites for political stability, even assuming we agreed on its definition. The immediately tempting thesis that economic and social betterment produce the desired result is hard to sustain;[1] it is easy enough to demonstrate how development can create dislocations that can lead to anything but stable politics. There is therefore as yet no satisfactory check-list of the essential pre-conditions for political stability against which to mark the Turkish case. Rather, the Turkish experience must be regarded as a case study from which, with others, political scientists may construct some tentative hypotheses. In this introduction it seems worthwhile, therefore, to describe very briefly those major characteristics of Turkish society that would appear to be significant for political stability, or instability.

There is the first fact that the Turks are increasing in number and at a good rate. From 28 million in 1960 they expanded to over 31 million in 1965. The population is also young, some 40 per cent being under the age of fifteen in 1965. These are population factors that suggest instability, but it is also in many respects a very homogeneous population. Over 90 per cent of the inhabitants are Turkish speaking, the only significant minority being that of the Kurds. The density of population is about half of that of Europe and is most concentrated in the coastal areas along the Marmara, the Aegean, the south-east coast along the Mediterranean and along the Black Sea. Situated in the central dry and

---

[1] See the excellent essay by S. P. Huntington, 'Political Development and Political Decay' *Political Modernization*, ed. Claude E. Welch (Belmont, Calif., 1967), pp. 207–45.

rather empty plateau Ankara, the capital, seems badly sited. It has, however, turned out to be quite a master stroke of Kemal Atatürk's to so place the capital. Remote though it is from any centre of dense population, it is at the hub of a wheel on whose rim are the densely populated regions. Ankara is therefore a centrally placed communications centre and an impartial unifying force—another factor that surely makes for stability in politics.

Another population factor may also be important. Towns have recently grown quite fast. In 1960 25 per cent of the population lived in towns of over 10,000 inhabitants, as compared with 18·5 per cent in 1950 and just over 16 per cent in 1927. Yet it is not the largest towns that have increased most rapidly. In 1960 only 17 per cent of the population lived in towns with more than 50,000 inhabitants.[1] Turkey is primarily a country of villages and small towns.

To take the village first, we can see that in a variety of ways the villager is much more in contact with the world than used to be the case. Yet this new contact with the world seems to generate in him a feeling of inferiority to townspeople, and in turn a certain hostility which replaces the indifference or traditional respect of the true 'traditional'. The widening of his horizons by contact with new ideas creates in the villager new demands. It is not so surprising if these demands are more for basic material needs and primitive luxuries than for the refinements of civilized life. The villages have never really known civilization, which in the Ottoman Empire could only properly belong to towns.

The towns may be said to have progressed further than the villages, but in the virtual absence of sociological studies of Turkish towns not very much may be said with confidence about them. It is generally accepted that small towns—which were more exposed to Ottoman civilization than the villages—are very conservative. They oppose modernism not with traditionalism quite, but with the values of another civilization not yet completely effaced. The artisans and traders of the towns are traditionally conservative groups with strong religious connections. Nor are they faced with quite the degree of material hardship that is the lot of many peasants and this may make them rather less susceptible to the material attractions of modernization.

[1] R. Keleş, *Türkiyede Şehirleşme Hareketleri (1927–1960)* (Ank.: Ank. Üniv. S.B.F., 1961), p. 12.

This brings us to the question of whether there are strong class divisions in Turkish society. The Atatürkist view that Turkey does not have any class conflict is not the same as saying that Turkey does not possess social classes. The purpose of the Atatürkist assertion was to deny the applicability of Marxism to Turkey.

It would be difficult to contend that there were just no class differences in Turkish society. There is quite obviously a large gap between the educated and the ignorant—and there must be very few men or women in high position in Turkish public, professional or business life who have not received a higher education. Yet differentiated by higher education though they are, persons in top positions may often be directly approached by the humble. They may be treated severely, but not generally with haughtiness or arrogance. The attitude is for the most part paternalistic. The arrogant minor official is arrogant probably because he feels he is only just a member of the educated class, but there is nothing specifically Turkish about this.

Other divisions in society may be observed beyond the basic one between the educated and the uneducated. In wealth, and probably now in prestige, the large landowners, the new industrialists and the businessmen come first. This is a new development. Until the decade 1950–60 pride of place was held by civil servants, university teachers and army officers of high rank, all of whom were in the vanguard of modernization in the Ottoman Empire and more recently formed the Atatürk elite. They now come second, or even possibly third. Their place is being challenged, if it has not been occupied, by the free professions of doctor, lawyer, engineer, architect and the like, though the situation is complicated by the large number of professional persons who are employed in the highest ranks of the civil service as administrators as well as advisers. Yet the free professions now seem to ally themselves more with the businessmen and industrialists than with the officials.

Below these high-ranking groups come, some way down—and reflecting their lower levels of education—the traders and shopkeepers of the towns. They are on about the same level as the lower public functionaries. These are the groups which have kinship connections with the villages, which they may not themselves have long left. Better off, but not substantial, land-owning peasants have about the same standing. Finally come the skilled, and then the unskilled, workers with groups like those of taxi drivers and owners occupying indeterminate positions.

Those who work on the land constitute the largest group in the population—about two-thirds. Given a very large peasant element in the population and an increasing class consciousness, land distribution is therefore a problem of first importance.

In Turkey land distribution is a subject of constant discussion, many promises and little effective action. Atatürk expressed benign sentiments about the lot of the land-hungry and landless peasant, but nothing much was done until after the second world war, when a law was passed allowing nationalization of privately owned land in excess generally of 5,000 *dönüms*,[1] but in certain areas of less plentiful land, 2,000 *dönüms*. However, distribution was to be undertaken only after uncultivated state lands had been shared out. Between 1951 and 1960 some 18·5 million *dönüms* had been distributed—no small achievement—but only 86,000 *dönüms* of this had actually been acquired from private land-owners.[2] In 1964 a moderate scheme of land reform was accepted by the government of İsmet İnönü, but the government was brought down before the necessary legislation could be passed.

The economic dangers of land distribution (the creation of uneconomic holdings) have to be considered by those who advocate a thorough-going land redistribution on grounds of social justice. That agricultural land is very unequally distributed is almost certainly the case. Information used by the planning authorities in 1963 (based on a 1952 study revised in 1960) showed that about 20 per cent of land-owning families owned some 60 per cent of the cultivated land. On the remaining 40 per cent the pattern is that of small proprietorship, but it may be noted that 75 per cent of farming families occupy only 30 per cent of the cultivated land.[3] A socialist party is not without telling facts to use.

---

[1] A *dönüm* is approximately a quarter of an acre.

[2] See Fikret Arık, *Türkiyede Toprak Reformu* (Ank.: T.O.D.A.I.E., 1961), and Suat Aksoy, *Toprak Reformunun Hukuki Esasları* (Ank.: 1966).

[3] See R. D. Robinson, *The First Turkish Republic. A Case Study in National Development* (Cambridge Mass., Harvard Univ. Press, 1963) pp. 275–6, where the figures are reproduced.

There is also the general economic fact that by the European standards by which Turks compare themselves Turkey is a poor country. The *per capita* gross national product in 1964 was $242, compared with $565 for Spain, $588 for Greece and $1,705 for Britain. Yet Turkey has made progress. In 1960 the *per capita* GNP was $171 after a decade which saw an average rate of growth of 5 per cent. This rate has been more than maintained (5·7 per cent) between 1960 and 1965, so there is reason for a measure of national confidence. It is also no doubt a significant political fact that agriculture has fared comparatively well in this process of economic development, with the result that the inequalities of land distribution stand out less prominently than they otherwise might do.

That Turkish politics is stable is certainly not because everyone is literate and can participate easily in political and social intercourse on a national level. The present illiteracy rate is 60 per cent. There are plans drastically to improve this position. By 1971 it is expected that all children will have at least a primary education (7–12 years of age) instead of the 70 per cent in this age group who received it in 1963. Apart from this group, the only other real expansion of the proportion of the population at school age is in the field of technical education. For the rest Turkey will be doing little more in the immediate future than keep her head above water on account of her population increase. Yet matters may work out better than the statistics suggest. The quantity, if not the proportion, of trained people will increase. Turkey may also avoid the dire problem of the pressures of rising expectations in an economic and social system that cannot afford to meet them. There is some merit in slow and steady development.

One of the most potentially disintegrative forces in Turkish society is often said to be that of religious 'reaction'. Islam is certainly a living force at village and small town level, where reports abound of the activities of the 'dervish' orders, notably the followers of Said Nursi, the *Nurcular*, who have long opposed the westernization of Turkey. Religion is now included in the curricula of the schools, but it is doubtful if this really helps much to keep popular religion alive. Villagers do not readily accept the validity of religious instruction offered outside the mosque by a lay schoolmaster who does not teach the ritual observances of

Islam or the modicum of Arabic that is necessary.[1] More indicative of the persistence of religious feeling is the increase in mosque
building and attendance since 1950 and the steady stream of
pilgrims to Mecca. Then too among even the educated—but
particularly among the technically educated, like engineers, who
have not been so immersed in western *culture*—there are many now
who exhibit religious feeling by observing *Ramazan* and in other
ways.

Nevertheless, the secular world is increasingly making its
presence felt, even now in the village; and there can hardly be
any doubt that popular religion will gradually decline. The modern
Turkish intellectual, in whom any real revival must surely be
based, does not seem to think deeply about religion, except to
ponder its potential threat to the secular state. He is not anti-
religious, if one may hazard a guess in this delicate matter, but he
seems to dispose of a great deal of his inherited religion as quickly
and completely as have many intellectuals in the West.

On the whole there seem to be more factors in the character of
Turkish society that operate for political stability than for instability. Even so, it is by no means the end of this complex
matter. It is often too readily accepted that a stable political
system is an unqualified blessing. The danger is that stability
may become confused with immobility. Turkey is a stable society,
but it is not immobile in a number of important respects and the
areas of movement, like popular religion, are potentially very
damaging to political stability. In the eyes of many Turks movement must, then, be contained within bounds; they sense the
perils lurking beneath the surface. A slow process of economic and
social development together with the influence for stability of the
other factors we have considered, have kept these dangers largely
dormant. But would they have remained so without the addition
of those Turkish political talents that are part of the Ottoman
and Turkish political tradition? We look first in this book at the
origins of Turkish political talents and the environment in which
they were exercised.

[1] Village attitudes have been observed by R. B. Scott, 'Turkish Village
Attitudes Towards Religious Education', *Muslim World*, LV, no. 3 (1965)
pp. 222–9. See also G. L. Lewis, 'Islam in Politics: Turkey', *Muslim World*,
LVI, no. 4 (1966) pp. 235–9.

PART I

Tradition, Achievement, Revolution

B

CHAPTER I

The Ottoman Tradition

It is not enough to examine present political and governmental practices without considering the political tradition as a possible source of explanation. Nor is it realistic to estimate current achievements without regard for what foundations have been laid in the past. The complexities of Ottoman history are, however, very great and no more can be attempted here than a summary of the Ottoman legacy.

Society

The westernization of the Ottoman Empire did not begin in any fundamental way until the French Revolution; and the reason the Muslim world was disposed to accept the ideas of the French Revolution was perhaps, because, they were secular and not religious. Before that time the Ottomans had adopted many important western techniques. They included printing and many innovations in warfare and they brought with them some acquaintance with the new western knowledge, but these earlier influences did not penetrate deeply. Europeans were regarded as clever and useful in practical matters, but not profound. Before the French Revolution the great movements in European ideas were a closed book to the Ottomans and not one they would have deigned to open.

It was, therefore, in what appears to us as an atmosphere of dangerous isolation—which is not, however, how they regarded it—that the Ottomans organized their political and administrative affairs until the nineteenth century. The ways in which they governed themselves were, of course, partly determined by the facts of their geographic environment, and their economic and social structure. To take the geographical factor first, we can see that the Ottoman Empire for a long period of its history stretched, north to south, from Hungary to the Yemen and, East to West, from Greece and Egypt to the Persian border. There were considerable difficulties in administering an area such as this without the benefit of modern communications—an area, moreover, which contained formidable mountain barriers and large expanses of desert. The problems for effective government posed by the geography of the area can be readily contrasted with the situation in the tight-knit states of Europe, even with that of European Russia.

To these difficulties were added the complexities of the social structure of the Ottoman Empire, which was divided into numerous communities whose ties with the central government were much weaker than would be permissible in a modern nation state. The communities with the slenderest connection with the central power were probably those of the Christians and the Jews, whose religious leaders were permitted to exercise (well-nigh complete) political power over their followers. Almost the sole condition for what was a quite formal recognition of autonomy was payment of a poll tax.[1] Other religious communities—chiefly those which were Muslim but of *Şiī*, not *Sünni*, persuasion—enjoyed a *de facto*, rather than *de jure*, autonomy, largely due to their inhabiting regions difficult for the government to control. The *Şiīs* of Iraq and various sects in Syria and the Lebanon, like the Druzes, were able to maintain a large degree of independence, particularly if they paid their taxes.

These basic divisions overlapped with other divisions in Ottoman Society. Most of the Christians and Jews were engaged in trade and industry, not in agriculture. Consequently, they lived in the cities, whose municipal organizations earned a measure of respect from the central government. Within the cities were the trade and craft guilds, which made powerful demands on the loyalties of their members. Moreover, many of the Muslim guilds had strong connections with the mystics of Islam, the *Sufis*, with the result that another range of loyalties was called into play.

The unorthodox religious beliefs of those communities which lived in inaccessible areas also coincided very frequently with the division between desert, or mountain terrain or steppe land on the one hand and the more prosperous sown land on the other. The central power had to contend with the problem of maintaining

[1] The general status of non-Muslims was nevertheless lower than that of Muslims. In their relations with Muslims they were restricted in various ways. For example in legal proceedings the evidence of a non-Muslim could not stand against the evidence of a Muslim.

the peace between settled peasant—or townsmen—and the tribal communities. This was never an easy matter, especially, when for reasons of economic hardship, valley sheep—or goats— were a dietary necessity, or when the commercial traffic on the trade routes became especially tempting.

The inhabitants of the settled agricultural areas, the peasantry, were essentially the 'subjects' of the Empire in a state where the main division was regarded as one between 'subjects' and 'rulers'. They were not, however, completely at the mercy of the agents of the central power. Their primary loyalties were to their headmen and to the feudal or other landowners.

It would be wrong, however, to represent the situation in any way as one in which the government was constantly seeking to aggrandize its power, but was prevented from doing so by the complexities of the social situation. Although officials were often arbitrary and rapacious, the aim of government was little more than to maintain a balance among the various classes of society. The basic concern was not to change society, but to preserve it. Where change was necessary it could only be justified as a means to re-establish what was deemed to be customary and to restore the balance. Change had to be approved by the guardians of tradition—by those who were learned in the true character of an Islamic community, namely the *ulema*, those learned in Islam. They formed a dominant part of what has come to be known as the religious institution. It was the interaction of the rulers, or ruling institution, with the religious institution that is the most distinctive feature of Ottoman government. To this we now turn.

Government. In theory the Islamic community has no need of legislative power. The laws to which the Ottoman 'state' was obliged to conform were regarded as already existing in complete and unalterable form in the Sacred Law of Islam, the *Şeriat*. The Sacred Law had been constructed during the early centuries of Islam by jurists and theologians from three sources; these were the word of God, as revealed to Muhammad and contained in the Kuran, the traditions of the prophet, as handed down and recorded, and the custom of the Islamic community that had been accorded general consent.

The immutable character of the Sacred Law presented a considerable obstacle to change, and the more so in that the law extended beyond the domain of religion in the western sense to embrace all social relations. A device in the Sacred Law which recognized an initiative to the monarch in the issuing of everyday orders did allow some measure of freedom, and these measures came to be embodied in *kanuns* or canons. The enactments contained in these canons were justified in the Sacred Law provided, however, they were to the benefit of the Islamic community and did not conflict with the provisions of the Sacred Law itself. Naturally enough when a new problem of government arose for which the Sacred Law provided no answer, it was necessary for the monarch to consult the religious leaders to determine the compatability of the proposed new measure with the Sacred Law. A restriction was in this way placed on the emergence of despotic rule.

This power of religious control was principally exercised by the head of the religious institution, the Chief Mufti (*Şeyhülislam*). In addition, the central administration was enmeshed at various levels with the religious institution and subject to its influence. The Chief Mufti had the great reserve power to issue a legal ruling that could sanction the deposition of the Sultan himself. As a counter-weight to this he could himself be dismissed by the Sultan, as indeed some were, but he possessed a great advantage over the slaves of the ruling institution in that the lives and property of religious persons were inviolate. It was a nice balance. The influence of the religious over the ruling institution could be, and at times was, very great. Yet this influence depended in the last resort on the strength of religious feeling in the Islamic community as a whole and on the *ulemas* being popularly regarded as the representatives of this feeling. Their corruption reduced the respect in which they were held and accounted for much of their later ineffectiveness. By the eighteenth century the moral influence of the religious institution had been significantly undermined by those same evils of patronage, nepotism and sale of office that had destroyed the efficiency of the ruling institution.

The ruling institution is a compendious term which includes the army, the navy, the imperial household, the central administration and the governmental machinery in the provinces. One of its important features was its recruitment of personnel of slave status for all its branches, excepting the feudal elements in the military. These slaves were obtained in various ways. Prisoners of war provided a valuable source of recruitment in the early days of the Ottoman Empire, but from A.D. 1360 boys and youths from among the Orthodox Christian subjects of the empire were taken as tribute and trained in special schools in Istanbul, where they were prepared for various tasks in the ruling institution. The majority went into the Janissaries, the standing army, but a number were selected for work in the imperial household and the central administration. In the heyday of the Empire its ruling institution was composed of these 'slaves',[1] who came to occupy under the Sultan the highest posts in the administration. Advancement seems to have been by merit. By making possible the promotion of pantry boy to grand vizier this widened the field of selection beyond that found in contemporaneous European states. Although members of the ruling institution might rise to the highest posts in the hierarchy, their slave status meant they could be as quickly and arbitrarily demoted as promoted. By the eighteenth century, however, the character of the personnel of the ruling institution had changed considerably. The suspension of the recruitment of Christian boys was one step in the capture of the ruling institution by free Muslims. As these latter had family and other connections in society, this meant in practice that posts in the ruling institution increasingly went to friends and relations. A liaison was being created between rulers and the more important elements among the Muslim subjects. As they came to appreciate the value of office, or having a friend there, the demand for governmental jobs increased. This led to bribery, purchase of office and much too rapid turnover of personnel.

One distinguishing feature of the Ottoman system was connected with the rise of the standing army. In the early days of the Empire the army was mainly based on the feudal system, but in contrast to the situation in Western Europe, none save the smaller tenants had hereditary rights to their lands. This prevented the emergence of a hereditary aristocracy that could rival the Sultan's authority. It also disinclined tenants to leave their lands on military service lest they be assigned to others in their absence. Not surprisingly, then, the feudal forces were not sufficient for the expansionist policies of the Ottoman state; but once the state had created for itself the means of recruiting a standing army, it

---

[1] In Islam a slave was a person with severely limited status, not a person devoid of status. He was nevertheless the property of his master, who had considerable powers over him.

could watch the decline of the feudal forces without much concern. There was no need to strengthen the social position of the feudal tenants. When in the eighteenth century powerful overlords made their appearance in the provinces, they were in origin rebellious servants of the ruling institution, not members of an entrenched feudal aristocracy. The inclusion of the standing army in the ruling institution was a very significant feature of the Ottoman state. It created the tradition not so much of military *interference* as of military *participation* in government.

To estimate the legacy of the Ottoman experience to the modern Turkish state is to assess the importance of certain practices and attitudes that linger on behind the modern forms. Such attitudes and practices are not readily demonstrable, but a student of Turkish politics cannot help but become aware of them as soon as he begins to penetrate Turkish political life.

There is the rich complexity of the Ottoman experience in government. The Ottoman Empire was not a simple traditionalist state. Decisions were made by a process of consultation and pressure in which church, government and army principally participated. These three great interests were also intricately interwoven in a fascinating pattern of institutional forms that cannot here be examined. Not surprisingly, then, the modern educated Turk has been exposed to a culture that has sophisticated attitudes towards authority. There is invariably an awareness of the complexity of politics, the need to take into account the presence of other social forces, to obtain a reconciliation with them and to engage their support. The modern Turk is the heir to a significant *political* tradition.

This point should not however be overstressed. It would be wrong to imagine the modern Turk is amenable to pressures from any direction. In the Ottoman Empire minority groups, like Christians or Jews, did not have the opportunity to participate in state decisions. They were outside the ring of established and recognized interests. The modern Turks can display a marked tendency simply to ignore new social forces whilst granting every opportunity to established groups to participate in the political process to the highest degree. Provided minority groups take an allotted place in the established order, however, there is a marked tendency to leave them to their own devices. If there is no political threat the dominant attitude is one of tolerance. To an extent this attitude defines the approach of the educated Turk to the peasant, who in Ottoman times was part of the eternal order of things and certainly did not have to be consulted. Modern Turks still find it difficult to adopt more than a rather distant attitude towards the peasant. The ruler and subject tradition dies hard.

It was important in this connection that the interests of the educated elite were centred on the capital. They did not have any roots in the countryside, no base from which to offer a leadership both natural and practical. Nor did the educated elite really establish themselves as a *noblesse de robe*. It was the institutions of government which brought deference to those who manned them; the persons did not confer the authority on the institutions. This is perhaps why modern Turks are so institutions conscious. Other nations could withstand the overturning of institutions much better than could the Turks.

The lack of social differentiation among the educated elite helps explain the underlying informality of relationships between its members and provides the opportunity for the continuation of the Ottoman tradition of promotion from pantry boy to vizier. The social equality of the members of the elite is really only affected by the office held, or more precisely, by the power that the office bestows. The competition for office can therefore be very keen, but the turn of fortune's wheel is accepted perhaps more philosophically than in other systems. Demotion is not so great a personal affront as it might be elsewhere. Foreigners who occupy places in Turkish administrative organizations can rather easily expose themselves to indignities that Turks are somewhat inured against by their tradition.

For all the concentration of the elite on government, for all the recruitment and training for office in Ottoman times of a special corps, the tradition is not one of high governmental efficiency. The corruption of the ruling and religious institutions in later Ottoman times partly accounts for this; and this corruption it is as well to remember, was not due to the undermining of traditional virtues by contact with the West. It has deeper roots than that in the Ottoman past. Yet, despite this there is in the modern Turks a real sense of the importance of government and a realization of its need. There is general support for firm government and the tendency is to look first to government to satisfy demands. Within the whole Turkish cultural tradition government occupies perhaps the most dominant position. The Turks have stepped into the modern age with a peculiar, but by no means inappropriate tradition of government. We must now briefly describe the nature of the Turkish achievement in their attempts to modernize the Ottoman state in the nineteenth and early twentieth centuries.

CHAPTER II

The Ottoman Achievement

The major task of the Ottoman Empire in the nineteenth century was to defend itself against Europe. The Treaty of Küçük Kaynarca (1774) was a portent of the future which could not be ignored; it had entailed the loss, not only of conquered Christian, but also of Muslim territories and it laid the foundation for Russian protection of the Orthodox Christians of the Empire.

The immediate danger was military defeat and perhaps even conquest by Russia, which had emerged as the most dangerous Ottoman adversary. The long-term peril was the disintegration of the Ottoman Empire by the force of nationalism working among the non-Muslim minorities, a process which European intervention generally assisted. These dangers were met in two ways.

First, the Ottomans allied themselves with the Western European states, notably Britain and France, but in the early twentieth century with Germany and Austria, which meant that the Ottoman Empire was brought into the arena of European politics. The days of self-sufficiency were over.

Secondly, the Ottomans saw that they had also to undertake a rigorous programme of reform in order both to increase their military strength and to improve the general conditions of life of the non-Muslim minorities. The main theme of the Ottoman Empire during the nineteenth and early twentieth centuries is, therefore, that of reform undertaken with the advice and assistance of the Western European powers, who were themselves interested in keeping the sick man alive and—to a degree at least—healthy.

The modernization of the Ottoman Empire was, however, a task beset by more than the usual difficulties. First and most important, the general attitude of the Islamic community was strongly antagonistic to those living outside whether French, British, Austrian or Russian. The new alliance with Western Europe was accepted with reluctance and in a mood often of truculent arrogance. Christians might be tolerated but their civilization could hardly be admired. By the early nineteenth century Islam had certainly not been prepared by any intellectual reformulation or reformation for a reconciliation of the values of European and Muslim civilizations.

In this predicament the natural solution was to attempt to copy only Western military techniques. As we have seen, military efficiency seemed to be the first necessity. The acquisition of these techniques could be justified by precedent, since the Ottomans had a long history of the adoption of innovations in military matters. They had long recognized that Christians could be clever in practical things even if fundamentally misguided and inferior. This narrow avenue to the West, however, soon broadened. In the first place it broadened of itself. Science and Mathematics were necessary to understand recent innovations in warfare. Foreign languages, chiefly French, were necessary to understand European books. Knowledge of language opened the doors to other forms of European thought and learning. Secondly, the sheer impact of the West after the middle of the nineteenth century and the dangers of national disintegration forced a deep interest in European politics and government. For it was evident that the effect of westernization, which in some ways was a means of strengthening the Empire, was in others leading to its downfall. Preserved from the aggression of their enemies, the Ottomans found themselves in danger from the subversive ideas of their friends. The ideas of the French Revolution, and particularly nationalism, led to the disintegration of an Empire composed of different religious and linguistic groups. The development of nationalism among the Empire's minorities in turn encouraged the Turkish element in the Ottoman Empire to develop its own national consciousness; and neither the theories of Ottomanism (the union of all Ottomans) nor of Pan-Islam (the union of all Muslims) could withstand the nationalist frenzy.

If reform was to be undertaken, however narrowly conceived, it could only be undertaken by the ruling institution itself. As we have seen, there was no developed industrial or commercial class—at least of Muslims—to take the lead. Within the ruling institution there was the question of who was to lead the reform, the Sultan or the Grand Vizier, who had long risen to prominence in the Ottoman State on the retirement of the Sultan from the active management of affairs. Then again the ruling institution had to reassert its authority against the provincial landlords who had arisen in the course of the eighteenth century, also against the *ulema* and, not least, against the Janissaries. The Sultan who really cleared the ground for the programme of reform was Mahmud II (1808–39). He destroyed the turbulent Janissaries (1826), and greatly restricted the powers of their quondam allies, the *ulema*, by controlling the revenues they obtained from their lands. Then he was able to discipline his provincial vassals with his new army, though they continued to exist as a powerful land-owning class in the countryside.

This consolidation of the power of the ruling institution was the prelude to active reform. It was now quite clear that the ruling institution was going to take the lead in modernizing the Empire. The classical balance was upset—new secular forces were gaining a momentum that would finally be released by the Atatürk Revolution.

The leaders of this great reform movement were the increasing numbers of western trained officials and army officers, but they did not have the field completely to themselves. By the end of the nineteenth century new elites influential in government had appeared. Lawyers were called into being by the new codes of law, journalists by the development of printing, teachers by the westernization of the educational system. Indeed some members of the elites developed a critique of the reforms which the Sultans and ministers were effecting and the ways in which they were being implemented. Writers like Namık Kemal and Ziya Paşa objected to arbitrary government and mechanical reforms that imitated Europe instead of adapting European ideas to Ottoman and Islamic institutions. It was a criticism both liberal and religious which sought a return to the democratic spirit of early Islam. But it did not rest, as in Europe, on the solid base of a developed commercial and industrial middle class. Despite this critique, which helped to give birth to the short-lived Constitution of 1876, it was finally the benevolent despotism of the Sultans and the not so benevolent despotism of the Young Turks (1908–1918) which won the day. The military/bureaucratic elite led the Ottoman Empire into the twentieth century; but it is a governing elite that has never been completely oblivious to the liberal point of view.

The reforms in economic and social life which occurred before 1918 cannot be described here in detail. It must suffice to say that during this period a number of the prerequisites of the modern state were created. Great strides were made towards strengthening the armed forces. Communications, principally railways and the telegraph, were developed—a process that entailed a not always welcomed increase in the effectiveness of the central government. Judicial and legal reforms were begun along western European lines, and included a monumental codification of Islamic law, completed in 1876. This code continued in force in Turkey until 1926. A scheme of secular education was developed which found perhaps its greatest achievement in the two important secondary schools of Galatasaray and Darüşşafaka in Istanbul, where the ruling elite sent their sons. In 1900 the University of Istanbul was finally established.

Politics

The landmark in the development of an opposition to the Sultan's rule was the setting up in 1865 in Paris of the first truly Ottoman political organization, the Society of Young Ottomans. Two groups subsequently emerged in Paris with differing ideologies. One group advocated a programme of Ottoman liberalism and decentralization, whilst the other inclined strongly towards Turkish nationalism and centralization. This latter group adopted the name of the Association for Ottoman Union and Progress. It was this group which entered into close contact with a revolutionary Ottoman Freedom Society set up in 1906 in Salonica by army officers and government officials, the society which organized and carried out the Young Turk revolution of 1908.

The political freedom which immediately resulted from the 1908 revolution brought political discussion out into the open. Three main tendencies in political thought appeared. First, there were those who wanted to westernize, but on the lines of a liberalism in which all other groups in the Empire could participate; this was essentially a faith in the self-energizing effects of liberty. Secondly, there were the Turkish nationalists, who were loath both to forgo the historical Turkish supremacy in the Ottoman State and who looked to a sense of cultural affinity among Turks to provide the essential driving force for a programme of westernization. Thirdly, there were the Islamists, who could accept some western innovations but rejected the cultural, religious and social ideas of the West as inferior to those of Islam. In their view the perilous position of the Empire was due to its deviation from the true Muslim path.

The officers and officials who carried out the revolution of 1908 came to embrace the nationalist solution and to lose much of their early liberal ardour. After the revolution they organized themselves into a secret Committee of Union and Progress which, first behind a screen of *ancien régime* politicians, and then openly as a political party, governed the Empire nearly all the period 1908–18. The liberals were not unsuccessful in gaining popular support and the sympathy of certain sections in the military, but they could not prevail. Their opponents were too powerful for them in the army and were unscrupulous and skilful in manipulating elections.

After the war, both Sultan and liberals showed they were prepared to work in conjunction with the allied powers, even to the extent of accepting the abortive Treaty of Sèvres (August 1920) which would have dissolved not just the Empire, but the heartlands of Asiatic Turkey. When the Sultan's government also declared holy war on the nationalists fighting for Turkish independence in Anatolia under Kemal Atatürk, it only required a nationalist victory for the Sultan and his liberal ministers to be completely discredited. In November 1922, shortly after the final defeat of the Greek invading army by the nationalists and the abolition of the Sultanate, Sultan Vahdettin left Turkey aboard a British warship. The sultanate was at an end.

It is clear from this very brief consideration of the course of later Ottoman political history that a great deal of political activity occurred during the closing years of the Empire and particularly after 1908. Numerous political parties were formed after 1908, though only the elections of 1908, 1912 and 1919 were contested by more than one party. The watchword of the 1908 revolution had been freedom, but the party of Union and Progress was authoritarian, whilst paying lip service to liberty. Yet so long as the Party did not make a positive target out of religion, or try to rend asunder traditional Ottoman society in other ways, there was little reason why its rule should not be accepted as legitimate. The 1908 revolution was in many respects hardly a revolution at all.

Institutions

Under Mahmud II institutions began to be shaped to direct the course of reform. As part of his policy to re-assert his sovereignty he took the important step of establishing the Chief Mufti in an office and thus converted the religious institution into a government department like any other. By this move Mahmud demonstrated its subordination to himself in the scheme of government. It was not fortuitous, therefore, that one of the first government departments established (1826) was one to deal with the administration of religious lands. It left to the religious institution only those revenues necessary for salaries, buildings and other religious purposes. The modern state was no less inaugurated when the new army was firmly placed under a Commander-in-Chief whose office was eventually to be converted to that of Minister of War. Another blow at the old order of things was the undermining of the position of the Grand Vizier as the Sultan's absolute deputy in all matters. Ministers began to be appointed with defined areas of administrative jurisdiction and often reported direct to the Sultan. The Grand Vizier began more to co-ordinate than to control. He was thus prevented from becoming a focal point for any organized ministerial opposition to the Sultan. The new organs set up for the management of the new reforms (like the Council of State) were similarly prevented from developing into centres of opposition to the Sultan's rule.

The attempt to curb the increasing power of the Sultan during the nineteenth century by institutional means was nevertheless persistent and may be said to have begun in 1839. Newly ascended to the throne, Sultan Abdul Mecid in that year issued the rescript of the Rose Chamber, a document which, besides elaborating various administrative reforms, also promised security of life, honour and prosperity, and equality before the law for Christian and Muslim alike. This promise of personal freedoms was repeated in more elaborate a form in the Imperial Rescript of 1856, the repetition itself being an indication that the 1839 reform had not been adequately achieved in practice.

The influence of the western powers combined with the pressures exerted by Ottoman liberals brought about these promises to safeguard individual rights. The need of the Ottoman Government to obtain the goodwill of the western powers in order to prevent a Russian war in 1876 gave liberal statesmen like Midhat Paşa their chance. Under their influence and after long and difficult discussion a 'fundamental law' or Constitution was drafted and finally promulgated which provided the Empire for the first time with a parliament. It was composed of two chambers, the upper of notables chosen by the Sultan and the lower of elected deputies. Two parliaments sat during the period March 1877 to February 1878, the second being dissolved when it showed itself too critical of the Sultan's ministers. The debates were often of very high quality.

The Constitution of 1876 is worthy of note not because it straightway made any changes in the exercise of political power— its effects were slight—but because it provided a framework that has deeply influenced subsequent development. In 1909 it was enough to amend the Constitution to achieve the supremacy of parliament. A new constitution was not thought necessary. The chief amendment was, not surprisingly, to make the Grand Vizier and the other ministers responsible to the Chamber of Deputies. Consequently the appointment of the Grand Vizier by the Sultan now lost its importance. The Sultan was no longer able to exercise his powers without the consent of his ministers.

The Committee of Union and Progress was at first content with this situation, partly because they were themselves not unaffected by liberalism, and still had as their aim to curb the power of the Sultan, but chiefly because the Assembly was in the beginning dominated by their own supporters. When they realized that nothing was to be feared from the pliant new Sultan, Mehmet V, and when their support in the Chamber began to evaporate, the Committee of Union and Progress began to press for constitutional limitations on the authority of the Chamber of Deputies. After many bitter struggles amendments were made which allowed the Sultan, purely under the control of the Unionists until 1918, much greater freedom in dissolving, convening, proroguing and prolonging parliament. It was the first imposition of dominant party rule that has since been the recurring pattern in Turkish politics.

There are two areas in the creation of the administrative institutions of the modern state where the Ottomans made real progress. One was in the machinery of government. The nineteenth century saw the development of new ministries to meet the

c

needs of the new age. In particular a reform of local government was undertaken—often under pressure from foreign powers anxious to protect minority groups. Foundations were laid for the future, but experiments in local democracy were not very successful. For the most part electoral devices came to be manipulated by the central authorities or by entrenched local interests. The government generally took the view that local populations needed the assistance of progressive civil servants if they were to govern themselves effectively. In short, weight continued to lie heavily with the centre, but a rational framework was created that was latently flexible enough to accommodate change in emphasis should it come. A new law in 1913 provided the basic framework for local government that largely persists to this day.

The other significant development in administration was the reform of the civil service. The first step was taken as early as 1838 when officials' salaries were made a charge on the Exchequer. This was a development of crucial importance. Another important step forward was taken in 1880 when all officials were organized into classes, subdivided into grades. The provincial organization was given its own range of ranks, as too were special bodies like the Council of State. The system was somewhat crude, did not generally apply, and no doubt did not bear a very close relation to the nature of the functions performed, but it must have provided a good measure of much needed rationalization. Probably it was of most value for the regulation of salaries, for a fixed salary was attached to each grade.

The tendency in recruitment during the period was increasingly to stress educational qualifications, despite a great deal of flexibility in the educational attainments required. Nevertheless, the principle was soon established of recruitment to different levels in the hierarchy on the basis of educational achievement; and a number of schools sprang up alongside those of the normal educational system with the object of training young men for government service. The most famous were the *Mülkiye* (Civil Government) School (1857) and the Law School (1871). From these two institutions have been recruited ever since the upper echelons of the Ministry of the Interior, including the provincial governors and sub-governors.

It is difficult to say how far the very numerous laws, ordinances and decrees ordering this or that aspect of the Ottoman bureaucracy were in fact carried out. Frequent repetition of earlier measures suggests that execution lagged behind intention and perhaps officialdom's chief concern was to ensure its own well-being. Yet when Turkey entered upon her new phase of moderniz-ation during the Atatürk Republic, it was with the help of an experienced and partly modernized bureaucracy. Modernization is a much less novel phenomenon in Turkey than visiting adminis-trative experts are sometimes aware. There is a tradition of ad-ministration which is not purely traditional but reflects the fas-cinating fusion of Ottoman and European ideas that occurred during the period of Ottoman reform.

It is quite clear that in administrative and other respects the foundations of the Turkish state were laid much before the time of Atatürk, but it is not clear that the reforms were heading in the specific direction taken later by the Atatürk new revolution. Certainly the temper of reform was authoritarian, as it was later under Atatürk. Certainly, too, the military was deeply involved in reform, as it similarly came to be in Atatürk's Turkey. We see too the beginnings of that alliance between liberalism and religion that was forced by the emergence of an authoritarian reforming state beloved of neither. It is an odd alliance that has persisted into modern Turkey. Yet without the loss of empire and the foreign occupation that were Turkey's fate after the first world war, it does not seem likely that in the normal course of history the Sultanate and Caliphate would have been jettisoned. For good or ill, that remarkable achievement was the work of the Atatürk revolution, to which we now turn.

CHAPTER III

Revolution and Republic

Politics and society

After the defeat of the Ottoman Empire in the first world war the allied powers occupied important parts of European and Asiatic Turkey. The Ottoman government in Istanbul under the Sultan Vahdettin accepted the abortive Treaty of Sèvres which, besides creating an independent Kurdistan and Armenia, made over large tracts of Anatolia to the French, Italians and Greeks.

Not all Turks, however, were prepared to acquiesce in the dismemberment of the Turkish homeland. In those parts of Anatolia and Rumelia left unoccupied a number of resistance groups emerged, known as the Societies for the Defence of Rights. These resistance groups were contacted by Turkey's most successful wartime commander, Mustafa Kemal, who had been posted by the Ottoman government to Samsun. With the support of other army commanders Mustafa Kemal gave a lead to these resistance groups, who demanded national independence and territorial integrity. Under Kemal's leadership they were formed into an Association for the Rights of Anatolia and Rumelia.

At first the nationalists attempted a rapprochement with the Sultan. As a result it was agreed to hold elections for a new parliament (the last Ottoman parliament as it turned out), in Istanbul. When the nationalist deputies voted for the 'National Pact', a declaration of Turkish independence and territorial integrity, the Allies declared a formal occupation of Istanbul and nationalist sympathizers, including deputies, were arrested. Parliament prorogued itself and was shortly afterwards dissolved by the Sultan (11 April 1920).

Mustafa Kemal, who had remained aloof from these attempts at rapprochement, was meanwhile directing the nationalist movement from Ankara, as chairman of the Representative Committee of the Society for the Defence of Rights. He now arranged the election of a new parliament under the title of Grand National Assembly in Ankara. Elected President of this new parliament, Mustafa Kemal led a war of liberation against the powers, of whom the neighbouring Greeks were the most detested and most strident in their claims. Mustafa Kemal also had to fight against the 'Army of the Caliphate', raised by the Sultan.

In the early stages of the struggle, the nationalists had their backs to the wall, but the severe conditions imposed by the Treaty of Sèvres signed by the Sultan's government brought them considerable popular support. They defeated the Greeks after bitter campaigns and more or less obliged the other Allies to forgo their claims. The result was the Treaty of Lausanne, 1922, which recognized almost all Turkish nationalist claims. It was an astonishing victory.

A fundamental political and social revolution now took place. The Sultanate itself, now much discredited for its supineness, was abolished (November 1922). On the assumption that Caliphate and Sultanate were not inseparable, the Caliphate was retained, but with the important proviso that thenceforth the Caliph was to be chosen by the Grand National Assembly, though as before from members of the Ottoman dynasty. The next move was the declaration of a Republic (October 1923) to which Mustafa Kemal was then elected President. This certainly prevented the assumption of any such function by the Caliph. Now that the Ottoman Sultan/Caliph's temporal responsibilities were well provided for, there would seem to be little reason for any further attack on the remaining Caliphate. It was, however, soon abolished (March 1924). There was some fear lest the Caliphate should provide a rallying point for political opposition; and if fundamental social reforms were to be undertaken, the power of religion clearly had to be nullified.

After the abolition of the Caliphate came the turn of the historic office of Chief Mufti and of the ministry concerned with the Holy Law and Religious Endowments. Then the administration of the Holy Law, which largely related to personal and family matters, was taken out of the hands of the *ulema*. With the closing of religious colleges and schools the state assumed complete responsibility for education. The Sacred Law itself was replaced when what was basically the Swiss Civil Code was adopted. The dervish convents were closed and their associations disbanded after the Kurdish revolt, of 1925, in which dervish sheikhs played a leading part. The symbol of the Muslim, the fez, was banned and in numerous other ways vigorous attempts were made to slough off the Islamic past. Not least among them was the language reform which, by the adoption of the Roman script in place of the more cumbersome Arabic, both broke a powerful connection with the Islamic and Arab heritage and made it easier to extend literacy. For all this fundamental reform the practice of religion was not banned and the implementation of the reforms in a largely agricultural and under-developed society could not be fully realized. Indeed the revolutionary reforms produced a ground swell of opposition that only awaited a chance for expression. The opportunity was not long in coming.

In 1924 a Progressive Republican party was formed by dissidents from the People's Party, the party of Kemal Atatürk. Whilst the Progressive Republican party supported the basic secular principles of the Republic, it soon attracted to it those who were opposed to the government's policies on religious and liberal grounds. As a concession to this opposition the liberal, Fethi Okyar, replaced İsmet İnönü, one of Mustafa Kemal's lieutenants, as Prime Minister, but this change of government coincided with the outbreak of the Kurdish rebellion of 1925 which, with its strong religious overtones, was doubly dangerous. The strong hand of İnönü was found again to be necessary. The Republican Progressive Party was suppressed.

The next wave of opposition, in 1926, took a more clandestine form in a plot to assassinate Mustafa Kemal. When this plan misfired the government took advantage of the law for the Maintenance of Public Order, passed in 1925, at the time of the Kurdish outbreak, to ferret out important personalities dangerous to the regime, a number of whom were executed or exiled. It was not a blood bath, but the opposition was intimidated into silence.

On the expiration of the Maintenance of Public Order Law in 1929, the opposition raised its head again. This time it received some encouragement from Mustafa Kemal himself, who as President was dissatisfied, it seems, with some of the policies of the Prime Minister, İnönü. A liberal party under Fethi Okyar appeared, only to provide the occasion for anti-government demonstrations. The heat generated by the experiment seems to have persuaded Fethi that Mustafa Kemal had actually turned against it. He dissolved his party, whilst other small parties that had appeared at the same time were then dissolved by the government.

In 1938, Mustafa Kemal, known since 1935 as Kemal Atatürk

(father of the Turks), died. İnönü became President of the Republic. The political atmosphere became more illiberal as Turkey found models to inspire, if not to be closely imitated, in the increasingly successful regimes in Italy and Germany. In 1936 a labour law which drew heavily upon the Italian code forbade labour unions or strikes. In 1938, before the death of Atatürk, various other measures had been passed which had the effect of preventing the creation of political parties and subjected the press to strict control. Police powers of arrest and detention were greatly strengthened.

It must be said, too, that the outbreak of the second world war presented Turkey with a number of problems which, in the absence of strong leadership, could have proved disruptive.

Towards the end of the war a more liberal atmosphere began to appear in Turkey when it became clear that the western democracies were going to win and when the dangers of war shifted away from the eastern Mediterranean. The victory of the western democracies persuaded the Turks that democracy was indeed an integral part of western civilization, of which, according to the philosophy of their revolution, the Turks were indisputably part. It was also becoming clear that the United States and Britain would again become Turkey's chief supporters against the traditional enemy, Russia—anything but friendly to Turkey at the end of the war. Very significant, too, was the emergence by the end of the war of a new Turkish middle class of merchants and businessmen (business and commerce before the Republic had largely been in the hands of Greeks, Armenians and Jews). These new elements were impatient with the heavy-handed paternalism of a government which showed little understanding and sympathy for business life. Moreover, the introduction by the government of a Land Reform Bill in 1945 brought firmly into opposition the large landowners who, by virtue of their financial gains during the war, were now a more prosperous and influential class. As ever, too, there were liberals to be found among the intelligentsia; and as always there was in the country a deal of religious feeling that looked for more expression than the government would allow. Not least the Turkish peasant was beginning to show signs of a more independent spirit; and was coming to resent the sometimes very heavy hand of arrogant officialdom. All these pressures amounted to a strong desire for change.

The government of the single People's Party was not oblivious of these new conditions. During the period 1945 to 1950 moderate and progressive elements gradually gained the upper hand in the People's Party. The first, and politically the most significant, step was to raise the ban on the formation of political parties. Among the many that sprang into being was the Democrat Party whose power was to grow and eclipse all the others. A single-party regime now converted itself into a multi-party system, but the law against communist and religious parties was strengthened. However, the press now became freer and police powers of arrest and detention considerably curtailed. One of the most important changes was the adoption in 1950 of a new electoral law which provided for a direct, to replace an easily manipulated indirect, system. At the same time the supervision of elections was transferred from the executive to the judiciary. In the first free general election of 1946 the Democrat Party won 64 out of 465 Assembly seats; in the 1950 general election they won 396 out of 487 and swept into power.[1]

The period 1945 to 1950 saw other liberal changes. Labour was now allowed to organize itself in trade unions, but still not allowed to strike. The universities were given a much larger measure of autonomy. The gendarmerie was made to bear less hard on the peasantry. The land law of 1945 was indifferently applied and modified in favour of landowners. In 1949 a small measure of religious instruction was re-introduced into schools, on an optional basis. (When the Democrat Party came into power in 1950 they required opting out in place of opting in.) In 1949 a Faculty of Divinity was opened, but significantly in Ankara, not Istanbul, in order to provide educated religious leadership. When the Democrat Party came to power there was a rush of mosque building, Koran reading on the wireless and a reversion to Arabic for the call to prayer. Yet these measures did not extend to dismantling the secular reforms of the Atatürk period. The Democrat Party's leaders came after all from the People's Party itself, where they had been leading personalities. Many had been in government office. Significantly the administration of religious

[1] The simple majority electoral system disguised the nature of the vote. The Democrat Party vote was approximately 4·2 million, but the People's Party vote reached almost 3·2 million. (The two parties shared nearly all the votes between them.)

endowments remained in state hands, and close to the Prime Minister, despite pressures from religious quarters. When in 1950–1 dervish sheikhs came out into the open with what seemed a large following they were vigorously prosecuted.

Economic life also began to be liberalized in the period 1945–50 under the government of the People's Party. Etatist policies, not adopted in Turkey for purely doctrinaire reasons, were modified in favour of private capital and enterprise; and foreign capital now began to be encouraged. In 1950 an Industrial Development Bank was set up with the advice of the International Bank and with capital from Turkish private and public sources, the International Bank and American 'counter-part' funds.

Although the foundations for this new liberalism were laid between 1945 and 1950, the Democrat Party after 1950 greatly accelerated the pace—in the economic sphere at least. Here they took the important step of encouraging foreign enterprise by measures culminating in a law of foreign investments (1954) that allowed foreign investors to transfer profits abroad and in the event of liquidation, capital. Many other forms of foreign aid in economic development began to be accepted as it became available for the less developed countries in the 1950's. A deal of this aid was channelled into agriculture, the sector somewhat neglected in the period of the People's Party's hegemony. Whilst private enterprise in industry and commerce was much encouraged, the existing state economic enterprises were not turned over to private capital and the state under the Democrat Party government continued to invest heavily in them. The economic policies of the People's Party and the Democrat Party differed in emphasis not in direction; and much the same might be said, as we have seen, of their social policies.

With politics the comparison is more difficult. The Democrat Party started off as the champions of liberty; but by 1960, after a decade of power, looked more like neo-Ottoman autocrats. They perhaps showed the first signs of an illiberal spirit when the government in 1953 dissolved the then third largest party, the Nation Party, for alleged complicity in reactionary religious plots. This was defensible on liberal (and Kemalist) grounds, but the People's Party alleged that the motives were narrowly political. It was defensible, but only just, to confiscate, again in 1953, the property of the People's Party itself on the grounds that government grants made to the Party when in office were a misuse of public money. The matter was eventually settled, but not without destroying almost all spirit of co-operation between the two major parties.

After their second electoral victory of 1954 with an increased majority the Democrats rather surprisingly sought to buttress their already strong position by firmly restricting political liberties. Just before the general election, in fact, a severe press law was passed by the Assembly; and this was strengthened further by amendments to the press and libel laws in June 1956. These laws now provided severe penalties, firstly for criticizing persons, particularly those in official positions (even satire was not excluded); and secondly for disseminating material likely to undermine the political and economic stability of the state. The laws applied to speeches at meetings as well as to the press and to radio. In order to increase its control over the press the government also began in 1958 to control the allocation of newsprint. The years from 1954 to 1959 saw many prosecutions of journalists, editors and newspaper owners unable or unwilling to control their feelings.

In 1954 two important amendments were made to the Civil Service Law. By one of these the government was empowered to retire judges and university teachers after twenty-five years service or at age sixty. A number of judges were compulsorily retired, including the President and Vice-President of the Supreme Court. The second important amendment allowed the dismissal of civil servants after a period of suspension. This was turned against university teachers and resulted in the dismissal among others of Professor Turhan Feyzioğlu, then Dean of the influential Faculty of Political Science, Ankara University. Although the political standpoints were very different indeed, Feyzioğlu's position might be compared with that, say, of Laski at the London School of Economics and Political Science at the time of Conservative governments in Britain. Only in a less developed society political criticism, no matter how much based on considerations of principle is less tolerable because, for one thing, it is more immediately influential.[1]

---

[1] For a detailed account of this episode see my 'University Autonomy and Academic Freedom in Turkey', *Science and Freedom*, Bulletin of the Committee on Science and Freedom: XII (October 1958), and W. F. Weiker, *The Turkish*

The activities of the other political parties were also quite severely curtailed, though they were not prevented from contesting elections and organizing electoral campaigns. One much-resented measure was an amendment to the electoral law to prevent the growth of an electoral coalition by the parties in opposition. Each party was obliged to contest independently the seats in each constituency in which it maintained an organization. Then again, although under certain conditions closed meetings could continue to be held, all public meetings and demonstrations were banned except when expressly permitted, or if they occurred in the forty-five day campaign period preceding a general election. The situation became very serious indeed when in 1960 a motion was moved in the Assembly to form a commission to investigate the activities of the opposition, accused *inter alia* of interfering with the army and with arming its own followers. The commission was set up with powers to suppress newspapers, subpoena persons and documents and to imprison for up to three years those who impeded its investigations. This raised the temperature dangerously high. When İnönü himself was temporarily expelled from the Assembly for vigorous opposition to such measures the pot began to boil over.

By restricting political freedom the Democrat Party governments maintained that their object was to prevent excessive political clamour and to provide a greater measure of political stability for the sake of continued economic development. (They ran into severe economic difficulties towards the end of their decade of power.) The effect of their restrictions seems, however, to have been to drive political strife out into the streets. The very dubious legitimacy of their own measures encouraged illegitimate means of action among their opponents. This was highly dangerous because the numerous street demonstrations that occurred could not be managed by the police alone. Their opponents were strong in the large towns and particularly amongst the students. It was necessary from time to time to call in the army; and the army, who made no bones about showing their sympathy with the old victorious general İnönü, could not be relied upon. In fact, in August 1960 the military stepped in to rescue the politicians

---

Revolution, 1960–61. Aspects of Military Politics (Washington; Brookings, Institution, 1963).

from themselves. Why did they need this rescue operation? Why, we might ask, did the Democrat Party cling so obstinately to power?

The phenomenon may of course require no explanation—power is not easily relinquished. Yet the Democrat Party started off with marked liberal slogans; the world's slow stain spread rather fast.

If explanation can be essayed, the first must be looked for in the character of the Democrat Party leadership. Its leaders, it will be recalled, had a long history of active participation in the authoritarian People's Party. They were not democratic by training so to speak, and this may be important.

Secondly, although the Party's leaders emerged from the People's Party they were not necessarily rebels by disposition. They left the People's Party because they were frustrated in their aims and ambitions within it. Particularly, they were unable to unseat İsmet İnönü. It is not too much to say that many Democrat Party members had an İnönü complex, a mixture of admiration and dislike that is still evident in the Justice and other parties today. When the Democrat Party restricted political freedom it was as much on a personal as on a rational basis. They had İnönü and the People's Party chiefly in mind.

Thirdly, it must be remembered the Democrat Party got into power and maintained itself in power by victory, often substantial, in the elections; and this gave them an excessive confidence in their own popularity and their own legitimacy. They felt—and rightly—that however illiberal they appeared to intellectuals, the peasants and workers would not care much. What mattered to the bulk of the electorate was more food, material goods, leisure, and, above all, little interference by the government with traditional and religious customs. They somewhat underestimated, however, the power of the opposition.

This opposition seems to have been centred chiefly in the educated sections of society—in the schools and universities, the civil service and the military officer class. For one thing, the purchasing power of the salaries of these sections of the community diminished as inflation accompanied economic development. More important, they began to feel themselves displaced as *the* elite in Turkish society. New centres of wealth and influence were arising and new and different types of persons were reaching influential positions in politics.[1] The former elite who led the Atatürk revolution and manned its institutions was being displaced from the centre of the stage. Their attack on the new forces rising in society was often harsh, didactic and patronizing. In such an atmosphere it was difficult to make democratic politics work. By the mid 1950's the military had begun to think of intervention and in 1957 a number of military plotters were arrested.[2] During 1958 and 1959 the conspirators within the military disposed their forces for an effective take-over. It seems that both senior and junior officers (including Gürsel) were involved, but the younger and more radical officers seem to have been the leading lights.

In the early hours of 27 May 1960 the long and well-planned coup took place under the direction of thirty-eight officers of the Army and Air Force, who named themselves the National Unity Committee. The transference of power was completed quickly and without fuss and without many casualties. The police force was generally loyal to the Democrat Party government but was in no position to try to offer serious resistance.

Why did the military intervene? Was it simply that they came to the rescue of an old and revered commander in İnönü, or to the rescue of his party—the party set up by Atatürk? Was it simply that the military, like the intellectuals, objected to the authoritarianism of the Democrat Party government? If they did, it must have been an objection to an authoritarianism different from that of Atatürk. This consideration begins to open up the horizons a little, but before discussing the fundamental reasons for the revolution we might look first at the members of the Junta themselves.

Three groups of officers may be distinguished within the Junta.[3] The first group is that of the 'pashas', composed of older

[1] They are more local than national in their interests and in terms of their occupations less bureaucratic and military. See F. W. Frey, *The Turkish Political Elite* (Cambridge, Mass., 1963).

[2] The two most important accounts in English of the military revolution are Weiker, *The Turkish Revolution 1960–61*, and Ergun Özbudun, *The Role of the Military in Recent Turkish Politics* (Harvard University Center of International Affairs, Occasional Papers in International Affairs, no. 14, 1966). This later monograph is able to draw upon information in the most informative Turkish publication, Abdi İpekçi and Ömer Sami Çoşar, *İhtilâlin İçyüzü* (Istanbul, 1965). For other studies see bibliography.

[3] This is an impressionistic division of the Junta derived from informal

and more senior officers of whom the Chairman of the N.U.C., General Cemal Gürsel, was the prime example. They were brought up in the Atatürk tradition, one element of which was the exclusion of the military from politics. Within this tradition—and to justify the exclusion of the military—lies a notion of politics that is simplistic, idealistic and basically nineteenth century. Competitive politics on the western model is essentially *the* civilized way of governing. There should be freely elected representatives who should oppose one another on the basis of different, but real and honest notions about the common weal; and, as a rider, political parties should not exploit peasant ignorance and prejudice (particularly religious) for electoral purposes. The Democrat Party government of Adnan Menderes was not observing these political rules. These officers would justify their intervention on the grounds that it was necessary to get the political system back on its proper foundations. Politics is too serious a business to be left to corrupt politicians still wallowing in Ottomanism. They need to be educated.

The second group, more nebulous and difficult to define, was on the whole younger and less senior in rank. They supported competitive, democratic politics but saw as the essential point in politics the discussion of the best and quickest means to economic and social development. They believed in a planned economy, with a large share for public enterprise, and a welfare state. They were less respectful about politics than the first group. To them it was more of a game. They stepped in as referee to see the rules were obeyed. They generally supported the first group, but sometimes the third. When, in November 1960, the third group was purged, members of the second group were not it seems, party to the decision and were presented with a *fait accompli*.[1]

The third group among the authors of the coup is most easily defined. They numbered at least fourteen out of the thirty-eight man Junta and accepted as their leader Colonel Alparslan Türkeş. Their chief characteristic was their comparative youth, but they

discussion with persons in academic and public life (including some members of the Junta) in 1960. My impressions seem to be confirmed by İpekçi and Çoşar, who also distinguish three groups. The second group supported a programme of social and economic reform but allied themselves with the first group because they distrusted Türkeş (Özbudun, op. cit., p. 33).

[1] See Özbudun, op. cit., p. 33.

were also for the most part of lower rank. They too, like the second group, wanted speedy economic and social reform; but they had little confidence in the abilities and the inclinations of any of the political parties to bring this about. Moreover, they thought that political controversy would inevitably centre around the principles of public ownership of industry and social reform, including, of course, land reform. This would foster socio-economic class divisions in Turkish society and thus destroy one of the sacred principles of Atatürkism, namely populism, or social unity. One of their proposals for the maintenance of social solidarity was, significantly a National Culture Union which would save the nation from schism, sloth, ignorance, etc. etc. etc. This was seen by the other members of the Committee, guided in their thinking by their allies among the intellectuals, as the harbinger of dictatorship. As we have seen, this group was purged from the N.U.C.

With some notion of the elements that made up the N.U.C. and their general attitudes, we are perhaps in a position now to examine the principal reasons for military intervention that have been advanced by students of Turkish politics. Some reasons for intervention will be seen to be more applicable to some members of the Junta than to others.

In the first place, there seem to be good reasons why the military should not intervene in Turkish politics. There is a wide consensus amongst the educated on the Atatürkist philosophy of the state and on the later development of multi-party politics. By those for whom these matters reach a conscious level the institutions of government are more or less respected. Moreover, since 1922, at least, there had, until 1960, been no marked crisis on the occasions when power changed hands. Then again, whilst there may not as yet be much of a range of secondary groups (private associations) in Turkish society, political parties are certainly well developed for a developing country. In other words, Turkey is at least on the verge of having a developed political culture.[1] In such a society military intervention is to be regarded as distinctly unusual.

It is often argued, too, that a highly professional and self-respecting army like that of Turkey is not likely to sully its

[1] For a clear analysis of what is involved in the concept political culture see S. E. Finer, *The Man on Horseback* (London, 1962) pp. 87–8.

character by military intervention. It will be satisfied to get on with its more ennobling function of defending the country. The difficulty with this argument is that professionalism, or any other quality, never exists in isolation. There are always other features in the military-cum-political situation that affect it. For instance, the Turkish military is professional and self-respecting, but by virtue of the supreme part it played in the War of Independence under Mustafa Kemal it regards itself as the guardian of the Atatürkist revolution, even though Atatürk did gradually exclude the military from politics. Moreover, with regard to the basic attitudes of the military towards the state, it is perhaps not too fanciful to remind ourselves that there was in the Ottoman Empire a long tradition of military intervention. The Ottoman army intervened in politics on many occasions in order to obtain more benefits for itself, or to replace the Sultan, or Grand Vizier, who were, from the army's aspect, primarily military commanders. The army did not, however, in any way seek to change the form of state, or even government. They demonstrated, mutinied and went on strike, in effect. Until the nineteenth century this caprice did not expose them to the dire penalties consequent upon disobedience in modern western armies. The Ottoman tradition is military intervention for limited purposes, with no intention to change the nature of the state or government, or even to capture it. The military is regarded as a legitimate component of society whose demonstrations are tolerated. There may be a trace of this tradition in the modern Turkish military's attitude towards politics.

One interpretation of the revolution is that it was merely an attempt by the military to recapture the influence they lost when Atatürk edged them out of power. Left in these bald terms the contention does not carry much conviction; there is no evidence to suggest that the military resented their exclusion from politics in the Atatürk era. A more sophisticated development of this suggestion arises from a discussion by R. D. Robinson[1] and is of more interest. It is contended that between 1950 and 1960 the extensive rearming and retraining of the Turkish military by the

---

[1] R. D. Robinson, *The First Turkish Republic, A Case Study in National Development* (Cambridge, Mass., 1963). See also D. Lerner and R. D. Robinson, 'Swords and Ploughshares: The Turkish Army as a Modernizing Force', *World Politics*, XIII (October 1960)

Americans re-established the military as the most progressive element in Turkish society, which it had gradually ceased to be under the one-party regime. This process of modernization created expectations that could not be understood, and therefore not met, by the more antiquated politico-administrative machinery. With the military again in the van, the tradition of military leadership of Turkish modernization, as exemplified by the Young Turks, could be revived, albeit under the guise of Atatürkism. A combination of frustration and renewed self-confidence could then be seen as an underlying factor that encouraged the military to intervene in 1960.

The difficulty with this view is that the elements in society in the 1950's generally regarded as most prestigious were not the military—nor the civil servants—but the free professions in law, medicine, engineering and the like; and it seems probable that these professions carried more prestige than the military not because they were more conservative and static but because they were more modern and dynamic.

Perhaps the most interesting reasons advanced for intervention in 1960—which are certainly the most pregnant with meaning for the future—flow from the social background and the social and economic views of the instigators of the coup. It is claimed that 'the groups that made and supported the 1960 revolution . . . sought to effect a more balanced economic growth and a more equitable distribution of wealth'.[1]

In the first place, it is argued that dynamic though the economic policies of the Democrat Party government were, social justice was not a main consideration; and evidence from statements made by members of the N.U.C. shows that many of them were discontented with the government's economic and social policies. For instance, of twenty-nine members of the Junta who were interviewed for the newspaper *Cumhuriyet* in 1960, nineteen 're-garded social justice and/or land reform as one of the most important problems of the country'.[2]

The reasons why the majority of N.U.C. members supported

---

[1] Özbudun, op. cit., p. 42.

[2] The quotation is from Özbudun, op. cit., p. 21. An English translation of the interviews noted by Özbudun is Cevat F. Başkut, Yaşar Kemal and Ecvet Güresin, *Interviews with Members of Turkey's National Unity Committee* (U.S. Joint Publications Research Service, 1960).

D

radical and socialist policies are seen to be principally two. First, the military were among those whose salaries suffered from the effects of monetary inflation in the 1950's; secondly, it is argued that a deeper cause of dissatisfaction stemmed from the social origins of the officer class. This view is based on the hypothesis that 'armies of lower- and lower-middle-class origins are more likely to be a progressive force than armies of feudal or upper-class origins'.[1] There is in fact no evidence available about the social provenance of the Turkish officer class as a whole, but we do know that most of the members of the N.U.C. came from 'lower-middle or salaried middle class families' and 'none of the members appeared to belong to the top political or economic elite'.[2]

This is a neat and seductive theory to which the facts seem to lend support, but something must be said about the methodological difficulties in the way of accepting the evidence, difficulties which Özbudun himself discusses. First, on the question of the attitudes held by the members of the N.U.C., it is of course extremely difficult to tell whether the attitudes they held amounted to reasons for intervention. Much must surely depend on how strongly these attitudes were held. They might create no more than a disposition to intervene and then again they may be to some extent self-justificatory. Secondly, what applies to attitudes and opinions applies even more to factors in social background. That the N.U.C. members' family background was lower middle class does not necessarily mean that they were in some real sense representative of the social, economic or political desires of that class. A connection between social background and impulsion to political action depends no doubt on many other factors, one of which is the extent to which socially mobile elements (like army officers in Turkey) continue to identify themselves with the class from which they have sprung. My own impression, subject to the research so necessary in this subject, is that they identify themselves with the class into which they have moved, namely the upper professional class of civil servants. They are certainly not deeply concerned with urging the claims of the lower elements in society against what might be called the Atatürkist professional and official establishment. Rather, like the civil servants and the intelligentsia into whose class they have moved, they are generally

[1] Özbudun, op. cit., p. 27.   [2] Ibid., p. 29.

opposed to landlordism, religious obscurantism and to the relatively uneducated entrepreneurs who are now forcing their way into prominence through business and commerce of various sorts. Interestingly enough, their opposition to this group is opposition to men of a very similar background to themselves, but whose route upwards has been very different. Many of the officers are undoubtedly the products originally of the military *lycées*, the only *lycée* education poorer parents could afford for their sons, because they provided free board and lodging.

On the whole, therefore, we perhaps need to be cautious about the intensity with which military officers in Turkey hold social and radical opinions. This is not to say that they do not have them, but to suggest that they may imbibe them more from the general discussion that goes on in Turkish educated circles than from any sense of injustice deeply ingrained in their original environments.

In sum, it is probably nearest the truth to ascribe military intervention in 1960 to a variety of causes, in different combination, and acting with greater or lesser force for this or that person or group. If obliged to name a combination most popular and persuasive, it would perhaps be made up of (i) resentment at the rise to influence of traditionalists and *nouveaux riches* (and of their means and style of authoritarian rule), (ii) a feeling that the military had to come to the aid of Atatürkism (and of its respected leader İnönü, an old army commander in some personal danger) and (iii) an awareness of the needs of the more lowly elements in society, whose plight indicated to the military mind a comprehensively planned and rigorously administered programme of development.

An important test of the reasons for the military intervention is of course the record of the Junta when in office. To this we now turn, but the test of action when in power is an imperfect one, chiefly because, it will be recalled, fourteen of the original Junta were purged in November 1960.

The N.U.C. was in power from May 1960 to October 1961. Its chief action, the trial of the members of the former regime, was spectacular, particularly when it resulted in the execution of the former Prime Minister, Menderes, and two other principal ministers, an action to which the N.U.C. was prodded by the military commanders. There were also two important purges, one of some 5,000 officers and the other of 147 university teachers, who seem to have been purged for a wide variety of reasons, few if any of which were valid.

Yet the N.U.C.'s real impact on Turkish politics was less than these dramatic and well-publicized actions suggest. To look first at the structure of government during the rule of the N.U.C., the first fact is that the N.U.C. did not rule directly, but through a largely civilian cabinet of politically uncommitted technocrats and intellectuals. Moreover, the civilian element was soon strengthened when, in January 1961, a Constituent Assembly was convened on the basis of a charter drawn up by a committee of five professors whose chairman, Turhan Feyzioğlu, was a former deputy of the People's Party. Under this charter the National Unity Committee became the upper house of a bicameral legislature with powers not confined simply to drawing up a new constitution. Both 'houses' had a veto. That of the Assembly remained theoretical, but the N.U.C. only exercised its right in one really important matter, namely to prevent re-instatement of the 147 dismissed university teachers. The N.U.C. exerted pressure over the Assembly in relatively few other matters. What it did clamp down on was any criticism of the revolution.

The N.U.C.'s secondary role in government was matched by its leniency towards political parties. Although their activities were formally suspended, they were from the beginning not completely restrained in practice and they soon found ways of obtaining publicity for their views. (The former Democrat Party, however, was closed down.) Then, as early as January 1961, official permission was given for the formation of political parties. This was all in accord with the N.U.C.'s early promise to bring about a speedy return to democratic politics. In doing this they had made it clear that there would be a constitutional court, a bicameral legislature and a system of proportional representation; but these had long been the chief demands of the political parties in opposition to the Menderes government. It is probable, however, that the chief opposition party, the People's Party, would not have carried out these changes had it come to power under the old Constitution.

As to economic and social policies, the N.U.C. achieved little of permanent importance, apart perhaps from the setting up of a State Planning Organization, which was also included in the Constitution—and which had long been one of the declared aims of the People's Party. Obligatory savings (3 per cent of salary), in the form of government savings bonds, was imposed on all earning more than £20 a month. This worked quite well, but the demand for Declarations of Wealth from all taxpayers raised an outcry and was not effectively followed up. Nor too was tax revision, although, it must be admitted, the principle of taxation of agricultural income was forced through, a tax that the Menderes government would never entertain. Land reform was not tackled in practice, but debates in the Constituent Assembly showed that the N.U.C. was strongly in favour of it. In fact, the N.U.C. forced out fifty-five large landowners in the east and confiscated their land for distribution.

Although the N.U.C. began to tackle some of the major political and economic problems, it really did not bite deep. What it did attempt it did not allow itself the time to carry out effectively, particularly its economic and social policies. It began very quickly to demilitarize its regime. The Junta acted, it has been justly said, 'more like orthodox politicians . . . than like non-political problem solving soldiers'.[1]

What is important, of course, is how the Junta did come to decide not to bite deep into Turkish politics. As we have seen, there was a strong radical group in the Junta, the 'fourteen' under Türkeş who, in November 1960, were expelled from the N.U.C. and exiled to embassies abroad. This was an important, and indeed probably the crucial step. The move against them was sudden, secret and swift. Gürsel felt moved to justify their expulsion at some length the following day in press conferences and on the radio. The road to minimal participation in politics by the Junta was now clear, provided the military as a whole stood by the rump of the Junta. That they did so suggests that the more radical socialist minded 'fourteen' were not typical of the officer class. A second coup—led by colonels and below—was a possibility, but did not occur although this was partly perhaps because the retirement of the 5,000 officers had alleviated discontents about promotion. In short, the Junta inaugurated a number of important economic and social reforms, but, particularly after the dismissal of the 'fourteen', does not seem to have had the strength or will to carry them through.

It is interesting that subsequently the Junta did get out of step

[1] Weiker, *The Turkish Revolution*, op. cit., p. 153.

with the military command. This is a more or less normal phenomenon in such situations. A Junta should logically consist of
all the highest military commanders if its governing authority is
to be accepted as legitimate by the military. Clearly for the sake of
stability—in order to avoid the danger of further coups—it is
necessary that the gap should be closed, or that the Junta should
rapidly civilianize its regime to reduce its reliance on military
support.

The Turkish Junta, however, was not bent on civilianizing
itself. It was restoring competitive democratic politics. This
necessarily meant giving a place to the supporters of the displaced
regime, who appeared now as members principally of the new
Justice and New Turkey parties. When this freedom resulted in
attacks in the press and in electoral speeches on both the military
and the revolution, the military commanders thought the N.U.C.
was being too lenient. The situation came to a head in 1961.
Members of the N.U.C. who held troop commands relinquished
them. The N.U.C. now passed under the control of the military
commanders. There was to be only one military voice. Given that
Turkey was on the road back to competitive politics, it was a
wholly beneficial crisis.[1] Supporters of the previous regime were
sharply reminded that the clock was not to be put back. The
legitimacy of the revolution was not to be questioned. The
military as a whole now showed it was prepared to uphold the
revolutionary and democratic tradition.

By October 1961, when elections for a new Grand National
Assembly were held, the military had formally bowed itself from
the scene. Its time in the sun had been very brief; and its impact
on Turkish politics had not in some respects been very great.
Was the coup then an attempt by the urban and professional
intelligentsia to get back to Atatürkism, to defend their own social
position against the new middle classes, to resist the effects of
democracy itself? Or was it forward looking? Was it an attempt at
economic and social reform that would make democracy safer?
It was perhaps neither—or better, it combined something of both
of these views. It was a forward- (not a backward-) looking
attempt by an intelligentsia as yet more social welfare than
socialist minded to make democracy work in a state whose basic

---

[1] It would not have been so if the Junta had been bent on civilianizing
itself along Atatürk lines.

Atatürkist principles would be respected. They were not opposed to democracy, but to what they regarded as its unfair manipulation by those they saw as political opportunists with scant interest in subordinating immediate gain to the long-term need of the Turkish state. Above and behind much else besides, the revolution was a moral protest.

Political institutions

We have seen how in 1920 the lower house of the last Ottoman parliament stood firm in the cause of Turkish independence and how this contributed to the full military occupation of Istanbul by the Allies and the arrest and deportation of a number of deputies.

Those deputies who escaped to Ankara brought with them to the new Grand National Assembly summoned there by Mustafa Kemal a continuity with the past, and thereby imported a measure of legitimacy. The new Assembly's principal claim to legitimacy lay in the contention that a parliament in Istanbul could not perform its proper duties under the influence of foreign occupation. Moreover, behind this scaffolding of legitimacy, an institution was being erected on the basis of a new idea in Turkish constitutional development—an idea designed to accord a new legitimacy. Mustafa Kemal had from the first lost no opportunity, to stress that sovereignty lay completely in the hands of the people.[1]

The Grand National Assembly which met in Ankara in response to Mustafa Kemal's call consisted of 232 newly elected members, to be joined in due course by 106 of the members of the last Ottoman parliament. An analysis of the occupational background of all the members shows that although nearly half were officials and officers, the remainder represented a fairly wide cross section of professional and commercial occupations.[2]

[1] The idea was stressed for instance in the Declaration issued after the Congress Mustafa Kemal called at Erzurum (1919) and was repeated at the Sivas Congress (September 1919). In calling for elections in the name of the Society for the Defence of the Rights of Anatolia and Rumelia (March 1920), Kemal envisaged a National Assembly 'with supreme authority to direct and control the affairs of the nation'.

[2] The most extensive study of Turkish deputies is by F. W. Frey, *The Turkish Political Elite* (Cambridge: M.I.T. Press, 1965). For other very interesting studies of this period, from which this information on the occupational background of deputies is derived, see T. Z. Tunaya, 'Türkiye Büyük

As soon as the new Assembly met, Mustafa Kemal was quick to remind it of its supreme authority, both legislative and executive. This insistence that the totality of power lay with the new Assembly both irrevocably involved its members in the revolution and prevented the emergence of an executive arm that could be regarded as deputising for the Sultan. There remained nevertheless the problem of government. It was temporarily solved when the Assembly accepted Mustafa Kemal's proposal for a government of eleven members elected by the Assembly from its membership. This produced a government, but not homogeneity in government. An amendment was soon accepted that gave the crucial right of nomination to the President of the Assembly, Mustafa Kemal.

In September 1920 the government submitted a programme to the Assembly containing a number of fundamental articles that unambiguously stated the basic constitutional doctrine of the new regime. Sovereignty was proclaimed as resting unconditionally with the nation; executive power and legislative authority resided in the Grand National Assembly, the sole and true representative of the nation. Government was to be in the hands of the Assembly, while the armed forces were to be responsible only to the Assembly, whose President was *ex officio* the President of the Council of Ministers—the government. In 1921 these principles were embodied in a Constitutional Law, with three important additions. The important doctrine was laid down that deputies were not representatives of their provinces but of the nation as a whole, a point that has subsequently always been insisted upon. Secondly the Council of Ministers was empowered to select its own President—without detriment, however, to the President of the Assembly's *ex officio* presidency of the Council. This device

---

Meclisi Hükûmetinin Kuruluşu ve Siyasî Karakteri', *İstanbul Üniversitesi Hukuk Fakültesi Mecmuası*, XXXIII, nos. 3–4 (1958) and his 'De L'Empire Ottoman au Régime de la Grande Assemblée Nationale de Turquie', *Annales de la Faculté de Droit d'Istanbul*, VIII, nos. 9, 10, 11 (1959) pp. 132–59. The figures for the 'official' element among the deputies are somewhat higher than those given by Frey, op. cit., p. 181. The differences are probably accounted for by the difficulties of occupational classification. A good study in English of this early period of the Republic is by Elaine D. Smith, *Turkey: Origins of the Kemalist Movement and the Government of the Grand National Assembly (1919–1923)* (Washington, 1959).

allowed Mustafa Kemal to divorce himself of responsibility for governmental shortcomings and maintain a more lofty eminence whilst reserving to himself the possibility of intervention. In conditions of multi-party politics since 1946—conditions that require a presidency above politics—the device has sometimes proved awkward. The President has been seen to be too much involved in politics. The third amendment was not destined to have much of a future, but showed the strength of religious feeling in this first Assembly. All laws, ordinances and other rules, it was laid down, were to be made in the light of the prescriptions of the Holy Law. This was a sop. No machinery was created to perform the complex task.

The fundamental principles of government of 1920 and 1921 were carried through to their logical conclusion in the following few years. With the abolition of Caliphate/Sultanate the demise of the religious institution and the Holy Law there was no rival to the authority of the new state.

Clearly the most important step was the abolition of the Sultanate. A republic followed logically from this move.[1] A purely spiritual Caliphate was a novel idea without wide support. Indeed, when the proposal to abolish the Sultanate was debated in the Assembly it was resisted just on these grounds that a spiritual Caliphate was not a meaningful institution. When the institution was created the new Caliph began, almost inevitably, to appear as a candidate for a constitutional monarchy. To divorce the Caliphate from temporal concerns was to run against a powerful historical tradition.

To some degree therefore the proclamation of a republic was no doubt influenced by the dangers that might arise from the existence of the Caliphate. Yet by itself the declaration repeated what was already implicit in the assumption that sovereignty resided in the nation and was exercised by the Grand National Assembly. Essentially the proclamation of the Republic was connected with—and to some extent disguised—another fundamental constitutional change, namely the creation of a President of the Republic (to be elected by the Assembly) who would supplant the President of the Assembly as the most important officer in the new state. A

[1] Mustafa Kemal almost certainly appreciated this. See the account of his interview with the Neue Freie Presse quoted in Lord Kinross, *Atatürk, the Rebirth of a Nation* (London, 1964), pp. 378-9.

practical advantage was said to derive from the new arrangements—the relatively simple method of selection of the Prime Minister by the new President—but this function could have been performed by the President of the Assembly, and cannot be said to constitute the real reason for the creation of a Presidency of the Republic. The real significance of the change is most probably that coupled with the office was the headship of state—not a function easily attached to the presidency of an assembly. The mantle of the Ottoman state now fell firmly on the shoulders of the new President, who not surprisingly turned out to be Mustafa Kemal. As Head of State he could command wider allegiance in society than as President of the Assembly, when it would be difficult to maintain the measure of dignity and apparent impartiality and concern for the common weal that seems generally to be expected of heads of state. In the new constitution that emerged in 1924, the theory of the concentration of legislative and executive power in the Assembly was maintained, but it is to the headship of the state that we probably need to look for the fount of power. The declaration of a republic ensured the occupancy of that seat by Mustafa Kemal. This process heralded a departure from a pure convention, or assembly, regime to one more parliamentary in character.

The principles which found expression during these early years were codified in the Constitution of 1924, which lasted until the new constitution of 1961. Some amendments of importance were made in later years, notably in 1928 when the statement that Islam was the religion of the state was removed, and later when the franchise was extended to women and the voting age raised from eighteen to twenty-two. In 1937 the principles of the single People's Party were incorporated in the Constitution—an indication of the fact that the most significant feature of the politics of the Atatürk republic lies with party, not with constitutional or parliamentary matters. Under the 1924 Constitution, Turkey was ruled by and through the People's Party until 1950.

Turkey's experience with political parties did not begin until the Young Turk period. In late Ottoman times political opposition groups were of two sorts. One element was intellectual and liberal and sought to bring about the end of absolute government by persuasion. The other element was conspiratorial and revolutionary, producing a motley of secret organizations. Sometime after the 1908 revolution the successful conspiratorial group, the Committee of Union and Progress, transformed itself into a political party. At first only the parliamentary party was known as the party, but by 1913 the whole of the organization was included. The party established a comprehensive organization which included provision for branches in the provinces. During this period other parties also appeared, but none was able to stand up against the Union and Progress Party except the Liberal Union, a parliamentary organization which enjoyed for a while the support of a group of army officers, the 'Saviour Officers'. After 1913 all parties but that of Union and Progress were suppressed.

After the war the party of Union and Progress dissolved itself, to be replaced under the Sultan's government in Istanbul by the revived Liberal Union, which provided a number of ministers for the Sultan's government. Meanwhile in the provinces political activity was dominated by the Associations for the Rights of Anatolia and Rumelia, which had as their nuclei the provincial organizations of the now defunct Union and Progress Party.[1] It is interesting, however, that the delegates at the Sivas Congress resolved not to revive the Committee of Union and Progress, now thoroughly discredited by its failure to avert national defeat.

The next stage in political party development occurred when the representatives of the Association for the Defence of Rights in the first revolutionary Assembly split into groups, one led by Mustafa Kemal, the other opposed to him. Since Kemal's group was supreme in the organization of the Association for the Defence of Rights, it held the upper hand. The Second Group, as the opposition was known, did not present candidates for elections to the second Assembly in 1923, and the Association, still under Kemal's chairmanship, issued a manifesto declaring that the Defence of Rights groups in the Assembly would henceforth be known as the People's Party. It then absorbed the organization of the Defence of Rights. Thus although the new party technically emerged from the Assembly, it really came into existence equipped with a local organization that owed something to the past. Significantly perhaps, the new party declared it was not the heir to Union and Progress, the immediate object in this no doubt

---

[1] See Tunaya, *Karakter*, for a brief but very interesting account of the emergence of these associations from Union and Progress provincial organizations.

being to prevent that party's former leaders from claiming a place in the new party as of right.

From 1923 the People's Party, known after 1924, as the Republican People's Party, enjoyed power without real break until 1950. It developed a broad political programme on the five principles of secularism, populism, etatism, republicanism and reform, principles that were incorporated in the Constitution of the Republic in 1937. This merging of People's Party and State was the distinctive feature of politics in the Atatürk era. In 1927 Kemal had been made permanent leader of the Party. In 1935 it was laid down that the Minister of the Interior should be Secretary General of the party and that governors of provinces (*valis*) should be the chairmen of the party's provincial organizations. In 1939, however, a liberalizing wind blew when an 'independent group' was created in the Assembly to act as an opposition, though within the Party. At the same time the close ties between Party and State were somewhat loosened.

In 1945 a real experiment with multi-party politics began. Dissatisfaction within the People's Party, reflecting criticism from outside, led to the establishment of a new political party, the National Resurgence Party. The really significant move, however, came when some other members of the People's Party presented to the parliamentary party proposals to restore some of the basic political freedoms. The four signatories of the proposal founded the Democrat Party in January 1946. This party quickly established a provincial organization in two-thirds of the provinces. In the general election of 1946 the Democrat Party won 64 of the 465 seats. The only other party of any real significance to emerge in the early post-war years was the Republican Peasant National Party, formed in 1948 by politicians expelled or resigned from the Democrat Party. The party did not do well in the 1950 general election and suffered a setback when in 1953 it was dissolved by the Democrat Party government on the grounds that it was reactionary and opposed to the Kemalist reforms. The party reconstituted itself almost immediately as the Republican National Party. In 1958 it joined a small Peasant Party that had emerged to become the Republican Peasant Nation Party. The Democrat Party gave birth to another political party, the Freedom Party, in 1955, composed at first of thirty Democrat Party deputies, some quite prominent. By and large they disagreed with the increasingly illiberal policies of the Democrat Party. Not at all successful in the 1957 general election, the party later joined forces with the People's Party.

By 1950 the People's Party had become much more liberal than before and during the war. In opposition it had greater opportunity to develop this new side of its personality, especially when after 1954 Democrat Party governments became more authoritarian. The other principal distinguishing characteristic of the party was the stress on the role of the state in economic development and the need for planning, to which the Democrat Party was opposed. The People's Party did not, however, wish to eliminate private enterprise. Perhaps the party's most convincing line was its claim, which could hardly be refuted, to be the most fervent supporter of the reforms of Atatürk. It was a claim, however, of more limited appeal than the party realized or liked to admit.

By contrast with the People's Party's new found liberalism the Democrat Party became more authoritarian. The style of its authoritarianism was not, however, Atatürkist. The party emphasized the leadership and encouraged the initiative not of the intelligentsia but of other middle- and upper-class elements, the landowners, business entrepreneurs and merchants. They did not, however, seek to impose the domination of these classes on the lowly, the poorer peasants and workers. They worked *with* them, wooing them with promises, partly kept, of economic betterment, greater religious freedom and a lighter and more responsive administration. In their use of landowners, richer peasants and entrepreneurs of various kinds they seemed to find a leadership that at local levels could really speak to the uneducated masses. They did not preach and they did not try to force the masses into new ways obnoxious to them. There is no evidence to suppose that peasants or workers had developed antagonisms towards the more prosperous elements of the Democrat Party. In this respect they reaped the benefits of the populism of the Atatürk era, the refusal to countenance any division of society along socioeconomic lines which prevented the dissemination of leftist doctrines. The Democrat Party's authoritarianism was directed towards its political opponents.

As we have seen, the Democrat Party was in power for the whole of the decade 1950–60. It remains now to try briefly to gauge the extent of their success by reference to the voting figures for the period. From 1950 a direct system of voting replaced the indirect system in use till then. The system was that of simple majority. Each party provided a list of candidates for all seats in each constituency it was contesting. The party with the highest number of votes obtained all the seats. This led to serious over-representation, especially as the constituency (which is the province) is large. Each province returned to the Grand National Assembly during the period on average nearly seven deputies.

However different on a strictly proportional basis the distribution of Assembly seats might have been, there is no gainsaying the Democrat Party victory in each of the three elections between 1950 and 1960. The following table shows the percentages of the vote obtained by the parties.

TABLE I

Grand National Assembly
Election Results, 1950, 1954, 1957
(Percentages of Valid Votes cast)

Party	Year		
	1950	*1954*	*1957*
Democrat	53·5	56·6	47·7
Republican People's	40·0	35·3	40·9
Republican Peasant Nation	3·3	4·9	7·2
Freedom	—	—	3·8

Source: Publications of the General Directorate of Statistics. This is the source for electoral statistics in subsequent tables unless otherwise stated.

The first point we may observe is that although the Democrat Party did not rout the People's Party, they defeated them roundly. The second point is that multi-party politics in Turkey resulted in a two-party system. The presence of two smaller parties could not have affected the outcome, save in 1957 when there was less than a 7 per cent difference between the two major parties. In this respect it is of some interest to observe that the Republican Peasant Nation Party did seem to take votes from the People's Party rather than from the Democrat Party; it also appears that the heavy Democrat Party losses in 1957 are not much attributable to the intervention of the Freedom Party, the offshoot from the Democrat Party in 1957.[1]

Administration

Central administration. The changes which occurred in Turkish administrative organization in the years following the war of independence were evolutionary, rather than revolutionary. By late Ottoman times an organizational framework had been created for the needs of the modern state that was broadly speaking adequate. The young republic did not have to start from scratch as some young republics have had to do. The basic pattern was French and its theory clear and logical. A consequence of its French origin was that problems of administration were largely approached through administrative law, and this may have been responsible for inhibiting enquiry into the real and practical, as opposed to legal and theoretical problems.

For all this, the attitude of the new republic to administrative problems was largely pragmatic. Administrative change was inspired by current need; and the need was not so very pressing in the early years.

During the period up to the second world war then, the Turks had a valuable opportunity to reform their administration without having to cope with pressures created by rapid modernization. During this early period they met a real administrative need by re-establishing the Council of State, abolished during the Empire on account of the political implications of its work. They further reformed the system of local government, avoiding in the process some of the inconveniences of the French model, which does not allow much of a distinction between town and country districts.

[1] These statements derive from an examination of constituency voting figures. By examining those constituencies which the R.P.N.P. contested in all three elections we find that the proportion of votes won by the People's Party was lower, and that by the Democrat Party higher, than is the case in the constituencies not contested by the R.P.N.P. The growing success of this party in terms of the proportion of the votes cast is largely due to its increasing the number of constituencies contested from about one-third in 1950 to nearly all in 1957. In the 1957 election the Freedom Party contested fifty-four of the sixty-seven constituencies. In the twenty-eight constituencies in which the Democrat Party lost between 10 per cent to 19 per cent of votes, the Freedom Party vote was little different from their average for all the constituencies contested.

Most important, however, of their reforms was perhaps their effort to reform the civil service, on which a start was made in 1926. Let us first review briefly the character of the reform.

The main purpose of the first measure of reform, the Officials' Law of 1926, was not to introduce novel reforms, but to apply to all officials principles that were for the most part already accepted —namely, recruitment by reference to educational qualifications and promotion based on a combination of merit and seniority. To these ends all public employees were now classified into those who were paid salary (*maaşlı*), a wage-paid category (*ücretli*) and auxiliaries (*müstahdem*).

The next important step in the ordering of personnel matters was a law passed in 1929 which applied in Turkey for the first time a *barême*, or schedule of salary grades.[1] The *barême* consisted of twenty grades and replaced what was little better than a dis-ordered array of some fifty-three grades. As the Minister of Finance at the time explained, the new grades were not decided upon after the examination of the importance and character of the posts, the procedure originally envisaged. The reorganization was merely an arrangement of officials into the new grades on the basis of the salaries they were receiving. This was crude, but was probably the only realistic way of proceeding. To have evaluated posts in terms of duties would no doubt have been too much for the resources of Turkish administration at the time and might well have resulted in no reform at all. The simplification of 1929 did to some extent match titles to salary grades.

This new *barême* did not apply to all civil servants, but only to those defined as salaried officials in the law of 1926. The condition of those paid wages, many of whom were in fact officials, was left in disorder. Of all those who were 'waged' those known as 'waged officials' (*ücretli memur*) were naturally the first problem. The real disadvantage in their position was not that in general they were paid less—it could be an advantage in this respect not to be included in the new rigid *barême* system—but that they did not rank for pension and, not being subject to the law of 1926, could be readily dismissed. Their numbers were considerable moreover. In 1931 there were half as many 'waged' as 'salaried' officials in the central administration.

[1] *Devlet Memurlarının Maaşlarının Tevhid ve Teadülüne Dair Kanun*, no. 1452, 8 May 1929.

One of the chief reasons for a new personnel law in 1939 (the next important stage in reform) was the need to clarify further the position of the 'waged' officials, particularly as the absence of restrictions on their salaries was encouraging a drift of salaried officials to the wage-paid category. The problem was partly solved in 1939 by regulating salaries and other conditions of employment of wage-paid employees by reference to the establishment norms for salaried officials. In 1944 they were transferred to the salaried official category, though only in the general budget offices.

This initial difficulty over the position of the wage-paid officials was a foretaste of the extensive trouble the Turkish civil service was to encounter after the second world war. Very sensibly the reformers wanted to keep the public service within bounds by establishing careers systems for its employees. Yet as soon as one gap was plugged another seemed to open. After the wage-paid officials came the turn of another category, the permanent auxiliaries, a class intended originally for posts of cleaners, messengers and so on. The discretion permitted in fixing salaries for these permanent auxiliaries was used to provide higher than normal salaries for persons employed, in fact, as officials. By 1960 the category of daily wage worker was being used to employ scarce professional and technical talent.

Why then did this attempt at reform of the public personnel system begin to run into difficulties during and after the second world war? The reason was that the reforms were not designed to cope with the stresses imposed by two connected problems that now began to appear, namely expansion and inflation.

To take the case of expansion first, we can see from Table 2, p. 50, how rapidly the Turkish public service expanded during and after the second world war. Clearly any system that did not take into account changes of this magnitude was bound to run into serious difficulties.[1]

[1] We also know something of the direction of economic and social development from the distribution of civil servants over the period. Between 1931 and 1938 such increases as there were occurred in education, public works, and health and social assistance. From 1938 to 1948 agriculture joined health and social assistance as one of the most rapid areas of development. Education was also well to the fore. The direction of this administrative expansion shows how, in its early stages, the Atatürk revolution was essentially political and social. Agriculture was comparatively neglected. Despised in Ottoman times, the Turkish peasant was idealized by the revolution as the

TABLE 2

Numbers of Civil Servants 1931–61[a]

Year	Central Administration (General and Annexed Budget Organizations)	Central Administration and State Economic Enterprises
1931	80,546	86,154
1938	74,183	95,782
1941	86,595	n/a
1946	119,769	170,202
1950	173,608	189,583
1955	190,206	230,336
1961	313,391	426,972

[a] These are numbers of positions, not all necessarily filled, and are based on budgets. Those for 1931 to 1946 inclusive have been obtained from publications of the State Statistics Office (formerly General Directorate of Statistics). The figures for 1950 and 1955 are those obtained by Professor C. Mıhçıoğlu from the State Statistics Office which appear in his 'The Civil Service in Turkey', *Ankara Universitesi Siyasal Bilgiler Fakültesi Dergisi XIX* (March 1964). The figures for 1961 are from *Devlet Personel Rejimi Hakkında Ön Rapor*. The figures should be treated with caution. They purport to give no more than a broad indication of the rate of expansion.

On the second problem, that of inflation, it seems that between 1929 and 1938 officials were more than able to maintain their standard of living. The cost of living did not increase and changes in the salary structure also improved the position of those in the lowest ranks. This meant that the difference in salary between the highest and lowest paid officials decreased, a development that always has to be watched carefully lest incentives for promotion are reduced.[1]

After 1939 the relation between salaries and cost of living changed considerably. By 1943, the real purchasing power of salaries was only about 20 per cent of the 1938 figures. This quite sudden and very considerable drop in purchasing power must have caused serious hardship. Gradually during the late 1940's

---

true Turk, but the revolutionary leaders, a bureaucratic and military class, found it difficult to get to grips with peasant problems. For the direction of administrative change see Gülgün Gönenç, *Türkiyede Âmme Hizmetinin Gelişmesi ve Devlet Personeli*, vol. 11 (Ankara, 1958).

[1] A publication by the Ministry of Finance is a useful source for figures on inflation, Maliye Bakanlığı, *Devlet Memurları Ücret Rejimi Hakkında Rapor* (Ankara, 1952). See also Gönenç, *Türkiyede Âmme Hizmetinin Gelişmesi.*

purchasing power crept up again, but in 1951 it only ranged from 33·8 per cent in the highest grade to 66·8 per cent in the lowest, of the purchasing power in 1938. The policy of reducing salary differentials between lowest and highest salaries meant that officials in the highest ranks were most affected. Between 1952 and 1957 purchasing power fell even further—to 31 per cent of the 1938 figures for the highest grade and to 57 per cent for the lowest. By 1961 officials generally were earning salaries worth about half their 1938 value. No wonder that higher grade officials on the *barême* scale sought to move into categories of public employ where remuneration was more flexible. They also appear to have moved into the public enterprises where salaries were often much higher. A 1951 survey also showed that higher civil servants were, even at that time, much less well-off financially than their counterparts in private enterprise.

The basic structure of the service became the chief preoccupation of students of the Turkish civil service during the period under review, but other changes of importance occurred during the period. For instance, 1930 saw a much needed clarification of the principles governing retirement and by 1949 all officials became eligible for pension. In 1936 the important Labour Law was passed which regulated relations between employers and employees and included the public service within its scope. Under this severe law officials were prohibited from forming trade unions and were denied the right to strike. By 1960 Turkish officials had real grievances, but no corporate means of obtaining redress. That they should mostly blame the Democrat Party government for their misfortunes was natural if not altogether just. We can see one set of reasons why, by and large, they welcomed the 1960 revolution.

PART II

The Course of Politics, 1961–5

CHAPTER IV

The First Coalition Government

We have seen how during 1961 the National Unity Committee bowed themselves off the Turkish political stage, not without some embarrassment and not without keeping a place for themselves in the wings as Senate life members.

The results of the elections of October 1961 were as follows:

TABLE 3

Grand National Assembly Election Results, 1961

Parties	Seats in Assembly	Prop. of Votes Cast %	Seats in Senate	Prop. of Votes Cast %
People's	173	37·6	36	36·7
Justice	158	34·8	70	34·8
R.P.N.	54	—	16	14·0
N.T.	65	—	28	13·7
Others	—	—	—	·8

It is obvious from the distribution of seats in the National Assembly that a coalition government was unavoidable. However, before a government could be formed the President of the Republic had to be chosen and this was the first task to which the new Grand National Assembly addressed itself on 26 October, the day of its first meeting. The decision on who was to be President was in fact decided before the 26th; but not without a flurry of excitement which set the tone for the future. It soon became apparent that certain members of the Justice Party preferred someone other than the former President of the N.U.C., Gürsel. They opted for a professor of Istanbul University, Ali Fuad Başgil, a man well known for his rightist views who had been closely acquainted with Menderes and Bayar. Professor Başgil, who was a member of the Senate, allowed his candidature to go forward, but he did not persist very long. After signs that the armed forces would not tolerate him as President he was obliged to withdraw and, moreover, resigned from the Senate. The affair was one indication of how matters were to develop, but it also brought up sharp the waverers, if not the extremists, in the Justice Party camp. Discussions between the army leaders and political parties subsequently resulted in a protocol signed by the parties in which the election of Gürsel to the Presidency was agreed upon.

After the election of Gürsel the next task was to form a government. After a period of intensive discussion among party leaders, İnönü was asked by the President to form a government on 11 November. It had become fairly clear during this period that the armed forces would not tolerate any coalition that would exclude the People's Party. The R.P.N.P. was disinclined to enter any coalition, especially one with the People's Party; the N.T.P. was fearful of the embrace of its big brother, the Justice Party, lest it should be absorbed into it. There was also serious concern lest a Justice Party/N.T.P. coalition should look very like a revival of the old Democrat Party, whose vote they had shared between them. To this the armed forces would object.

The most satisfactory coalition might perhaps have been between the People's Party and the N.T.P., but the leader of the N.T.P. declined. It was clear that such a coalition would allow the Justice Party to create a powerful image of itself as *the* Opposition Party—and romp away with the old Democrat Party vote. The alternative was, then, a coalition between the People's and Justice parties, which at first seemed unthinkable. However, it did satisfy the armed forces' hankering after a truly national coalition; and the Justice Party contained a large number of moderates who were prepared to forgo revenge. Whether the party would join was very touch and go. The Justice Party's parliamentary party divided equally and left the decision to the party executive, which in the end decided to join with the People's Party. Under İnönü as Prime Minister offices were divided equally between the two parties. The Chairman of the Justice Party, Gümüşpala, did not, however, take office. It was a move which left him freedom to manoeuvre later. Tactically the Justice Party had been quite successful; it was necessary for the party to keep out of the company of the two minor parties for a while, particularly the N.T.P.; solitary opposition would have suited the party best, but coalition with the People's Party was a passable substitute.

The seemingly strange coalition of People's and Justice parties was as close to a national coalition government as could be obtained. It survived until June 1962, when the government re-signed over disagreements on the question of an amnesty for those sentenced for political offences after the revolution. The amnesty question was the most persistent issue at dispute between the two parties forming the coalition; but they approached so close to an understanding on it, that it is doubtful whether this is the issue that really divided them. However, the amnesty question was the first major point of dispute to arise. It began to raise its head in early December when the parliamentary groups of both the Justice and N.T.P. parties discussed the matter with some heat. The Deputy Prime Minister, a Justice Party minister, ex-plained the government's attitude, which was that any proposal should emanate from the government; and that in three or four months' time such a proposal would come. A question for verbal reply in the Assembly was put down by a N.T.P. deputy, but otherwise the parties showed every sign of developing a united front on the matter and admitting that initiative should in fact come from the government. Yet however possible it might have been for the moderates in all parties to agree it was difficult to prevent the demands of the more extreme from creating reper-cussions outside the parliamentary circle. In a declaration on 14 December the Turkish National Students' Federation declared, 'We absolutely do not, and will not, accept that the guilty shall be pardoned.'[1] The students of the Law Faculty of Ankara University also rejected what now seemed a certain amnesty and used more extreme language. One 'natural' senator (formerly a member of the N.U.C.) put the military view in picturesque language. 'Some trees put forth their leaves too early thinking summer has come. Trees which are taken in like this are deprived, however, of the chance of producing fruit.' Although Gümüşpala accused the life senators of clouding the minds of youth, and some of the parties' youth organizations attacked the students for interfering in politics, there for the time being the matter rested. İnönü replied to the parliamentary question himself, making the now familiar points that the government had an amnesty in mind as a measure to heal old wounds, but that it was not a matter of first importance. Discussion of the matter would do more harm than good and the parties had agreed when signing their protocol in October that the amnesty could not be definitely promised; and

[1] *Cumhuriyet*, 15 December 1961.

they had agreed also not to use the amnesty question in a matter of political dispute. A joint meeting of the Justice Party's parliamentary and general executive committees agreed to let the matter rest—first round to the moderates.

This skirmish plainly showed how political forces were arranged. People's Party and Justice Party moderates were in control and enjoyed the tacit support of the armed forces; but within the Justice Party and to a lesser extent within the smaller parties there were elements who had little liking for the revolution and wanted to undo it. There are indications that a number of local party organizations prodded their representatives in this direction. On the other side, the students' organizations were the most ardent supporters of the revolution; but there were signs that the military as a whole was probably not prepared to be as extreme or uncompromising as the former members of the N.U.C. in the Senate.

In this situation the government was able to make a start on its governmental work. A certain amount of progress was made in getting through legislation to reform taxation and the difficult question of an increase in officials' salaries was taken up. Some governmental legislation, however, could hardly be anything but extremely contentious. There was general agreement among those of moderate views that some of the acts of the revolutionary government had gone too far, but to amend them was likely to offend extremists on one side or the other. For instance, the release of the fifty-five landowners from forced residence in the west and their return to their estates in the east taxed the magnanimity of the former N.U.C. members and led to strong protests from the students. The legislation allowing for the return of the 147 university teachers dismissed by the revolutionary government had to be carefully handled. İnönü exerted himself in stressing the innocence of the N.U.C. in the matter without being able to indicate who were the guilty!

Another matter which tested the strength of the spirit of cooperation and also had repercussions outside was the dispute which developed over the salary of deputies, senators and members of the government. The problem arose because, while the Constitution states that the salary of members of the Grand National Assembly should not exceed that of a government official's in the highest salary grade, the National Assembly's

Constitutional Commission interpreted salary to include extra-ordinary additions of various kinds made to certain civil servants. This enabled the Assembly's Finance Commission to recommend a higher salary for deputies and senators than that laid down for officials in the highest grade. Discussion in the Assembly became very heated. An element of tragi-comedy was introduced when two deputies announced that they did not have enough money to last the year out. When this was eagerly relayed by the press to the general populace ridicule took over. Mock appeals for members of parliament were held, and students went round with their hats. The prestige of parliament was hardly increased. This was dangerous at a time when belief in the efficiency of the democratic institutions was essential if a democratic system was going to be retained. It did not escape notice that most of those who advocated an increase were from the Justice Party and N.T.P. It is usually left-wing parties who press for more salaries, which suggests the move was intended to embarrass the government and discredit parliamentary work. If this was so the stunt was certainly successful.

The stir about salaries of members of parliament was over by the beginning of January 1962, but January was not without its incidents. It began to look as if the students were not all unshakeable devotees of Atatürk and the 1960 revolution. A group of right-wing students demonstrated in Istanbul, accusing certain liberal left-wing newspapers and periodicals of communism. Counter demonstrations were induced which led in Ankara on 13 January to several scuffles between 'reactionaries' and Atatürkists.

To this general disruption the affair of Nuri Beşer added its share. Nuri Beşer, a Justice Party deputy, made some very offensive and unprintable remarks about army officers and their wives in an Ankara night club. He was knocked down in the club, but this was not enough as it is an offence under Turkish law to insult the armed forces. He had subsequently to face trial, his parliamentary immunity having been quickly removed by the National Assembly. The affair left Ankara talking for a day and provided another opportunity for the students' organizations (and the Federation of Turkish Women) to convey to the army their respects and sympathy. Although the Justice Party did not defend Beşer, and indeed expelled him from the party, some Justice

Party members raised their voices on his behalf. In this lowering atmosphere İnönü visited Istanbul in order to learn at first hand the feeling of different classes in the capital, and did not neglect the army in this research tour.

In the National Assembly friction easily developed into violence if the honour of the military was at all sullied. But other problems also arose to disturb the peace. One of the most trying of the government's problems was what do do about the High Investigatory Council and the High Council of Justice which had, respectively, prepared and tried cases against the members of the former regime. All those in office on 27 May 1960 had long been investigated and tried; and those convicted were serving sentences in jail in Kayseri, but investigations into ministers and officials previously in office were still continuing. Whilst on the one hand some politicians were demanding immediate amnesty for those already imprisoned, on the other often quite important personages of the former regime were being arrested and committed for trial. It was a very odd and contradictory situation which was not improved by the right of the High Investigatory Commission to make arrests without declaring the reason. For instance, on 13 February orders went out for the arrest of three former Democrat Party Ministers. The next day six other persons were arrested, one of whom was another former minister. The Constitutional Commission of the National Assembly, under a Justice Party chairman, refused to recognize the legality of the High Investigatory Commission and the High Council of Justice —an attitude which prevented the Commission from considering government draft legislation which sought to modify the High Investigating Council's powers of arrest. A deadlock resulted that was broken only by a great deal of heart-searching by the Justice Party and resulted in their expelling the offending chairman of the Constitutional Commission. After this it proved possible for the government to get through legislation preventing automatic arrest by the High Investigatory Council.

By this time hope had been given up of creating national political stability. Every minor squabble seemed to lead to a storm liable to destroy the coalition. Consequently during January and February of 1962 it became necessary for the President and the moderate politicians to appeal again and again for some degree of political unity that would enable more attention to be given to the country's social and political problems, which were very grave. The late autumn of 1961 saw near famine conditions in the eastern provinces, whilst under the guarantee of the constitution now a number of strikes occurred, a novel and rather alarming experience for Turkey. More important than the right to strike however, was the opportunity to work; and political instability did not encourage a high level of economic activity. Yet the response of the parties to calls for political moderation and unity was generally good, if short-lived. The Justice and New Turkey parties, where the extremists were most prominent, made real efforts to tighten up their discipline, to the point of expelling or threatening to expel extremist members. In the Justice Party a very real conflict developed between the party's executive committee and the less tractable parliamentary groups.

On 21 February the National Assembly approved the National Defence budget. Members of all parties, including the spokesman of the Justice Party, avidly seized the opportunity to express undying devotion to the armed forces. This was not so much a straw in the wind as a hayrick. Since October the armed forces had had to stomach a crescendo of insinuations and criticisms of their revolution. They had witnessed the annulment of many measures passed during the period of military rule, attacks on the judicial institutions they had set up, slights on their honour and efforts to get an early pardon for those so roundly condemned but twelve weeks previously. Some lost all patience. The late afternoon of 22 February the tank battalion of the Armoured Forces' School, supported by a few other units including some from the Presidential Guard regiment, began a movement under the direction of the officers of the War School, among whom was the Commandant of the War School, Colonel Talât Aydemir. They threatened the government with military action unless, according to newspaper reports, two hundred members of parliament were dismissed and the Grand National Assembly dissolved.

The military movement failed for a number of reasons. First the attempt to capture the government failed. On the afternoon of 22 February the Council of Ministers and the President were meeting in the President's residence. They could easily have been held there by the Presidential Guard. The loyalty of that unit, however, to the military movement did not rise to the occasion. It was broken, largely it seems, by the courageous action of a major commanding the mounted troop. The government was thus able to take shelter with the air force. The second reason for the failure was the immediate and very resolute support of İnönü by the air force, under İrfan Tansel. This would have made it extremely perilous for the bulk of the army to support the revolutionaries, if they had wanted to do so. (The attitude of the army command was not clear.) This situation helped to reinforce the very firm attitude taken by İnönü, who played for time in discussion with the leader of the military movement, while not conceding their demands. Finally, on both sides there was extreme reluctance to spill blood. An undertaking by İnönü that no action beyond retirement and re-posting would be taken against the insurgents if they surrendered also encouraged the less enthusiastic units to fall away. When this happened the confidence of the leaders of the movement declined and they surrendered. In less than twelve hours it was all over; and İnönü was given a great reception in the National Assembly. A successful coup against a tough and wily former general who is also a military (and national) hero must always be very difficult to achieve. From the fact that the fire was extinguished so quickly, it should not be too hastily assumed that it was only a small blaze. That it had a real chance of spreading was evident from the fact that the C.-in-C. Land Forces resigned the day after the event. (It was reported he claimed to have knowledge of the affair before it happened.)[1] The Ministry of Defence in a statement on 3 April said that sixty-nine officers had been retired in connection with the affair of 22 February, but that no further retirements would be made.

What difference did the military movement make to Turkish politics? In the short term its effect was to make the government stronger, but in the longer term, rather oddly, it seemed to have left the government weaker.

Anxious to mollify the armed forces and in recognition of their support, the leaders of the parties announced jointly that draft legislation would be brought to the Grand National Assembly without delay to prevent any sort of attack on the legitimacy of the 1960 revolution and the new constitution. Their joint declaration soon crystallized into a law which made it an offence to attack the legitimacy of the revolution, the legal decisions of the revolutionary period, or to praise those convicted during that period

[1] *Cumhuriyet*, 25 February 1962.

for their crimes. Nor was it permissible to commend the former Democrat Party, nor to claim that any party was its successor. Propaganda which belittled the democratic system in Turkey or claimed that democracy would not work in Turkey was also not to be permitted; but more than this, no activity or propaganda that would give rise to, or further incite, feelings of enmity was to be allowed. Wide interpretation was clearly possible and maximum penalties ranged from two to five years. Although all party leaders supported the law, if not all with marked enthusiasm, there were those in all parties who did not continue to do so as the effect of attempted coup wore off. The occasion lent itself to the expression of liberal objections of the purest sort, though not in every camp from the purest liberal quarters. If the 1960 revolution saved democracy, it now began to look as if democracy had to save the revolution. The most common view was that this legal prohibition could not solve anything; but this sort of view is not as realistic as it sounds—if only because a Turkish prison is quite a deterrent and slack enforcement of the criminal code not common. What was more realistic to argue was that all that had been done was to cork the bottle; and it could be claimed that this forced the extremists in the Justice Party to make a bid for control of the party, and so eventually to break the coalition with the People's Party.

In any event the pill was made more bitter for the rightists to swallow by the continuing activities of the High Investigatory Council, deprived though it now was of the power of automatic arrest; and by the opening of investigations by parliament into alleged misdeeds of certain members when they held office before the revolution. Yet it was not those on the right who had every occasion to complain, for an ugly controversy began to occupy the fore-front of attention during March 1962, which seriously perturbed not only those concerned with social justice, but all those concerned with the health of the Turkish state. This was the affair of the Sub-Provincial Governor (*Kaymakam*), Mehmet Can.

Mehmet Can was one of forty-nine sub-provincial governors reposted on 29 March, for, it was said, the normal reasons of promotion, seniority, health, and so on. Mehmet Can's case, it soon appeared, was not, however, regarded as normal by everybody, including many of the inhabitants of Kadirli, the administrative centre of Mehmet Can's district. They voiced their protest to the Ministry of the Interior and followed it up with a delegation to Ankara to see İnönü and Gürsel. The students of the School of Political Science, Ankara University, lent their support to Can, a former student, in a declaration which stressed their anxiety at what appeared to be the core of the matter, namely that those in the highest government posts should be influenced by illegitimate local pressures. The students' protest was of more than general importance because the main source of recruitment for the higher provincial governmental service is the School of Political Science. The gist of the complaint against Mehmet Can's transfer was that it was arranged because he had pushed through a number of developments of various sorts in Kadirli in which he had fallen foul of some of the richer and more influential landowners.[1] The Ministry of the Interior, on the other hand, claimed that his transfer was in accordance with the regime imposed by the revolutionary government, that all provincial subgovernors should spend part of their service in primitive parts of the country. The position was complicated by the fact that relatives of the Minister were involved in the group of landowners who wanted the *kaymakam*'s removal. One People's Party deputy was also closely involved on the side of the landowners. It was a classic case of the frustration of the modernizer by local established interests. The People's Party's coalition government with the Justice Party gave the impression it was prepared to defer to traditionalism. Thenceforth the more Atatürkist and socialist elements in the People's Party wanted to break the coalition. This sort of compromise left them disillusioned with their own leaders.

In playing down this incident the government was anxious of course not to arouse issues that could further upset governmental stability. That was now rocked, however, by a revival of the amnesty question.

The amnesty question reappeared when the government introduced legislation to prevent any legal action being taken against those involved in events of 22 February, this being in accord with its promise to the insurgents that if they surrendered they would not be prosecuted. On 5 April, however, the day following the appointment of a new executive committee of the

---

[1] This is a rough rendering of the word *ağa*. Most peasants in a village would own land. The *ağas* are the richest and most respected landowners.

Justice Party, the party leader Gümüşpala announced he could not sign the draft law for the absolution of those involved in the military movement unless it was extended to include all those who had offended against the Constitution, namely those condemned at Yassıada.

So the challenge was thrown down once again. After a tour of army units the Minister of Defence declared that politicians who sought an amnesty would learn without doubt that an amnesty was a dream; and everyone took it he was expressing not just his own, but also the view of all the armed forces. Members of the Justice Party resented such strong language and so the political temperature rose once more, the students again not neglecting to make their views known. By the time it came for the government's draft legislation to be brought to the National Assembly near crisis conditions had been reached. The Justice Party was by now coming much more under the control of the extremists; and in both the Justice Party and the People's Party there was talk of breaking up the coalition. However, the Justice Party decided on 21 April to support the government's legislation, the majority in favour in its executive committee being surprisingly large considering how near the brink the party had gone.

By early May it appeared all parties had agreed on the principle of amnesty by stages. This was something, but it proved not to be enough for agreement. The Justice Party would not give a really firm undertaking that it would leave the date for an amnesty to the government. Yet it was sufficient for the moment to encourage the People's Party to stay in office; and it gave the Justice Party the chance to bring the matter before a meeting of party provincial chairmen on 20–21 May.

The differences between the two parties were in fact not so very considerable. The essence of the government's view (and the Justice Party ministers subscribed to this) was that, while the time of an amnesty should be left to the government, if pressed it would undertake a first stage by the end of October 1962. The Justice Party essentially wanted the first stage before the parliamentary summer vacation, and a second and final stage releasing all remaining prisoners in November 1962. An attempt by moderate members of the Justice Party to get a compromise solution—to which the government expressed agreement—was

F

unsuccessful, and this because the moderates failed to carry the party. The end came when, on 29 May, the National Assembly group of the Justice Party rejected a proposal close to the government's ideas and instead repeated the Justice Party's basic proposal for settling the pardon question before the parliamentary summer recess. Seeing that there was no hope for agreement the government resigned. It had lasted just over six months.

The first and not unexpected result of the resignation was to split the Justice Party. In the cause of political stability this could have been a powerful stroke. The question was would the moderates now be able to show how right they were and finally quell the extremists? For a few days the battle waged fierce within the Justice Party, and ninety-two Justice Party senators and deputies demanded the resignation not only of Gümüşpala (now regarded as thoroughly influenced by the right wing) but also of the party's executive committee and the executive committee of the National Assembly group. If these demands were not met, they threatened to resign from the party and seek coalition with the People's Party. In the face of this very serious threat, judging rightly that time was on their side, the rightists in the National Assembly group used the tactic of not attending group meetings in order to prevent there being a quorum. On 6 June, the party executive committee resigned, the moderates having persuaded the founder members of the party to appoint a new executive. Yet even this new executive turned out to be unsympathetic to the moderates, who finally gave up hope after the congress of party provincial chairmen condoned the action of Gümüşpala and the rightists; indeed, the moderates were hardly given an opportunity to present their case. Apart from some subsequent rowing in the party group of the National Assembly it was all over; and resignations of moderates from the Justice Party began.

The party whose unity was now put to the test was the R.P.N.P. Its leader, Bölükbaşı, now led twenty-nine of its seventy parliamentary members out to form a new party, the Nation Party, because the rest of the R.P.N.P. was prepared to enter into a coalition with the People's Party. The New Turkey Party, which had experienced great difficulty, but had shown much resolution and success in controlling its rightists during the life of the first coalition government, not surprisingly weathered the June storms best of all.

In this atmosphere İnönü was entrusted by the President with the task of forming another government. The parliamentary party of the People's Party agreed that they should form part of another government and left İnönü with full authority to go ahead in his efforts to do so.

The only possible combination seemed to be with the N.T.P. and the R.P.N.P., but one of the worries of the People's Party was whether a coalition with these two parties would stay the course. Defections from them could easily lead to the overthrow of a coalition. Consequently the People's Party was anxious to include in any such coalition as many 'independents' as they could. As to differences of view between the People's Party, the N.T.P., and the R.P.N.P., they did not seem so great as to prevent broad agreement and all seemed set fair for a new coalition government to emerge when negotiations unexpectedly broke down. The snag seemed at first nothing to do with principles or policies in definite matters. The dispute was that the N.T.P. wanted to have the Ministry of the Interior and they objected to a third deputy prime minister from the People's Party (in addition to one each from the N.T.P. and the R.P.N.P.). The question involved in their objection to a People's Party Minister of the Interior was clear enough; it was the fear that the People's Party (which must still live down its record for oppressive administration in the period of one-party rule) would use the apparatus of internal government for illegitimate ends. İnönü objected strongly to the mentality underlying such views. The second point was a little more subtle, and more to do with principle. If there were a third deputy prime minister from the People's Party he could be charged to look after the State Planning Organization. Otherwise the task would fall to Ekrem Alican, leader of the N.T.P. whose views were anything but etatist—as the People's Party well knew.

With the collapse of negotiations gloom descended. The Justice Party seemed to be preparing itself off stage for a grand re-entry, while the most pessimistic fancied they heard the sound of a none-too-distant drum. Then it appeared that Gürsel had not accepted İnönü's resignation and he was to try again. This time he succeeded quickly. The N.T.P. agreed that the People's Party should have the Ministry of the Interior and a deputy prime minister, but—and this was the concession the People's Party had to grant—Alican, as one of the three deputy prime ministers, would be given responsibility for economic and financial matters —in a word for planning. The new government was formed on 25 June. The process had taken nearly a month.

There are indications to suggest that a coalition with the N.T.P. and R.P.N.P. was not at first encouraged by many of the People's Party. It was generally expected that there would have been some seventy to eighty resignations of moderates from the Justice Party; and that with their support a strong government could have been formed in which the initiative would have remained with the People's Party. In this event it would probably not have been necessary for the party to lose any control of the planning organization. As it happened, very few resigned from the Justice Party.

In review, what can be said of this apparently crucial testing period for Turkish democracy? Was it a failure? Did it give the lie to those who thought that a new constitution and the new device of proportional representation would save democracy?

The first point about this six-month period of trial was that it was very unusual by any nation's experience. The alliance of the Justice and People's Parties was its most surprising feature. Partly convenience, particularly for the Justice Party, it was in effect that most interesting of experiments, a coalition of moderates of the two major political parties in the contest for power. As might be expected, the moderates from both sides managed to co-operate quite well; and there is every reason to believe they could have provided effective and positive government that would have satisfied that most watchful of all spectators, the military. Indeed the army—and particularly the air force— prevented the attempted coup of 22 February. In this respect the coalition was broadly a success. Yet this very success convinced some of the right wing extremists that the events of 22 February were a great bluff and that the armed forces would never intervene again. Thus they became more intransigent.

The trouble really lay in the wings of each of the major parties and particularly in the Justice Party. It was a very difficult political situation. Initial fear of the military made a coalition of moderates inevitable. Yet the gathering strength of the more extreme elements in the two parties made the coalition unworkable.

One of the great merits of this short, passionate and very crucial period in Turkish politics was that its high emotional tensions did sort out the moderates from the extremists in the minor parties and could therefore provide the People's Party's moderate leadership with possible groups for another coalition. It is to the next coalition that we now turn.

CHAPTER V

The Second Coalition

On the morning of 25 June 1962 the first coalition government held its last cabinet meeting. After the meeting İnönü gave the former members of the government a farewell lunch in a nearby restaurant; and then hastened to preside over the first cabinet meeting of the new government, of whose twenty-two members, including İnönü, eight had been members of the first coalition government. A measure of continuity was therefore preserved.[1]

On 7 July İnönü presented his new government's programme to the National Assembly and obtained the expected vote of confidence. The Justice Party and the new Nation Party voted against the government. Of the now eighteen independents twelve supported the coalition. The government in sum obtained a sufficient majority, one which compared quite favourably with that of the first coalition.[2]

The vote in favour of the coalition was not, however, achieved with the ease which a bare recital of the facts might suggest. All trouble was not over when the participating parties had settled their differences about which party should hold which posts. The parties had to get the coalition's programme approved by their parliamentary groups; and for the People's Party in particular this proved quite troublesome. Within that party's parliamentary party a group sixty-three strong emerged which saw the new coalition with the 'rightish' minor parties as a betrayal of principles of 27 May and of social justice.[3] Nearly half of these sixty-three in fact voted against the coalition in the parliamentary group, although they did not carry their dissatisfaction so far as to vote against the coalition in the National Assembly. This 'revolt' was sparked off by the publication by the three coalition

[1] İnönü dropped three former People's Party ministers and appointed four new ministers from his party. The government was made up as follows: People's Party 12, N.T.P. 6, R.P.N.P. 4, Independents 1.

[2] See *Cumhuriyet*, 8 July 1962, for details.

[3] The group was made up of senators and deputies. In the parliamentary groups' meeting referred to (which comprised deputies and senators) twenty-nine of the thirty-one who voted against the coalition were deputies.

parties of a protocol containing the basic principles of the government programme. A large minority group in the party obviously would have preferred not to participate in a government with other parties. They would have preferred to remain in opposition until such time as new elections should bring them fully into power. To do so, however, would perhaps have encouraged a recurrence of military intervention, since the Justice Party, with its provocative extremist wing, was as yet unacceptable to the armed forces. So the argument of political responsibility weighed heavily against the People's Party.

The features of the coalition bargain which most irritated this left-wing People's Party minority were as follows. First there was the agreement not to use the Declaration of Wealth as a basis for taxation for 1961, but to return unopened the declarations already made. It was laid down, however, that these (highly unpopular) declarations of wealth which are used, with dubious effectiveness, as a basis for taxing middle-class businessmen, would be employed in subsequent years. Secondly, the understanding that private and public enterprise would march along together and that the state would not interfere with private enterprise also seriously disturbed the etatist-minded left wing. The programme envisaged that the state would assist private enterprise by the formation of a capital market and by the provision of technical assistance. It is interesting that these matters disturbed the People's Party minority more than did the agreement on the amnesty.

These errors of commission were, however, only part of the complaint. There were the alleged errors of omission as well. For instance, there was no firm agreement on the character of land reform, merely a general agreement that it was of first importance. Nor was there any mention of recreating the village institutes that Atatürk himself had set up, nor of plans for village self-development, nor any details of the means to be taken to preserve forests (a major problem in Turkey). There was only general reference to the problem of the general decline in the use of the railway system, in which so much capital had been sunk; and not least, there was no agreement on taxation policy. The untaxed farmers might get away with it still. The protocol and the government's programme in no way amounted to a programme of revolutionary action which subjected private gain to the test of public good. What was left, it was asked, of 27 May?

The majority of the party followed İnönü's arguments for realism; and in the end the objectors gave their support in the Assembly. They acquiesced in what was after all the mixture as before, a coalition of moderates, but with the difference this time that the moderates in the parties in coalition with the People's Party were not hampered by a strong right wing. This could make it possible for this second coalition of moderates really to carry out positive policies of economic and social development. One chief complaint against the first coalition had been not that it did the wrong things; but that it did nothing of any importance for the future of the country. A new hope stirred.

This very guarded optimism began to show some beneficial effects. Steps were taken to provide the chairman of the Assembly with more powers to discipline unruly members, as a result of quarrels and near fights in the Assembly between deputies at the time of the debate on the government's programme. More important, the fourteen exiled former members of the National Unity Committee decided at a meeting in Brussels at the end of July to go their separate ways; and the political pundits envisaged the entry of about half of them into politics when, in November, they would be free to return to Turkey, as the most likely outcome of the business. Rumours of possible collusion between the fourteen and the instigators of the attempted coup of 22 February went the rounds; but ex-Colonel, and ex-Commandant of the War School, Talât Aydemir, was very careful to deny all such suggestions. Altogether the new government of moderates was no more popular on the left than on the right; but after a shaky start the government appeared strong enough certainly to undermine the confidence of extremist opponents of the democratic system itself.

The confidence of extremist opponents *within* the system was affected but little. At summer provincial congresses the rightists of the Justice Party received much applause. The two general principles around which the party seemed to revolve were hatred of İnönü and an immediate and full amnesty. There were signs that the moderates were not routed, but for the present they took a back seat. The party was very active in publicizing the alleged evil acts of its opponents, but this seemed to sap energies that might have gone into forming a coherent opposition policy. The party's opposition at this stage was primitive and not at all constructive. Much the same can be said of the Nation Party under Bölükbaşı. The government, on the other hand, realized that a programme of action was urgently necessary.

The State Personnel Office now presented its awaited report on the Turkish public service to the Council of Ministers. The Council also agreed on the draft legislation on strikes and lock-outs. Some details were worked out of the proposed law on local elections; and the Minister of State in charge of religious affairs announced a scheme of training in provincial centres for *imams* (prayer leaders) and other persons performing religious duties, and a promise of better pay. The Minister of Finance outlined a proposed new scheme of income tax, which included *inter alia* a tax on agricultural profits, although the exemption limits were generous. Again this was the product of coalition compromise; but here another factor began to enter into the situation—the views, strongly held, of the planners of the State Planning Organization. There were reports of disagreements between the planners and the government on where and how the money was to be found for the investment necessary for a 7 per cent growth rate. Certainly the Planning Organization was perturbed by the Ministry of Finance's announcement of the new principles of taxation and it might appear to the general public that the Planning Organization approved the Finance Minister's proposals. The State Planning Organization was indeed ordained by the Constitution; and more important perhaps, was looked upon with considerable favour by the armed forces who had set it up after the revolution. Yet its members were appointed by the government, to whom they were responsible. It was as yet, however, too early for a show-down.

The Turkish Grand National Assembly reassembled on 5 September 1962 for a session regarded by many as crucial for democracy in Turkey. Could, and would, parliament provide and support a government that could heal old wounds and still do something positive for Turkey's future development? If this attempt to achieve development under democracy failed, there might well not be another chance.

At first the wind seemed set fair. The Justice Party showed a certain amount of moderation by not supporting those motions moved by its own more extreme members, including one for an immediate pardon for all political prisoners.

The coalition seemed strong enough; so much so that in early September the government was able to weather the storm produced when the N.T.P. voted against it in the Assembly on whether investigations should be opened into the case of a former Democrat Party Minister. At least the N.T.P. members of the government did their best to persuade their followers to fall in line. Of course, the coalition was difficult for the N.T.P., some of whose members had correctly perceived that by joining with the People's Party they were handing over the inheritance of the Democrat Party to the Justice Party.[1]

The programmes of action which the government had promised were begun in a not too forbidding atmosphere, and even although a succession of storms developed the legislative work went steadily on, thanks to the steadiness of the government. The Five Year Plan was announced (8 September) and was through the Assembly by the end of the year. Laws regulating trade unions, collective bargaining, lock-outs, strikes, meetings and processions were pushed through most of their stages and without suffering a great deal of amendment.[2] A good, though belated, start was made on a new law governing political parties and on a local election law, made necessary by the new Constitution. The principles of the new Land Law, a moderate measure as expected, were released in May 1963. Activity in the cause of administrative reform was evident when the government accepted (12 April) the principles to govern the reorganization of the personnel system, and received (7 May 1963) the report of the Commission set up to examine the distribution of functions in the Turkish central administration. The legislative and administrative record of the second coalition cannot be said to have been a bad one in circumstances that soon became less propitious. After a while governmental activity was carried on against a

[1] The N.T.P. and Justice Party were at this time vying for the support of the landowners of the eastern provinces exiled to the west at the time of the revolution who were now allowed to return to their lands. They were warmly welcomed back by local organizers of both parties.

[2] It was sometimes difficult to obtain a quorum in the National Assembly for the discussion and enactment of weighty topics such as these. The press was not slow to notice the disinclination of many members to devote their energies to these exacting tasks.

background of disturbances, many of so important a character as to make it a matter of wonder that any constructive government at all could have been carried on. The disturbed atmosphere resulted from a series of major and minor crises.

The crisis which was most fundamentally linked with the government's programme was that which occurred over planning. In September 1962 the Under-Secretary (*Müsteşar*) of the Planning Organization and the heads of the three basic departments of Economic Planning, Social Planning and Co-ordination resigned; since they persisted in their resignations they were accepted by İnönü, who professed to be baffled at their reasons for resigning. The basic dispute was that the planners were not prepared to accept changes in the internal financing of the plan. They had no confidence in the existing taxation system as a means of providing the necessary internal financing. Consequently if the plan was to be viable, they felt it was part of their job to amend the taxation system. The government, on the other hand, was very certain that this was its own job; and the text of the law establishing the State Planning Organization certainly does not make the Organization anything but advisory. Moreover, decisions on which parts of the community shall pay tax, or the proportion of taxation they were to contribute, are everywhere—and not least in Turkey—political questions of the first importance. The planners could easily be shown to be in the wrong; they had simply offended against the 'morality' of the democratic system, which assumes that the holders of political power represent the will of the majority and that public servants therefore have no contribution to make, in this regard. Yet the planners merit some sympathy. Are they to be expected to stand by and take some responsibility for the plan when they think it will fall down by reason of what, in their expert view, are inadequate and unsatisfactory modes of internal financing? This last point was made very clearly, albeit without the political overtones which are, in practice, difficult to avoid, by the new head of the Economic Planning department appointed by the government when he, too, resigned at the end of January 1963, after only a few months in office.[1]

[1] In his letter of resignation the Head of the Economic Planning Department, Dr Atilla Sönmez, points to disagreements in the administrative, not political plane. He resigned because, as he said, the 1963 economic plan was

The troubles concerning the State Planning Organization largely coincided with troubles which emanated from the amnesty question. During September 1962 the government coalition parties agreed on going ahead with a partial amnesty which would release some 180 of those convicted at Yassıada, the necessary legislation being introduced on 8 October. The timing of this partial amnesty—coincided—unavoidably since delay was not possible—with the anniversary of the handing out of the Yassıada sentences, which included of course, the hanging of Menderes, Zorlu and Polatkan. A small number of right-wing newspapers recalled the events of September 1960 by articles and photographs which offended against the law passed after the abortive coup of 22 February 1962, protecting the revolution against attacks of all sorts. The editor of one newspaper, *Zafer*, was arrested and others questioned. The following day saw fisticuffs in the Senate during the discussion of a law passed by the lower House to pay state pensions to those convicted at Yassıada. The indignation of some senators, notably those who were former members of the N.U.C., could not be contained. In a declaration these 'natural senators' reaffirmed the legitimacy of the revolution. The army was put in a state of readiness and the students' organizations announced once again their determination to defend the revolution and their impatience with democracy, at least of the local variety. Called to its duty by the students the government declined, however, to allow itself to be hustled into extreme action, even when street demonstrations, which, it seems, were instigated by small right-wing groups, led to some ugly scenes, including attacks on the Justice Party and some right-wing newspaper offices. İnönü was also criticized within his own party for his weak handling of the affair, but the policy adopted was firm enough to preserve the government (and democracy).[1] Alarmed by the

---

being made to fit the budget, and not the budget to fit the plan. The basic practical point was that the government insisted on inserting into the plan for 1963 the Ministry of Finance estimates of revenue which the planners thought very optimistic. (Text of letter of resignation in *Cumhuriyet* 1 February 1963.)

[1] Most commentators saw the disturbances as the result of a rightist plot to create chaos and thus discredit the government. The role of the Justice Party is not very clear. Their leader Ragıp Gümüşpala reproved the right-wing newspapers, but he allowed mass party meetings to be held in Adana, Izmir and Balıkesir which were interpreted as a means of increasing the

force of the reaction against the rightists, the Justice Party found a moderate voice with which to join with the other parties, on 11 October, in reaffirming their support for the revolution. The next day the partial amnesty law was passed by the lower house, only five members voting against. On 18 October, the release of the 280 prisoners began. (Surely the agitation against the revolution would now decline.)

The events next to have some impact on the political scene were the annual congresses of the two major political parties—for the Justice Party its first. At the Justice Party's Congress, which began on 30 November, the air was thick with demands for an immediate general amnesty (which would release remaining prisoners convicted at Yassıada), criticism of the People's Party and also of those responsible for the attempted February coup. It was during this congress that the Commander of the Air Force, İrfan Tansel, gave obligatory leave to four generals and seven colonels, the official reasons being that they were in disagreement with Tansel on certain matters. The officers in question then resigned. Exactly what was at stake is obscure, but Tansel stated that there were political connections and Talât Aydemir asserted that one natural senator had been in touch with the officers. The general view is that the affair was political. If this is so it is tempting to see it as a reaction to the disturbances in general and to the hostility shown to the armed forces and the revolution. This hostility was evident, at the Justice Party Congress, where, moreover, the election of the party's executive committee had resulted in defeat for the moderates.

The generally troubled atmosphere at the Justice Party Congress did not bode well for successful democracy. In any event, it might be said, the People's Party would not founder. Yet in early December the temperature also ran high even there when the party sought to expel four noted older personalities as a result of their having voted against the partial amnesty in the Assembly. The three most notable were expelled for a year from the party. Not unnaturally this was a provocative prelude to the General Congress where unsavoury quarrels resulted. In the general estimate the prospects for democracy declined a little further.

---

general disturbance. Probably he could not prevent these meetings from being held.

All this was as nothing, however, compared with the events which followed. First the Justice Party in February 1963 renewed its demand for a general pardon on grounds of political stability. The government refused the request protesting that it was those intent on revenge who upset political stability. This exchange was enough to keep the pot boiling until at the end of March it boiled over once again. The former President during the Democrat Party regime, Celal Bayar, who of all the persons convicted at Yassıada had successfully maintained his contempt for the revolution, was released from prison for six months for medical treatment. Unlike the other former politicians released in October 1962, Celal Bayar did not sensibly efface himself from the political scene. His unrepentant attitude, which included a visit to the Atatürk mausoleum and criticism of the Yassıada decisions, soon aroused demonstrations against him and all he stood for. During the demonstrations Bayar was soon confined to hospital where, after a half-hearted attempt at a hunger strike, he did not cause any further trouble.

Accused so often of weakness, the government held a general discussion of the events in the National Assembly, where to a crowded house and packed gallery the Justice Party was accused by the government of fomenting the disturbances. Moreover, enquiries were begun into the cases of ten Justice Party deputies for offences against the law protecting the revolution from attack; with the result that the National Assembly was asked to lift their parliamentary immunity. For technical reasons to do with the time of their alleged offences it was only possible to proceed further in the case of one Justice Party deputy, Özarda. The Justice and Constitutional Commissions of the Assembly, required to meet jointly in such cases, decided to remove Özarda's immunity, the government using its majority. When the Joint Commission's recommendation came to the Assembly, however, the government lost by ten votes. Although some Justice Party deputies did not attend, the 121 who did voted against the Commission's recommendations. Some N.T.P. and R.P.N.P. deputies also voted against the motion.

The crux of the matter was not the principle of parliamentary immunity; there was hardly any argument about the principle. What was at stake was whether the political parties, particularly the Justice Party, and to a lesser extent the R.P.N.P. and N.T.P., were prepared to surrender Özarda to the judicial authorities as proof, as it were, of their approval of the revolution and the armed forces who made it. Surrender of Özarda would have been a gesture, almost a symbol of the politicians' acceptance of the armed forces; and proof that it really was a crime for anyone to attack the democratic regime in which the army, having re-established it, wanted to believe.

The day after the voting on Özarda, İnönü announced (14 May) that the situation was 'very grave' and had discussions with Gürsel and the Chief of the General Staff, Cevdet Sunay. He told the parliamentary group of his party to be prepared for elections; and called back hurriedly from Erzurum the head of the N.T.P., Alican.

The general expectation was that a military *emeute* was imminent; and this was not unnatural since on 23 April ten officers had been arrested in Istanbul who called themselves the 'Young Kemalist Officers'. They were charged with distributing documents inciting to rebellion and with forming a secret society. The centres of the activity were the naval and military schools in Istanbul.

By the time of İnönü's warnings this particular movement had, however, been snuffed out, though the tension remained high for a few days, during which one natural senator suggested a 'legal revolution' with İnönü as a Turkish General de Gaulle.[1] To some extent İnönü had to eat his words by explaining his serious warnings related to the state of the coalition; but there was really no need to backpedal, for on 21 May, Ankara awoke to gunfire.

The details of the events of 20–21 May need not concern us much. The centre and only real participant in the attempted coup was the War School in Ankara. Their former Commander, ex-Colonel Talât Adyemir, donned his uniform once more to lead the cadets. The Ankara wireless transmitting station was at once occupied by the cadets; but government forces soon restored order, though not before six loyal troops and two cadets were killed.

It was a bloody affair in comparison with that of the previous year, yet it was less important. Consequently, the punishments meted out could be greater; and this was really a sign that so far

---

[1] The senator was Mucip Atakli who, according to Talât Aydemir, was closely connected with the eleven Air Force officers who in December 1962 were given forced leave and subsequently resigned from the Air Force.

as the military threat went the regime had grown in strength. Nevertheless the government now imposed martial law in Ankara, Istanbul and Izmir, one result of which was that newspapers had to be careful what they printed. Some of them were prevented from publication for short periods.

Those accused of participation in the coup were tried by military courts, of which one confined itself to the trial of the War School cadets. Of the 1459 War School cadets tried only seventy-five received substantial prison sentences (four years two months each). Of the remainder, ninety-three received a sentence of three months; the rest were declared innocent. It was a different matter for the other suspects, of whom there were 106. They were described in fierce tones by the public prosecutor as having stabbed the Turkish nation in the back and as having tried to overthrow the Atatürk Republic. The sentences demanded (including twenty-eight death penalties) were heavy. The Court's verdict was not equally severe but included seven death penalties, and twenty-nine sentences of life imprisonment. About half of the remaining sentences were from four to five years. Included in those freed from suspicion was Alparslan Türkeş, the erstwhile leader of the fourteen members expelled in 1960 from the National Unity Committee. The sentences were subject to appeal, the final result of which was that only two, Talât Aydemir and Fethi Gürcan, were executed.

Under the protective umbrella of martial law in Ankara, Istanbul and Izmir—which prevented any public discussion of the trials—the army put itself to rights.[1] The trials therefore passed remarkably quietly, but they had two rather surprising repercussions. First, they led to further arrests and trials,[2] which included that of a distinguished woman medical scientist, in the field of cancer research, Dr Perihan Cambel, who was sentenced to three years' suspension from public service. Among the most

---

[1] One of the measures taken was to revise the organization of the Cadet War School. The political education of the Army was to be given needed attention. It now became possible for the War School to employ university teachers, a very revealing development.

[2] İnönü on 22 August 1963 announced that they were seventeen in number. They were said to be of persons of the extreme left wing who wanted to save those accused in the trials. See Sancar's statement, 19 August 1963, in the Ministry of the National Assembly for that day. *Cumhuriyet* 20 August 1963.

respected persons in Turkey are distinguished women eminent
in public service. They are very few; they are living symbols
almost of the Atatürk revolution.

The second repercussion was on the People's Party. As we have
seen, that bastion of Turkish stability had its troubles with a vocal
opposition which included prominent men like Kasım Gülek
and Nihat Erim. It now emerged from the trials that some members of the party had had connections with those being tried for
the events of 21 May. İnönü made it clear the party was not
prepared to tolerate such adventurers; the three deputies involved were sent up to the Party's Court of Honour (responsible
for questions of discipline) by the Party's Council with the recommendation for expulsion. The occasion was seized to recommend
the expulsion of Kasım Gülek, Nihat Erim and Turgut Göle.[1]
The proceedings dragged slowly on.

Despite the military trials, the arrests, the crisis in the People's
Party, drastic ministerial changes, and a few other disturbing
events besides, the main political interest of the period now became the crucial one of maintaining the coalition in existence. The
trouble lay in the relations between the People's Party and the
N.T.P. The third party, the R.P.N.P., managed to share in office
without great strain—the effect, no doubt, of the hiving off of its
former leader, Bölükbaşı and its less co-operative members, to
form the Nation Party.

There is no question that the N.T.P. tried hard to make a go of
the coalition. That is really to say that the party leadership under
Alican was firmly in favour of the coalition and the party's leaders
did not restrain their efforts to hold the party to the coalition.
This was much more satisfactory than the Justice Party, whose
leadership had swung this way and that between right and centre
during its period in office. The People's Party did not complain
so much about the N.T.P. as it had about the Justice Party during
the previous coalition; it was the N.T.P. which complained about
the People's Party. In this it resembled the Justice Party, but
the nature of its complaints was different. The Justice Party, more
or less devoid of a set of constructive political principles, created
crisis conditions by its demands for an amnesty. The dissatisfaction of the N.T.P. was at once personal and also based on a deep
cleavage of principle.

[1] They had already been expelled for one year for opposition to the party.

G

In early August 1963 Alican sent a memorandum to İnönü complaining of the treatment of the N.T.P. in the coalition. The tension increased when İnönü and the People's Party appeared to be giving scant attention to the memorandum, and it rose still further when Alican walked out of a meeting in which the Prime Minister was in the chair. Gürsel came to the rescue and the coalition continued in existence.

The chief issue at stake was the status of the N.T.P. in the coalition. The government was beginning to appear like a People's Party government assisted by representatives of two minor parties, not like a true coalition. This was very dangerous for the N.T.P., which could see that its apparent subservience to the People's Party was leaving the field to its rivals, the Justice Party, as the principal opposition party. A section of the N.T.P. wanted more than ever to withdraw from the coalition.

Moreover, if the N.T.P. stood for anything distinctive it stood for private enterprise—a part of its generally liberal outlook. It was, therefore, important that it should have a firm say in economic planning; and to this end Alican had, successfully, argued for responsibility as Assistant Prime Minister for planning, although the People's Party was not unnaturally eager to keep its own fingers on so important a subject. In fact the People's Party Assistant Prime Minister was still responsible for a number of economic functions including negotiations for Turkey's entry into the Common Market; and this led to a demarcation dispute between him and Alican. There were other complaints, too, largely to the effect that the N.T.P. leaders in government were kept out of the picture in relation to discussions with the military chiefs, the appointment of highest officials and reports prepared by the internal security authorities. Behind all this lay the usual suggestions that the administration was 'partisan'. The N.T.P. always insisted that a People's Party Minister of Interior could not be impartial in his administration.

The second crisis arose over just this question of the type of direction of the Ministry of the Interior by the People's Party Minister, Hıfzı Oğuz Bekata. Some deputies of the N.T.P. called for a general discussion in the Assembly on Bekata's administration. He was criticized *inter alia* for not having prior information about the attempted coup of 21 May, for not preventing the escape to Greece of a former Democrat Party politician and minister Zeki Eratman, condemned to life imprisonment at Yassıada, for not preventing the robberies and general disturbances which were occurring in the east, and for not taking seriously complaints against officials of his ministry.[1] Old style, heavy handed secretive, People's Party government was not to the liking of the N.T.P., and mere traces of it could easily be exaggerated.

On 2 October, Bekata in a speech in the People's Party's parliamentary group responded to these criticisms by attacking the N.T.P. Minister of Health and Social Assistance, Yusuf Azizoğlu, chiefly by accusing him of an anti-revolutionary mentality. One thing led to another until Bekata, in the Assembly, after asserting a connection between the Minister of Health and Social Assistance and the escaped former Democrat Party politician Eratman, let it be known he had documents in his possession which he suggested incriminated the Minister of Health in other ways. For these attacks on a fellow minister Bekata was then forced to resign. Back in the ranks again, he then made life so difficult for Azizoğlu that he too resigned.

The dangers to the coalition in this dispute were obvious, as each side ran to the defence of its champion. On the whole, however, the attempts by moderates to keep the affair at the personal level were successful. At least the now cotton-thread coalition still hung together. It was probably because the local elections were in the offing that the coalition did survive. That would be the time for the minor parties, at least, to decide finally what to do.

So the local elections to be held on 17 November were awaited with some eagerness—and trepidation. These were elections for provincial general councils, municipal councils, the chairmen of municipal councils and for village headmen. The elections for provincial general councils were considered a guide to electoral chances in the general elections due in 1965, although personality factors may play a larger part in provincial councils than in the parliamentary election. Moreover, these local elections would be

---

[1] Turkey suffered from general lawlessness in the eastern provinces in 1963. Complaints were also rife during this time, in many parts of the country, of the heavy-handedness of the gendarmerie in their dealings with the peasants. Relations between the peasants and the gendarmerie were improved after 1950, but they are clearly not perfect yet.

the first time the Turkish electorate had been able to give expression to its views since October 1961.

The results of the election for the Provincial General Councils compared with the voting in the 1961 general election are given in Table 4.

TABLE 4

Provincial General Councils' Election Results, 1963

Party	1963 Elections (Provincial General Councils) % of Votes Cast (75·5% participated)	1961 (Parliamentary Elections) % of Votes Cast (81% participated)
Justice	45·9	34·8
People's	37·0	36·7
Republican People's		
Peasant	2·8	14·0
New Turkey	6·5	13·7
Nation	3·1	—

The immediate deduction from these figures is that the N.T.P. and R.P.N.P. had both lost heavily in favour of the Justice Party. The two minor parties of the coalition gloomily read the dreaded writing and did not delay action long. The R.P.N.P. was the first to withdraw, on 26 November, closely followed next day by the N.T.P., unpleasantly surprised at having lost the initiative. On his return at this juncture from the funeral of the late President Kennedy, İnönü announced he was not intent on making another experiment. On 2 December the government resigned.

It had been quite a worthwhile coalition which had in the circumstances achieved a great deal of legislative work. There was still a lot to be done and much legislation had to be postponed that the Constitution itself required should be passed within two years. By the summer of 1963 the coalition was really breaking up and if there had been no local elections it is not likely to have lasted any longer, if as long. As with the first coalition the signs of disintegration began to appear shortly after an attempted *coup d'état*. After those events both the Justice Party and the N.T.P. seemed to become bolder and more intransigent. They felt more sure that the army was now firmly in its barracks. One effect of the declaration of martial law after the 21 May attempted coup was to prevent the right wing of the Justice Party from inflammatory speeches and publications which, it had been seen, could set all politics alight. It may be due to this that during the latter part of the second coalition period the Justice Party quietened down considerably, but probably most important was the continuing release of the imprisoned members of the former Democrat regime. The major political issue was fast disappearing.

CHAPTER VI

İnönü's Third Government

The second coalition had raised real hopes for a measure of political stability. When it fell only one possibility for stable government with an adequate majority in the lower house seemed to exist, namely coalition between the Justice Party on the one hand and the minor parties on the other; and no party save the Justice Party wanted a general election. There was some talk at first, but not much hope, of a national coalition (essentially a People's Party/Justice Party coalition), but this fell through before the situation exploded in Cyprus at the end of the third week in December 1963. Had the Cyprus situation developed earlier there might have been a slim chance, but having ranged itself against and beaten the minor parties, the Justice Party saw its basic interest was now to appear always in opposition to the People's Party.

The difficulty about Gürsel's asking the Justice Party to form a coalition with the minor parties was obviously the attitude of the army. Clearly the Justice Party must have been on good behaviour long enough to make this feasible. The President asked Gümüşpala to try, but he had to report failure when the minor parties refused to come in. The main reason they refused was that they were still afraid they would be swallowed up and had not as yet given up all hope of capturing some of the former Democrat vote—their only hope. After all, in the local elections just held they had lost to the Justice Party; their adherence straightway to a coalition led by that party might look like abject surrender.

So the ball rolled back to İnönü, who now announced he would try again. The R.P.N.P. refused outright and although negotiations began with the N.T.P., disagreements were too great. The N.T.P. was concerned to keep its hands on planning and wanted a large say in the appointment to the Ministry of the Interior—the same problems as before. A new condition was that their leader Alican, did not propose to enter the government, a situation İnönü could not accept after the experience of the first coalition with the Justice Party, when Gümüşpala remained outside. The

N.T.P. was also not friendly disposed towards the independents, on whom İnönü intended to rely, and sought to limit rather strictly the number of portfolios to be given to them. With expectation of support from twenty to twenty-five of the independents, of whom there were now thirty-three, and with pressure behind him from the Party to go it alone on a more reformist programme, İnönü did not show much inclination to bargain. It is difficult to see how things might have turned out but for the urgencies of the Cyprus situation, which demanded that Turkey should have a government to speak with authority. Together with the independents' votes the People's Party (175 deputies) could muster only some 200 votes in the National Assembly. The N.T.P. then decided to support the government, but not to participate in it. On 4 January, İnönü received a vote of confidence in the Assembly. Out of a possible 441 votes (there being by now nine vacant seats) his government received 225 votes. This by no means represented solid support and was a most unsatisfactory solution forced by national crisis. The N.T.P. votes might be withdrawn at any time.

That the governmental crisis was temporarily solved was then really due to the emergence of the Cyprus situation. That the solution was brought about by the N.T.P. reflected that party's desire to re-assert itself in the eyes of the electorate. In permitting the formation of a government it could claim to be more patriotic and responsible than any other party save perhaps the People's Party; it also held the whip hand over the government since its defection would bring it down. Yet the party paid a price. A number of its right-wing members resigned, though not as many as might have been expected. It was thus further weakened in the Senate and National Assembly;[1] but it seemed to have made up its mind to drop its right wing and concentrate on becoming a moderate right of centre party. Whether this was a wise move would only be apparent in the next general election to be held in October 1965.

[1] Changes in N.T.P. membership of Senate and National Assembly between 11 January and 29 February 1964 were as follows:

Senate	15	13
National Assembly	45	39
	60	52

As for the new government, younger and more reformist than either of the first two, it had to cope with the Cyprus situation. Yet it continued, and somewhat accelerated the flow of activity leading up to legislation, including the new political parties' law, which proved very controversial.

It was not long, however, before domestic quarrels upset whatever unanimity the common Greek enemy provided. Towards the end of January 1964 the National Assembly had to consider appeals against the death sentences passed on four of those involved in the attempted coup of May 1963. There was not much dispute about the sentences, only one of which was not accepted by the Assembly,[1] but a speech by a Justice Party deputy indirectly attacking the Army and its part in the 1960 revolution set the house by the ears; and had the usual effects outside, resulting in the now customary declarations by student organizations. So the domestic atmosphere was kept unduly warm.

For a moment it boiled over once again when, inspired perhaps by the recent assassination of President Kennedy, an unsuccessful attempt was made on 22 February to assassinate İnönü. Police investigations did not reveal the existence of deep-laid plots originating from high quarters, but the event was indicative of the depth of feeling against İnönü and the People's Party in some sections of society.

Thereafter, Cyprus continued to occupy the centre of the stage and damped down internal political activity to some extent. Yet government had to be carried on, and one of the conditions of this was adequate revenue. The budget was passed with the provision that some of the necessary revenue would be raised from a new agricultural income tax. The legislation for taxation was, however, not yet passed; and İnönü made it clear that unless it was passed in a form acceptable to the government he would resign. With Cyprus in the foreground, which more or less prohibited the disruption that would be caused by a general election, the threat worked. By the middle of May, but only after acrimonious discussion, the legislation was more or less through parliament. The most controversial parts of it were those establishing the agricul-

---

[1] The house considered on appeal the report of its Justice Commission on the death sentences passed on Talât Aydemir, Fethi Gürcan, Osman Deniz and Erol Dinçer. The appeal was successful only in the case of Erol Dinçer. The other sentences were confirmed with considerable majorities.

tural income tax, although this was a modest enough measure. Rather surprisingly, the Justice Party did not turn out in full force to oppose the measure. Completely tax-free farming is not to the liking of all members of the Justice Party.

If the opposition to agricultural tax legislation had been pushed by the opposition parties to the limit, the government would probably have received adequate support from members of the N.T.P. to carry the measure. The N.T.P. would not want the onus of bringing down the government. Yet the effect on the N.T.P. itself of its general policy of support weakened the party still further. An 'Extraordinary Congress' held on 9 and 10 May resulted in the re-election of Alican as chairman, but in much criticism of his passive leadership and in the subsequent resignation of four more deputies.[1]

Another test of party strengths was to occur, however, on 9 June, when one-third of the membership of the Senate was due to retire. All parties, except the Justice Party, wanted this test of party strength in the full daylight of proportional representation. To this end the Electoral Law, which specified simple majority voting for senators, was changed, but not without determined opposition from the Justice Party, which stood to gain from the existing system.

Taking into account other vacancies also to be filled the election was for fifty-one seats and embraced twenty-six of Turkey's sixty-seven provinces. The elections were likely to be a good gauge of opinion and a pointer to the general election to be held in 1965. Outstanding success for the Justice Party would also make government by the People's Party even more difficult, as the Senate could exercise a delaying action on legislation from the Assembly that could slow down even more the working of the parliamentary machinery.

It will be seen from Table 5 that the election represented a considerable victory for the Justice Party, since it appears it obtained most of the votes that had previously been given to the N.T.P. and R.P.N.P. The extent of the decline in the vote of the minor parties is shown on page 90. Table 6 compares their vote in the constituences both parties contested in 1961 and 1964.

One effect of the Senate elections was to lower the morale of

[1] This was popularly known as the *Kader Kongresi* or congress to decide what the fate of the party would be.

TABLE 5
Results of Senate Elections in 1961 and 1964
in twenty-six Provinces[a]

Party	1961			1964		
	% of Valid Votes	Seats	No. of Con- stituencies Contested	% of Valid Votes	Seats	No. of Con- stituencies Contested
Justice	34·64	26	23	49·78	31	26
People's	36·06	14	26	41·16	19	25
New Turkey	14·93	9	20	3·81	—	12
Republican People's Peasant	14·34	5	18	·99	—	14
Independents	3·69	0	6	2·26	1	5

[a] The comparison in the table is not exact, because the number of seats for competition for the twenty-six provinces in 1961 was fifty-four, compared with fifty-one in 1964. Normally the 1964 election would have been for fifty Senators (one-third of the 150 elected senators), entailing elections in twenty-four provinces. However, as one seat was that of the President of the Senate and not subject therefore to re-election, the number of seats to be filled was forty-nine. (As the seat of the President of the Senate was one of the four Balikesir seats, the number of provinces where elections were to be held remained at twenty-four.) Elections in two other provinces were however necessary (Çorum and Eskişehir) where vacancies had arisen, raising the total of provinces voting to twenty-six. As (1) these last two provinces voted for their *full* quota of seats (two each) in 1961, and (2) the President of the Senate's seat was not contested in 1964, there are three more seats shown in 1961 than in 1964. The proportion of the electorate voting was 80·1 per cent in 1961 and 60·2 per cent in 1964, another reason for caution in comparing the two elections. Although in 1964 a proportional representation system was used, it did not, of course, apply to thirteen of the twenty-four provinces, which could return only one senator each, nor to the elections for one seat each in 1964 in Çorum and Eskişehir.

TABLE 6
Senate Elections 1961 and 1964, R.P.N.P. and N.T.P.

Party	1961			1964		
	Votes Cast	Total Valid Votes	% of Votes Cast of Total Valid Votes	Votes Cast	Total Valid Votes	% of Votes Cast of Total Valid Votes
Republican People's Peasant	445,436	3,700,942	12·03	83,400	2,756,275	3·02
New Turkey	567,827	3,700,942	15·88	96,427	2,756,275	3·45

the People's Party. It was perhaps on account of the latent weakness of his party that İnönü decided to ask for a vote of confidence from the National Assembly before going to the United States to discuss the Cyprus question. The opposition parties preferred that he should not ask for a vote of confidence; and announced that if the government persisted they would not give it.[1] At this juncture, a warning from the President on the need for national unity in the face of the Cyprus crisis may have been influential. Nevertheless, about a third of the members of the small parties and a small number of Justice Party deputies did not participate in the proceedings. With the help of sixteen independents defeat was avoided. It was not, however, much of a victory[2] and İnönü it seems, was disinclined at first to regard it as satisfactory until prevailed upon by his party.

Attention was focussed now on İnönü's talks with President Johnson and the general preoccupation with Cyprus was punctuated only by two glum reminders of what lay beneath the surface. On 27 June Fethi Gürcan was executed for his part in the May 1963 attempted coup, to be followed by Talât Aydemir on 5 July. Their executions did not attract much attention. The authors of unsuccessful coups are soon forgotten.

The results of the Senate elections were of course not lost on the political parties. In particular the smaller parties played with the idea of amalgamation but, as in earlier attempts at unification, two questions seemed unanswerable, namely who should be the leader and what would the new party's name be. Towards the end of August the minor parties appeared to be finding a new saviour. There were intriguing reports that the fourteen expelled members of the National Unity Committee were acting as brokers for a new political party.

The effect of the Senate elections on the Justice Party seemed to be wholly beneficial. The party's tone became more moderate whilst the setting up of a party research bureau and the greater inclination shown by the party to make contact with intellectual

---

[1] Half the *normal membership* is needed to overthrow the government, i.e. 226 out of an actual membership of 439 at this time, made up as follows People's Party 181, Justice Party 166, other parties 64, Independents 28. A vote of no-confidence was a real possibility.

[2] The result was that 194 voted no-confidence, 200 supported the government and 2 abstained. *Cumhuriyet*, 20 June 1964.

circles bespoke a more measured approach.[1] By contrast, the People's Party at its Istanbul Provincial Congress held at the beginning of August became a battlefield of factions.

By the autumn of 1964 the Cyprus crisis had blown over. The atmosphere there was uneasy, but the government could claim to have come out of the affair with some credit. This release from external pressure now meant that domestic politics could come to the fore again. They did so with a vengeance.

At first things went well for the government. Under constitutional and legal provisions permitting the release of prisoners on grounds of good behaviour, ill health or old age, practically all the remaining Yassıada prisoners (some 50 out of an original 400) were released.[2] Henceforth the Justice Party could perhaps keep on a more even keel.

The government and the People's Party now began, however, to show very obvious signs of weakness and unpopularity. There was an unpopular decision that forbade pupils in schools who had failed in just one examination at the end of one year from continuing to a higher class. The problem was small in itself but affected many middle-class parents, to whom education of their children is as important as to parents everywhere. There were demands for the resignation of the Minister of Education.

Another problem in the educational field arose when students of Istanbul University, denied the opportunity to speak in the university's opening ceremony, made public their criticism of the university. The significant feature of the students' demands for reform was that they were showing dissatisfaction not with the Justice Party this time, but with the situation as it had developed under People's Party rule. Clearly the İnönü government was losing support among the students. They remembered that in 1960 the military had shown courage to purge the universities.

The military also complained again. The complaint was the familiar one that Justice Party politicians had been attacking the

[1] Noticeably at the Istanbul Provincial Congress of the party held in July.

[2] Under Turkish law those serving sentences may be conditionally released for good behaviour (except for life sentences) or they may be released for a period on health grounds. In addition there is the hitherto little-used device (Article 97 of the Constitution) whereby the President may reduce or abolish a sentence in cases of permanent sickness, infirmity or old age. Even those who did not petition for release were nevertheless freed, including Celal Bayar, the former President.

1960 revolution and the role of the military. This time, however, the military dropped a bombshell when on 12 November the Chief of the General Staff, Sunay, in a letter to the president of the Grand National Assembly, threatened military intervention unless something was done before 22 November about certain deputies.[1] With what looked like undue haste the Ministry of Justice requested the National Assembly to lift the parliamentary immunity of seven Justice Party deputies. The military obviously felt that the government had been dragging its feet in the prosecution of Justice Party deputies openly critical of the military. The affair led to a great deal of criticism of the slackness of the Minister of Justice in the People's Party's joint parliamentary group, there even being the possibility of a censorship motion in the Assembly. Although saved from this the minister decided to resign.

In this unhappy atmosphere for the government the political parties now began to do battle in earnest in a number of matters vital to the general election to be held in 1965. A second 'summit' conference with Gürsel in early December laid the foundations for agreement among the parties on the Political Parties Law. On the proposed changes in the Election Law there was anything but agreement.

There was first of all dispute about when the next general election had to be held, a disagreement based on different interpretations of the legal and constitutional provisions. The Justice Party wanted to force an election before October 1965, the generally accepted latest date. This raised enough heat, but nothing like that raised by the government when it introduced into the electoral system the device of 'national remainder'.[2] The ostensible purpose of this was to strengthen the minority parties in order to prevent Turkey from developing once more into a two-party system, which is often held to divide the country into two very hostile camps. It was alleged by the Justice Party that the real reason for introducing the 'national remainder' device was to prevent a strengthening of their vote, since the evidence suggested

---

[1] The alleged text of the letter is given in *Cumhuriyet*, 18 November 1965; but Sunay later denied that any period was stipulated for action against those who had been insulting the military. For Sunay's statement see *Milliyet*, 19 November 1964.

[2] See below, pp. 182–3, for an explanation of the principles involved.

that losses of votes for minority parties were gains for the Justice Party, more than for the People's Party. Another amendment to the Election Law was also resisted by the Justice Party. This amendment introduced for the general election a joint voting paper on which all parties' candidates were shown. This replaced a system of separate voting papers for each party which, it was maintained, was easily open to abuse. The new system was criticized by the Justice Party (and by many others) on the grounds that ignorant peasants left alone in the booth with a composite voting paper would probably spoil it—or vote for the wrong party. The Justice Party alleged that as it drew more strength from the peasants than did the People's Party, they would suffer most; and that this was the intention of the government's amendment. The amendments to the Election Law were nevertheless passed. The minority parties welcomed them.

Distracted until now by foreign affairs, internally divided, deeply affected by the resounding victory of the moderates in the Justice Party under a new and modern leader, Demirel, and thinking now, perhaps, that it must finally take a firm step to the left, the government published its proposed land reform law.[1] Indeed, the government put the proposal directly to the Assembly without going through its parliamentary group and, moreover, tried in the Assembly to have the draft bill referred to an *ad hoc* commission in order to avoid the delays of normal procedure. This move to accelerate matters failed, however, some of the People's Party deputies significantly voting against its own government's proposal.

Another move by the government that was interpreted in some quarters as a move to the left was a quite sudden and unusual warmth in Turco–Soviet relations, although it seems to have been founded in a desire to use the Soviet Union as a counter-weight to the United States in the Cyprus affair. A step to the left by the government that involved closer relations with Russia was inevitably viewed with disquiet by large sections of Turkish society, for whom Russia is the traditional enemy.

In this atmosphere of uncertainty the Justice Party now decided to try to overthrow the government. To this end Demirel,

---

[1] It was a moderate measure which included the restriction of the size of agricultural holdings to a maximum of 2,500 *dönüms* half the amount in previous proposals.

the new party leader, entered into close and, as it proved, successful negotiations with the small parties, amongst which the position of the N.T.P. was crucial. The opposition chose as its occasion the vote on the budget—not the issue, it was widely felt, that the most responsible would have chosen since it involved some disruption of economic affairs. On 13 February 1965 the government's budget was rejected by 225 votes to 197; and as a result İnönü decided to resign.[1] After consulting political party leaders the President then called upon Fuat Hayri Ürgüplü to form a government. Ürgüplü was a respected independent senator, who had entered the Senate on the Justice Party list and had till recently been president of the Senate. Gürsel's choice was criticized on the grounds that he should have left the choice of a new Prime Minister to the normal democratic processes of a multi-party system, in which event a member of the Justice Party should have been asked first to form a government.[2] Ürgüplü was successful in forming a four party coalition of all but the People's Party. Demirel became Deputy Prime Minister, each of the other three parties providing a Minister of State. By 23 February the new government was in office.

With so little time to go before a new general election, why did the opposition parties decide to overthrow the government? We shall have to wait for history for a definitive answer; but some suggestions may be made.

The first reason is the possible desire of the Justice Party and other parties to frustrate land reform, which the People's Party now seemed eager to push through. This is a motive that can only be tested by later Justice Party policies.

A second and disturbing reason is said to have been direct American pressure. The new friendliness between Turkey and Russia may well have caused some disquiet; and visits paid by the American Ambassador to the Justice Party and the R.P.N.P. not long before the overthrow of the government were most unhappily timed if no influence over Turkish internal affairs was intended.

---

[1] There is no device in the Turkish Constitution for an automatic budget if a government is overthrown on its budget. A new budget must await a new government.

[2] See below, pp. 217–18, for a discussion of the role of the President in selection of the Prime Minister.

Another reason for the overthrow of the government may be the İnönü complex. A widespread attitude among politicians of dislike and admiration for İnönü really meant that the opposition parties feared to let him set the stage for the general election. By taking popular decisions in the last few months before an election and in other ways governments improve their image, and their chances. The Justice Party was not so sure of itself that it could contemplate with satisfaction the prospect of İnönü's leading the country into the general election; and the national remainder and combined voting card issues no doubt affected their confidence in electoral success.

Perhaps the most significant cause of the combining of the opposition to overthrow the government was that this was the first time since 1961 that a government without the People's Party (and İnönü) really seemed feasible. There was some sign now that the Justice Party could control its right wing. The release of the Yassıada prisoners and just the passage of time had also taken some of the bitterness out of political dispute.

Whichever reasons were uppermost, February 1965 was as important a month as the February three years before when the military was restrained by İnönü. It was a sign that Turkey's political life could start again. It was a moment of sadness, but also of victory for İsmet İnönü and the moderate politicians. Their overthrow was a measure of their success.

CHAPTER VII

The Caretaker Coalition

On the formation of the new government under Ürgüplü the four coalition party leaders signed a protocol.[1] The document was remarkable because it contained no suggestion of any new policy of substance. Apart from many platitudes and broad and well-nigh meaningless statements of principle, the protocol did little more than re-enumerate the long-term policies of the İnönü government. In particular, land reform was to be speeded up, planning and a mixed economy were to be retained, the necessary effort was to be made to get the Personnel Law through and to reorganize the state economic enterprises. At the time of its overthrow the previous government had been showing some energy in these matters and indeed, as we have seen, in the case of its draft Land Reform Law the government's desire for accelerated treatment in the National Assembly had been frustrated by the opposition parties. Nor was there evident any ideological shift in the new government. It was as definite in its aversion to extreme left and right as its predecessors had been. Moreover, there was a hint that the now more friendly relations with the Soviet Union would continue to be developed; and indeed for the whole of its period of office the Ürgüplü government did maintain the new warmth with Moscow.

The new government's programme did not seriously depart from the principles contained in the protocol. The really surprising feature of both protocol and programme was that it would obviously take years to bring to completion the long-term policies they contained. After all, the government would come to an end in October. There was, however, the feeling about at this time that the Justice Party would not be so successful in the election as to command an absolute majority in the National Assembly and that coalition government along the present lines

[1] It was only after much discussion, it seems, in the party's executive committee that the Justice Party agreed to an independent Prime Minister. *Cumhuriyet*, 16 February 1965.

was going to be necessary for a long time. The likely effects of the national remainder and joint voting card innovations in the electoral system were perhaps exaggerated.

A puzzling feature of the new coalition is why the minor political parties agreed to form it. At this time their image in the forthcoming elections was all important. Clearly, as always, a coalition of People's and Justice parties would have suited them best; then they would have appeared as the only opposition parties at election time. Certainly the R.P.N.P. was very loath to join. The N.T.P. leader, Ekrem Alican, later put forward the view that the country had now become accustomed to coalition government without the participation of the People's Party.[1] The voters would therefore see no need to concentrate on one party (the Justice Party) in order to prevent the People's Party from getting into office. This view, somewhat sophisticated for the majority of the electorate one suspects, rested on the premise that the People's Party was the big bad wolf. It also ignored, what was later to appear very prominently, the fact that the Justice Party was not to be satisfied with less than an absolute majority. The Justice Party was really the big bad wolf for the smaller parties. Perhaps the small parties were indeed putting too much faith in the new electoral devices that had been introduced.

The R.P.N.P. joined the coalition under Ürgüplü, but immediately began to prepare itself for the coming election in a quite spectacular way. During the period the party was successfully taken over by Alparslan Türkeş. Türkeş joined the R.P.N.P. at the end of March, together with four other former members of the 'fourteen'.[2] After much internal turmoil, Türkeş was elected leader by the national congress. The party had also been joined by three deputies of the Justice Party, whose complaints that the Justice Party had become a party of capitalists and employers had

---

[1] Reported in *Cumhuriyet*, 25 October 1965. In the same speech Alican also advocated strengthening the executive. This was criticized as leading back to authoritarian government, but was consistent with Alican's view that coalition government had come to stay—which could mean that the National Assembly would be more powerful than in conditions of two-party government.

[2] During the middle of June four more members of the 'fourteen' joined the R.P.N.P. Early in May three others of the 'fourteen' joined the People's Party, not altogether an unmixed blessing for that party always at pains to prevent allegations of implication in the 1960 revolution.

received scant attention. The R.P.N.P. now began to develop a strong policy which stressed national unity.[1]

As for the Nation Party under its colourful leader Bölükbaşı, it seemed to have joined the Ürgüplü coalition only to criticize it. It seems Bölükbaşı strove to cut a figure for himself in the public eye without going quite to the point of trying to overthrow the government. The issue that he principally chose was that of the alleged partisanship of political broadcasts on Turkish radio. This and the other chief issues with which the Ürgüplü government had to struggle may now be briefly reviewed.

Political issues. The question of the political impartiality of Turkish wireless broadcasts was thrown into the political arena very shortly after the Ürgüplü coalition government took office. The storm arose when Turkish State radio was accused of showing a lack of respect for national politics when it did not immediately report both the new government's programme when it was read in parliament, nor the deputies' speeches arising from it. When the report was finally given governmental speeches were quoted *verbatim* in what looked like a too studied attempt at impartiality. These and other relatively minor points were used as a starting-point by the Nation Party for a campaign that brought that party into the limelight at a crucial time, but grossly exaggerated the shortcomings of Turkish State Radio.[2]

Another controversy that came to the fore was the recurrent question of parliamentary salaries. The Senate accepted a report from the Joint Senate and National Assembly Commission on Petitions to increase substantially the salary of a certain senator. They did so on the familiar grounds that members of parliament were entitled to the salary of civil servants in the first grade and

---

[1] See below, pp. 158–62 for an account of the 'take-over' by Türkeş and of the policy of the party.

[2] The Minister of Touring and Information in the new government, Zekai Dorman, was from the Nation Party, but the Ministry's control over radio was limited. The Radio Organization was certainly displeased with the new government when it tried, unsuccessfully—since the measure had already been published in the Official Gazette—to withhold an increase in salaries to officials in the Radio Organization approved by the previous government. The Minister tried to have the Radio Organization inspected by his ministry, but this was refused by the Council of State. The matter eventually subsided without conclusive result.

that if, as could be shown, a certain first-grade civil servant received additional payments, so too should a member of parliament. Of course this meant that every member of parliament could claim the same right. This decision of the Senate also passed the lower house.[1] It was not a law and therefore could not be appealed against to the Constitutional Court; but it would be necessary to make provision in the budget law soon to be introduced in order to meet the extra cost of the increase in salaries. The affair created considerable resentment in some parts of the press and among the students. The President made it clear he regarded the increase as unconstitutional, whilst the president of the National Assembly declared he would refuse to use his executive power to apply the measure if passed in legislation. It was passed, as an amendment to the budget, though this time the People's Party deputies were marshalled to vote against the amendment. Now that the measure was law it could be appealed against to the Constitutional Court. The People's Party took a lead in this, but the Justice Party and the Nation Party also requested its annulment. This was very odd procedure on the part of the two last-named parties whose votes could have killed the budget amendment in the Assembly. They did not try to do so, it seems, in order not to press too hard on their party deputies and senators and thus create a rift between the party central organization and the parliamentary parties. Yet in doing this they did allow the initiative to slip into the hands of the People's Party in a matter of some significance for the party image. The People's Party could pose as guardian of the public purse. On 12 July the Constitutional Court did in fact declare the increase unconstitutional.

Perhaps the issue that caused the greatest stir in domestic politics during this last coalition was the demand that arose for the nationalization of the petroleum industry.

Under a law passed in 1954 foreign capital was encouraged to participate in the development of the Turkish oil industry.[2] A number of foreign firms were attracted by the terms offered, but only two large foreign firms, Mobil and Shell, have found oil in

[1] The decision of the Assembly was arrived at by the employment of the practically unused device of 'secret vote'.

[2] The law was drafted with the advice of American oil experts, a source of dissatisfaction to Turkish critics of the oil regime.

commercially profitable amounts. The foreign firms entered a field then dominated by the Turkish Petroleum Corporation, a jointstock company more than half of whose capital is held by state economic enterprises. The complaints against the foreign firms were chiefly (i) that the foreign companies did not produce enough in comparison with the Turkish Corporation, (ii) that they did not wish to produce more since it was profitable to them in conditions of a world surplus of oil to sell to Turkey than to produce oil within Turkey, (iii) that by means of small subsidiary companies they obtained more exploration licences than they were really entitled to, (iv) that they sold crude oil to Turkey at excessively high prices, (v) that the conditions governing transfer of profits abroad were excessively generous, and (vi) that unlike most oil-producing countries Turkey was entitled to *at most* 50 per cent of the produce, not to *at least* 50 per cent.[1]

The two foreign oil companies chiefly concerned responded to this barrage with technical arguments showing, for example, the difficulties of exploration and transportation and Turkey's need for special types of imported crude oil not available at less than the prices they asked. The Justice Party in this matter were sympathetic to the foreign oil companies and were not enthusiastic about amending the law. Proposed amendments were still in commission when parliament rose in mid-July. The government did, however, enter into discussion with the oil companies on the price of imported crude oil. The government pressed for a 20 per cent reduction on posted world prices, but could not persuade the companies to move beyond the 18·5 per cent reduction which they had already made. For the People's Party and for the Worker's Party the oil question came to the fore most opportunely in view of the forthcoming general election. The cry was raised that the concessions to the foreign oil companies were new 'capitulations'—a word that raises national pride and indignation in every Turkish breast.

In not undertaking any legislation in the oil question the government could—and did—point out that amendment of the Petroleum Law was not a matter included in its aims. Nothing

---

[1] The case against the foreign oil companies is contained in Muammer Aksoy, *Türkiyenin Petrol Faciası ve Çıkar Yol.* (Ankara 1965) and in the many articles that appeared in the press and journals. Senator Süphi Karaman contributed significantly to the discussion. (See *Cumhuriyet,* 21 May 1965.)

like this could be said, however, about land reform, about which in the government parties' leaders protocol (but not in the government's subsequent programme) it was stated 'we think it necessary that investigations should be made by the government to see whether there are possibilities of reducing the period of reform to less than the twenty-five years mentioned in the previous government's draft law and of increasing, with effect from the year following the enactment of the law, the amount of 100 million liras to be provided (for the purpose) from the budget'.[1]

The government's programme omitted these proposed measures and was content to promise to pursue the matter without delay. In June the government did indeed bring out a new draft Land Reform Law, but one that differed quite substantially from that of the previous government—and in favour of landowners. The maximum holding of fertile land was doubled by this proposal from 2,500 to 5,000 *dönüms*. The previous government's recommended maximum for fertile land was raised from 125 to as much as 400 *dönüms*. When the force of opposition to the new draft provisions was felt the government, unsure of its partners it seems, took the surprising step of allowing the previous government's amendment to form the basis of discussion in parliamentary commission while reserving its own opinion. This seemed to amount to an abdication of governmental responsibility; and, as in the oil dispute, drove home the point that this was only a holding government. Discussions rumbled on in parliamentary commission until the end of the session.

The general election. By July the main focus of interest was certainly the forthcoming campaign in which the Justice Party got off to an early start. It was soon apparent that the struggle between the two main parties was going to be presented as a difference between left and right. By its opponents the People's Party was pushed further to the left than its next slogan 'Left of Centre' intended. Even by the beginning of July, before the election campaign proper had begun, the political temperature was unduly high. There were angry demonstrations against the Worker's Party's Congress held in Bursa, and one People's Party senator, perhaps looking for political capital, went so far as to telegraph the President and the Prime Minister to the effect that the Justice

[1] *Liderler Protokolu*, in *Milliyet*, 22 February 1965.

Party campaign was dividing the country into two camps and bringing the country to the verge of civil war.[1] The government took these allegations calmly and was proved justified in doing so when early election fever subsided of its own accord.

After a vigorous but, in its later stages, quite calm and orderly election campaign Turkish voters went to the polls on 10 October 1965. The Justice Party, which had been advocating a return to a simple majority electoral system in order to produce strong government, obviously surprised itself by obtaining a clear majority under the system of proportional representation. In one sense the 1960 revolution seemed to have been in vain. Certainly the object of preventing political domination by any one party was not attained and, worse, the party that had come to power was that which had most successfully inherited the Democrat Party mantle. Many attributed the success of the Justice Party to general disillusionment with the working of coalition government. Whether the coalition period was successful depends on the criteria by which it was judged. A single-party government might have governed more positively and have got more done, but would it have provided sufficient opportunity to represent, and meet, the many political demands that were made during this period of re-settlement after the revolution? The coalition system did not in fact break down, which meant there was no successful challenge to the democratic political system itself. Looked at in the broad, the period 1961–5 was one of marked political success.

[1] Süphi Baykam, Assistant General Secretary to the People's Party. See *Cumhuriyet*, 1 July 1965.

PART III

The Political Organization

CHAPTER VIII

The Turkish Constitution

Constitutions are important in politics because they contain the rules by which the political game, or battle, is to be fought. They are effective only if those who participate in the political competition are prepared to obey the rules. This they can be expected to do if they agreed to the rules when they were being made, or if they are obliged to keep to the rules by the force of public opinion, or by some powerful pressure group or groups, of which the most powerful in less developed states is often the military.

The present Turkish constitution was born during the period of military rule from May 1960, to October 1961. The military promoted it and, it can be argued, have ever since protected it, but in any serious way they were not its authors.

As in so many military coups and revolutions, the Turkish National Unity Committee promised a speedy return to constitutional rule. They also very speedily took steps to give effect to this sentiment by almost immediately appointing a commission to draft a constitution. This commission came to be known as the 'Onar' Commission under the name of its Chairman, Professor Dr Sıddık Sami Onar, of the University of Istanbul, a very distinguished and senior scholar in the field, particularly in administrative law.[1]

[1] The other members of the Commission were eminent scholars in the fields of constitutional and administrative law and political science with a legal approach to politics predominant. Two members, less legal in approach, were removed from the Commission, namely, Tarık Tunaya and İsmet Giritli of Istanbul University, on account, it seems, of dissension with the Commission (see Weiker, *The Turkish Revolution*, op. cit., 64–72, for an illuminating account of the politics of constitution making). The membership of the Commission when the Report was presented (October 1961) was, in addition to the Chairman, as follows: Muammer Aksoy, Bahri Savcı (both of the Faculty of Political Science, Ankara University), İlhan Arsel (Faculty of Law, Ankara University), Lûtfi Duran, Ragıp Sarıca, Naci Şensoy, Nail Kubalı, Hıfzı Velidedeoğlu and Vakur Versan, all of the University of Istanbul. The Commission is often referred to as the Istanbul Commission. The predominance accorded to Istanbul University was not readily conceded as just by the Faculties of Political Science and Law in Ankara

As part of its work the Commission distributed widely a questionnaire inviting suggestions. The reply of the Faculty of Political Science, Ankara, ran to a draft constitution which differed in many respects from the draft constitution eventually submitted in October 1961 by the Istanbul Commission. Members of the National Unity Committee, being in Ankara, were also more open to the influence of the School of Political Science group.

One of the recommendations of this group was for a Constituent Assembly, in preference to a draft constitution to be submitted to a referendum, the method proposed by the Istanbul Commission. The National Unity Committee decided, in the upshot, to convene a Constituent Assembly. The Constituent Assembly appointed a Constitution Committee of twenty members under the chairmanship of a distinguished historian, Professor Ziya Karal, who could not be regarded as belonging to either the Istanbul or Ankara group. Those who represented a more legal approach to constitution-making were in a minority in this committee.[1]

The making of the Constitution[2]

Before the revolution of 1960, critics of the way in which Turkish government was developing often recommended the creation of

University, whose representatives on the Commission were not the most senior. The two Ankara faculties' members were more involved in politics than their counterparts in Istanbul; and the National Unity Committee had to be careful not to show any political bias.

[1] Of the Istanbul Commission there were four members on the Commission set up by the Constituent Assembly. Only two of these four were from Istanbul, namely Professors Sarıca and Velidedeoğlu. One of the two Istanbul University members dismissed from the Istanbul Commission, Professor Tunaya, was a member of the Constituent Assembly's Commission. Six of the remaining members of the Commission were deputies representing the People's Party.

[2] The drafts of the Istanbul Commission, the Faculty of Political Science, Ankara, and the Constitutional Commission of the Constituent Assembly are contained in Server Feridun, *Anayasalar ve Siyasal Belgeler* (Istanbul, 1962), which also includes the final text of the 1961 Constitution, previous constitutions and important laws; and standing orders and programmes of the political parties in 1961. A useful work of comparison of constitutions is Rona Aybay, *Karşılaştırmalı 1961 Anayasası* (Istanbul, 1963). The Faculty of Political Science, Ankara, draft constitution was published by the Faculty, together with a discussion of the principles involved and reflections on elec-

an upper house in the legislature, a constitutional court and a system of proportional representation. The first two of these devices, it was hoped, would prevent a government from using its majority to become despotic, whilst the third, by increasing the number of parties in the legislature, would make single-party government unlikely and would prevent the division of the country into two hostile camps, a condition widely attributed to the two-party system. Indeed, immediately after the revolution, General Gürsel announced that a new constitution would provide for these three changes.[1]

The principal differences among the draft constitutions are to be found between the drafts of the Onar Commission and that of the Ankara Faculty of Political Science Group. The Karal Commission generally steers a middle course, but does make some changes of its own, as we shall see. The National Unity Committee had an opportunity to review the draft accepted by the Constituent Assembly on the basis of the Karal Commission, but significantly not all its amendments were accepted.

The chief area of disagreement between the Onar Commission and the Ankara group was the organization of the legislature. The Onar Commission provided for an upper house elected

toral systems in *Siyasal Bilgiler Fakültesi Idarî Ilimler Enstitüsü 'nün Gerekçeli Anayasa Tasarısı ve Seçim Sistemi Hakkındaki Görüşü* (Ankara, 1960). A valuable analysis of developments leading up to the making of the Constitution is by Bahri Savcı, 'Yeni Anayasa Rejimine Doğru Gelişmeler', *Ank. Üniv. S.B.F. Derg.*, xvi, nos. 1 and 4 (1961) 62–101 and 93–145, xvii, no. 1 (1962), 21–87. Professor Savcı was a member of the Onar Commission and was associated with the Ankara Group. In one of these articles, Professor Savcı examines the extensive comments made by the People's Party in reply to the widely circulated questionnaire from the Onar Commission asking for suggestions for the new Constitution. The People's Party agreed with proportional representation and a two-chamber parliament. It was opposed to election to the upper house by institutions and professional groups, but envisaged a single-member constituency system. Of the two houses, the lower would be supreme. The president would be elected jointly by the assemblies and would not be responsible. Save in very exceptional circumstances ministers would be chosen from the legislature. The basic system of the 1924 constitution was not to be changed. An illuminating digest and analysis of points made in a series of seminars on the Constitution held in the School of Political Science, Ankara, from October to December 1960 is contained in Nermin Abadan, 'Siyasal Bilgiler Fakültesi Anayasa Seminerlerinde Belirli Esas Düşünceler', *Ank Üniv. S.B.F. Derg.*, xvii, no. 2 (1962), pp. 251–80.

[1] Weiker, op. cit., p. 66.

partly by the general electorate and partly by the most important institutions in Turkish economic, social and political life,[1] with, in addition, life members and members selected by the President. The normally elected members would number some fifty to sixty, and the other elected members eighty-five, there being altogether some 150 members.

For this Senate, the Onar Commission provided some influence over legislation. Disputes between the two houses were in the last resort decided by the Grand National Assembly (the two houses sitting together). The Ankara draft provided for an upper house completely elected on an adult franchise, whilst ultimate decision in disputes was to lie with the lower house. The Karal Commission—and the final version—accepted the supremacy of the lower house, the National Assembly, together with direct election of senators on an adult franchise, but allowed life membership of the Senate for members of the National Unity Committee and for a small number of appointments to membership by the President.[2]

When we turn to the National Assembly, the lower house, we find that the Ankara draft provided for dissolution of itself by the National Assembly before the expiry of its four-year term, a measure not contained in the Onar draft. There was also in the Onar draft the requirement of at least primary school education for membership of the National Assembly, a requirement reduced to an ability to read and write by the Ankara group. The Onar Commission included proportional representation in the Constitution for the election of members of the lower house but, in the Ankara group draft, this was to be left to a subsequent law, as it was finally.

In all the drafts, votes of confidence in the government were to be taken in the lower house only, but the Onar Commission's draft allowed censorship motions in either house.

In the selection of the Prime Minister and the other ministers there were some differences, but in all drafts the government was

[1] There were to be representatives of judicial, military, educational, economic and legal institutions, of professional organizations, trade unions and artisan groups.

[2] The Karal Commission recommended ten presidential appointees, a figure raised to eighteen by the National Unity Committee, but reduced to fifteen finally.

made responsible to the lower house. The Onar Commission envisaged the possibility of selection of the Prime Minister and the other ministers from outside the Grand National Assembly. The Ankara group added that prime ministers and ministers should satisfy the conditions of eligibility for candidates for election to the National Assembly. The Karal Commission (and the final version) accepted this, but stipulated selection of the Prime Minister from among the members of the Grand National Assembly. The 1924 Constitution had required selection of all ministers from among the members of the Grand National Assembly.

The draft provisions for the new Constitutional Court showed that the Onar Commission seemed to envisage more initiative by the Court than did the Ankara group.[1] The Onar draft empowered the Court to examine alleged illegalities in the election of members of the legislative assemblies and the election of the President. The final version of the Constitution adopted the Karal Commission's recommendation and instead set up a High Election Council to control elections. The Ankara group would have been content to leave the matter to be regulated by law.

There were very few differences on the form of the Presidency of the Republic; and the position was maintained, as in the 1924 Constitution, that the President should be chosen by the Grand National Assembly but should not be responsible to it.

However, there were differences about the crucial question of the relation of the armed forces to the government and the state, a matter affecting the Presidency very much. The Onar Commission sought to have the Commander-in-Chief of the armed forces appointed by the President, on the recommendation of the Council of Ministers from three names submitted by the High Military Council. The appointment was to be for three years and the Commander-in-Chief was directly responsible to the President. The Ankara group's draft envisaged the selection of the Commander-in-Chief by the President on the recommendation

[1] The Onar Commission draft described one of the functions of the Court as 'to control the conformity to the Constitution of laws, standing orders of the legislative organs and every type of decision made by them' (Article 173); whereas the Ankara group's draft described this function more narrowly as 'to examine complaints that the laws or decisions of the Assemblies were contrary to the constitution'. The Onar wording formed the basis of the final version.

of the Council of Ministers from among officers of high rank; the High Military Council was excluded from the process. The Karal Commission still made the Commander-in-Chief responsible to the President. The National Unity Committee wanted to have him as close to the top as possible; they preferred him to be responsible to the Prime Minister rather than to a not-very-powerful President. The final version in fact provided for this and in this also reflected the views of the Ankara group, who thus again demonstrated their trust in the more-or-less unimpeded working of politics.

Other points made by the National Unity Committee were in the direction of increasing the number of Senate members to be appointed by the President, providing a seat in the Senate for the Chief of the General Staff and strengthening in minor ways the role of the Senate in legislation. The Ankara Group differed from the Onar Commission's views in a number of other ways. For instance, the Onar Commission's draft is not at all firm on the need for planning, whereas the Ankara group states bluntly that national development will be planned. The Onar Commission includes provisions for ensuring that political parties and trade unions are run in accordance with democratic principles. The Ankara group prefers to leave these matters to be provided for by law. The final result in these matters was largely a compromise between these two sets of views.

Underlying principles

The differences in constitutional drafts noted above suggests basic differences in approach to Turkey's political problems—and particularly as between the Onar Commission and the Ankara group.

The basic political conviction underlying the Onar Commission's constitutional proposals, it seems, was a deep disquiet about the working of democracy in Turkey—and in particular a distrust of political parties. To this end an upper house was envisaged weighted in favour of responsible professional persons. Although the principle of national sovereignty was seen to be essential—and was represented exclusively in the lower house—it was to some extent to be constrained in its operation. Elected deputies would be obliged to pay heed to the advice of experienced public personages.

Secondly, the deputies who would appear in the Grand National Assembly would have been elected on a system of proportional representation—a device the Onar Commission wanted to have included in the Constitution. The expected—and desired—result of this would be no party large enough to establish a one-party dictatorship.

Thirdly, the Onar Commission's distrust of political parties led them to be concerned to ensure that political parties were democratically governed and in other ways effectively disciplined. A political party in the grip of unchanging leaders does not seem to advance the interests of democracy; yet sometimes the extent to which, in fact, an oligarchic political party does nevertheless feed in demands to the political system can be overlooked.

In its treatment of the relationship between the government and the military, the Onar Commission also departed to a degree from strict democratic principle by making the Commander-in-Chief directly responsible to the President, but it did so in order to make it more difficult for the military to be brought into politics by the government and to encourage the military itself not to enter into politics.

Basically, the Onar Commission had deep reservations about the working of democracy in Turkey. This involved them in trying to introduce numerous devices into the Constitution for the sake of democracy—and this then threw them open to the charge of being legalistic in approach. The charge was just, but the situation unavoidable. The Onar Commission was not undemocratic in spirit; it tried to preserve democracy from the dangers within itself, but began to look undemocratic in doing so. It is an old dilemma.

The Ankara group came down firmly for pure democracy and no nonsense. Sovereignty rested in the *elected* representatives of the nation. The upper house should therefore be elected like the lower and natural members even (the members of the National Unity Committee) were not to be admitted. The Onar Commission's upper house, it was claimed, was undemocratic in principle and its professional composition was a manifestation of the corporate principle often found in undemocratic states. Moreover, professional organizations, it was held, were not really 'developed' in Turkey; the persons of the high calibre expected would not be obtained. Then again—a powerful argument—the adoption of the

I

Onar Commission's scheme would result in the politicization of the professional organizations, not the reduction of excessive political strife. As for a referendum on the Constitution, the ill uses to which that seemingly democratic device had given rise in history were only too well known.

The Ankara group had a complete faith in political parties as necessary agents of the democratic process. It was recognized that the necessity of party discipline rendered difficult parliamentary control of the government of the dominant party, but the educational effect on public opinion of parliamentary discussions was stressed.[1] The Ankara group did not want to include in the Constitution provisions to ensure the internal democracy of political parties—partly on the grounds of not cluttering up the Constitution with detail. There was also perhaps discernible the feeling that political parties should be left to their own laws of nature, or that control through the Constitution would anyway be ineffective.

A considerable concern of the Ankara group was for the retention of the means for strong government. To this end, doubt was expressed about any system of proportional representation that encouraged an insufficient majority in the National Assembly. The proper course, it was said, was not to produce weak governments but, rather, strong means of control through encouraging a vigorous opposition in parliament and the participation of the public in the discussion of political issues. There were also, of course, the legal and now the constitutional remedies. Strong government, it was argued, was necessary in a developing country like Turkey. In more developed societies decisions affecting economic and social development could be taken to a far greater extent than in Turkey by the existing non-governmental social and economic institutions, which, by definition, were fewer and less developed in Turkey. When a government has to do so much it must be strong. Moreover, it is argued darkly, if a strong government does not emerge from the democratic political pro-

---

[1] It is very difficult to estimate the value of the reporting of parliamentary discussions on public opinion in Turkey. Much depends on what is reported. The better-quality newspapers include the better-quality discussions, as is the case everywhere—and by and large, coverage of parliamentary affairs in Turkish newspapers is more extensive than, say, British parliamentary affairs in the British press.

cess it will break through in some other—and less desirable—form.

The Ankara group seemed more modern, less legalistic and more optimistic about the prospects for democracy than the Onar Commission. They seemed to be looking to the future, not harping on the recent past. They were building a new ship, not just plugging the holes in the old one. Yet in one sense they were more conservative than the Istanbul group. Their ideas were much closer to the principles of the 1924 Constitution; they were perhaps less realistic, after all, than the Istanbul group in their insistence on real democracy. It is odd that they did not much try to bar the road to the re-emergence of single- or dominant-party government. It certainly did not seem at the time that any single party would arise to inherit the mantle of the fallen Democrats; and there was their keen awareness of the dangers of legislating for the past instead of for the future.

The main features of the Constitution

The Constitution is arranged in six parts, in addition to a short Preamble, and consists of 168 articles. One part (Part V) consists of Temporary Articles, of which there are eleven; the Constitution may be said then for practical purposes to have 157 Articles in five parts. It is well above the average length of constitutions.

As might be expected, the Preamble stresses the tradition of freedom in Turkey and firmly places the 1960 revolution within this tradition. The Turkish people also expresses its dedication to national independence, sovereignty and the reforms of Atatürk. In addition to democracy there is also expressed the desire to establish social justice.

Part I of the Constitution is a statement of general principles. The Republic is described as nationalist, democratic, secular and social (Article 2). 'Social' and 'democratic' are not in the 1924 Constitution, while 'populist' and 'revolutionary', which appeared in the old Constitution, are now omitted. A significant change in the new Constitution is the omission of the principle that 'the Grand National Assembly of Turkey is the sole representative of the nation on whose behalf it exercises the rights of sovereignty'.[1] There is now no possibility of urging the argument that the Grand National Assembly may supplant the nation as the source of

[1] *The Turkish Constitution*, official English translation (New York, 1945).

sovereignty. Another important change in the principles underlying the Constitution is the division of legislative and executive power between the Grand National Assembly on the one hand and the President and Council of Ministers on the other. Legislative and executive power are no longer concentrated in the Grand National Assembly. Turkey has moved further from an assembly, or convention, system to a parliamentary one. Finally, the principle is now stated that laws should not be in conflict with the Constitution; and as we shall see later, a Constitutional Court is created to act as judge.

Part II of the Constitution sets down fundamental rights and obligations. Its fifty-two rather long articles replace the twenty rather brief articles of the 1924 Constitution. This development has principally occurred for two reasons. First, the previous Constitution did not establish the traditional liberties of the citizen in much detail, tending to leave this to law. This led to abuse by the government, most notably in respect of the freedom of the press. The present Constitution strengthens these basic rights by attempting to state the grounds on which liberties may be curtailed and how far restriction may go. For example, Article 22 says in regard to freedom of the press; 'Freedom of the press and the obtainment [sic] of information can be restricted by law only in order to safeguard national security or public morality, to prevent attacks on the dignity, honor and rights of individuals; to prevent instigations to commit crimes; and to assure proper implementation of judicial functions.'[1] On the law that shall regulate the publication and distribution of newspapers, the Constitution indicates the extent to which the law may go by saying (Article 23) that 'Such law shall lay down no political, economic, financial or technical restrictions liable to curb or coerce the free dissemination of news, ideas and opinions.'

The second reason for the increased attention given to rights and obligations of citizens is the introduction of a section on social and economic rights and obligations, very little developed in the previous Constitution. The individual's right to own and inherit are recognized; but a number of limitations on economic freedom are admitted in the Constitution. Chief among these are

[1] *The Constitution of the Turkish Republic*, translated for the Committee of National Unity by Sadık Balkan, Ahmet E. Uysal and Kemal H. Karpat (Ankara, 1961).

(i) the obligation of the state '. . . to provide land for those farmers who either have no land or own insufficient land . . .' (Article 37), (ii) to nationalize 'where it is deemed necessary in the public interest private enterprises which bear the characteristics of a public service. . .' (Article 39), (iii) the right of employees and employers 'to establish trade unions and federations of trade unions without having to obtain prior permission . . .' (Article 46), (iv) the right to bargain collectively and to strike (Article 47), and (v) the right to social security and medical care (Articles 48 and 49). The state's duties in respect of the social and economic objectives stated in the Constitution are limited by the level of economic development and the financial resources available (Article 53). The Constitution gives a firm indication of the direction of future development in regard to social rights and duties.

Part III lays down the basic organization of the Republic.

The legislature (the Grand National Assembly) is composed of the Senate of the Republic and the National Assembly. The Senate consists of 150 elected members, fifteen members appointed by the President, the members of the former National Unity Committee and former Presidents of the Republic. These three last categories of members are known as 'natural' members; they forfeit their *ex officio* membership of the Senate if they join a political party. The same basis of universal adult suffrage is used for the elected members as is used for the election of all members of the National Assembly. One-third of elected and appointed members of the Senate retire every two years, the term of office of all elected and appointed senators being six years. The National Assembly has 450 members; its term of office is four years. Senators have to be at least forty years of age and to have had higher education. Deputies need only be thirty and be literate.

Although the two houses are elected on the same basis, it was decided, after long discussion in the Constituent Assembly, not to give them equal powers, but to make the lower house supreme. It was clearly wise to avoid the possibility of conflict between two houses which could each claim the legitimacy accorded by democratic election. It was also logical to give supremacy to the lower house because it was larger and likely to be more representative than the Senate on account of its system of election by proportional representation.

The National Assembly is, therefore, given supremacy in four crucial matters. First, in normal legislation the first and last voice is that of the National Assembly. Only the National Assembly initiates discussion of Bills or other legislative proposals, and in the event of dispute between the two houses the lower house has the final authority. Secondly, while the budget is first considered by a mixed Senate and National Assembly Commission in which representatives of the lower house are in a majority of twenty, the final debate and vote on the budget lies with the lower house. Thirdly, interpellation or censure motions are debated and motions of no confidence may be made only in the National Assembly. Fourthly, votes of confidence on the reading of a new government's programme lie only with the National Assembly, as do votes of confidence requested by the Prime Minister at any other time.

The influence of the Senate is not, however, reduced to nothing. In ordinary legislation if the Senate rejects a draft bill *in toto* by a majority vote of all its members or by two-thirds of their votes, its acceptance similarly by a majority or two-thirds majority of total membership of the National Assembly is required. Then again the Senate enjoys, like the National Assembly, the right to control the government by questions, general debates and parliamentary enquiries. The Senate also joins with the National Assembly in joint session to decide on parliamentary investigations into the Prime Minister or any other minister, the investigation being conducted by a mixed Commission drawn equally from either house.

The greatest change from the previous Constitution is, of course, the creation of the Senate itself. Other important changes are the introduction of two devices to increase parliamentary control over the government, namely, 'general debates' and 'parliamentary enquiries'. These two devices arose from a desire to find means of controlling the government not as extravagant as censure nor as restricted as the parliamentary question.

The second section of Part III is devoted to the Executive Power. Under this heading come the President, the Council of Ministers and the Administration.

The President is elected for seven years by a two-thirds majority of the Grand National Assembly (in plenary session) from among their own members who are at least forty years old.

A President is not eligible for re-election, but it will be noticed that his term of office is three years longer than that of the members of the Grand National Assembly. He has to disassociate himself from any political party.

The President is Head of the State: he presides over the Council of Ministers wherever he deems it necessary, though he is not responsible, his decrees being signed by the Prime Minister and the ministers concerned. The President promulgates laws and although he may return a Bill to the Grand National Assembly, if it is insisted upon, he has to promulgate it as law. Finally, the President chooses the Prime Minister; who must, however, submit his government's programme for a vote of confidence in the National Assembly. He also appoints fifteen members of the Senate and two judges of the Constitutional Court.

The form of the Presidency differs from that of the 1924 Constitution in certain important respects, reflecting a tendency to make the President an arbiter in the political struggle. He is said now to 'represent the Turkish Republic and the integrity of the Turkish nation' (Article 97). His longer term of office (he was elected for the Assembly's term previously), his ineligibility for re-election and the requirement of political neutrality all make him more distant from the Grand National Assembly than formerly. Yet the break from parliament is not complete. After all, he is still elected by the Grand National Assembly from among its members.

The Council of Ministers is the real executive. The Prime Minister, who is appointed by the President, has to be a member of either the National Assembly or the Senate. The other ministers, who are appointed by the President on the recommendation of the Prime Minister, may be from parliament or from outside (provided they would qualify for election as deputies). The Prime Minister's authority is now mentioned; he is to promote cooperation among the ministries and supervise the implementation of the government's general policy; his authority was not described in the previous Constitution. The general view is that Menderes was much more than *primus inter pares*. In conditions when coalition government is very probable there is some point in giving some guidance as to the role of the Prime Minister. The provision allowing appointment of ministers from outside parliament is also new and reflects the need for highly qualified administrators, particularly in technical fields, sometimes not available in parliament.

The administration is regulated in the Constitution in some detail. One addition of significance is the clause which states 'No act or procedure of the administration shall be immune from the review of law enforcing courts' (Article 114). Another is the elaboration of the procedure to be adopted when disciplinary action is taken against government officials and employees of quasi-official organizations. Government officials are also not permitted to join political parties. Attention is given to the problem of the impartiality of the radio by requiring, *inter alia*, that radio stations should be regulated by law as autonomous public corporate bodies. The autonomy of the universities is also underlined and spelt out in the present Constitution. The important principle is established that only the universities, not the Ministry of Education, may dismiss university staff. Moving rather away from central administration, we find that professional organizations are required to conduct their affairs in democratic ways. Perhaps the most important of the many administrative innovations in the present Constitution—most of which try to prevent some former flagrant abuse—is the establishment of a State Planning Organization. It is laid down that 'Economic, social and cultural development is based on a plan. Development is carried out according to this plan.' It may be mentioned at this point that both the Council of State and the Court of Accounts are carried over into the new Constitution.

Section three of Part III deals with the Judiciary. One of the principal complaints against the Democrat government was that it interfered with the independence of the Judiciary. The present Constitution, therefore, seeks at every turn to protect judicial functions from executive influence. The 1924 Constitution had left a great deal of the organization and many of the functions of the Judiciary to be regulated by law. The strongest constitutional guarantee was contained in Article 54 in which it was stated: 'The magistrates of courts are independent in the trial of all cases and in the rendering of their verdicts they are free from all kinds of interference and are dependent only on law.'[1] Legal prescription is, presumably, not interference, but in conditions in which the

---

[1] *The Turkish Constitution* (1945), Article 54.

legislature is not really separate from the executive the touchstone of law is not enough.

The present Constitution stresses in firmer language the independence of the courts and seeks to block the ways by which the executive has in the past exerted influence over the Judiciary. It is now unequivocally laid down that judges may not be dismissed or retired, unless they so wish, before the age limit nor deprived of their salaries if a court, or a position therein, is abolished. Of course, the Constitution has to recognize that there may be cases of justifiable retirement or dismissal (e.g. ill-health or inefficiency) and clearly these exceptions to the general rule of permanent tenure could be abused. To attempt to ensure they are not so abused is one of the principal objects in establishing in the Constitution a High Council of Judges, which has the power to decide about all personnel matters of judges. The High Council is composed of eighteen members of whom two-thirds are elected by, and from, the higher ranks of the Judiciary, whilst the remainder are chosen by the National Assembly and the Senate separately, each electing three members from among persons who have served as judges in the higher courts or are qualified for membership of such courts. Constitutionally, the Judiciary seems to be in a watertight compartment. Any future attack on their independence would require an amendment of the Constitution. If they develop into a conservative closed corporation this will have to be done unless the six members elected by Parliament are enough to bring flexibility, which seems unlikely. It is the old problem—of how to exclude the chill air, but not the fresh.

The other large innovation within the boundaries of the Judiciary is the creation of a Constitutional Court, in response again to the passing of laws by the Democrat Party government, claimed by many to be unconstitutional.

The Constitutional Court has a complex membership. The essential principle is, however, to supplement persons of judicial integrity and competence with those knowledgeable about the economic, social and political conditions of modern Turkey. Eight of its fifteen members are from the Judiciary, including the high administrative courts. One of the President's appointees is on nomination by the Military Court of Cassation. The Senate and the National Assembly have to appoint from outside their membership, one of each of their appointees being nominated by joint sessions of the teaching staffs of university faculties of Law, Economics and Political Science—in practice a very cumbersome arrangement.

The principal function of the Constitutional Court is to review the constitutionality of the laws of the Grand National Assembly and its Standing Orders. In addition, the Court acts as a High Council to try the President of the Republic, the Prime Minister and other Ministers and the highest legal personages for offences arising out of their duties. Suits for annulment of laws and standing orders of the two houses of the Grand National Assembly may be initiated by certain specified persons and bodies including political parties represented in the Grand National Assembly, and those with at least 10 per cent of votes in the most recent elections. The Court also decides suits for the closing down of political parties.

In Part VI of the Constitution, the procedure for amending the Constitution is laid down.[1] This does not differ essentially from the position under the 1924 Constitution. Proposals for amendment have to be by at least one-third of all members of the Grand National Assembly; adoption of a proposal for amendment is by at least two-thirds of all members of each house.

To consider the Constitution generally, we might say that the Constitution derives from three main sources. There is, first, the legacy of the Constitutions of 1876 and 1924; secondly, the experience of contemporary democratic states; and, finally, Turkey's present social needs.[2]

To take first the historical legacy, it can be argued that the 1876 Constitution, by creating an elected parliament and by giving place to individual rights (limited though they were), really gave recognition to the idea of limitation of the Sultan's powers in the name of the people. In 1876 this amounted to no more than *participation* of the 'people' in a system dominated by the Sultan, but it was an important beginning. There is also evident in 1876 the emergent principle of division of powers, to replace the con-

[1] Part IV contains a small number of miscellaneous provisions. Part V is devoted to temporary provisions covering the transition from the government of the N.U.C. to government under the new Constitution.

[2] For this approach to the general character of the Constitution see Bahri Savcı, '1961 Anayasasının Müdir Prensiplerine ve Müesseselerine Mukayeseli Kısa Bir Bakış', *S.B.F. Derg.*, XIX, nos. 3–4 (1964) pp. 11–36.

centration of all legislative, executive and judicial powers in the hands of the Sultan. Again, the idea was far from being realized.

The 1924 Constitution might be described as a victory for principle of popular sovereignty at the expense of the separation of powers. Sovereignty was now firmly invested in the nation, but with the potentially dangerous rider that the nation's sovereign rights were exercised on its behalf by the elected Grand National Assembly. To underline the fact that only the nation and its representative, the Grand National Assembly, possessed authority (and certainly not any Sultan or Caliph) the Grand National Assembly was said to be the source of executive as well as legislative power. Development towards the separation of powers was in this way made difficult. The Sultan had been exchanged for a Grand National Assembly. In theory this was acceptable; but in practice it was difficult to avoid a large measure of arbitrary rule through the domination over the Assembly of the single party (up to 1946) or the preponderant party in a two-party system (1950-60). The trouble was aggravated by the inadequacy of the 1924 Constitution in providing means for deciding whether laws made by the Grand National Assembly were unconstitutional.

The present Constitution now provides in greater degree for the separation of powers by creating conditions for a more impartial Presidency, though the close tie between legislature and executive is not in fact broken. What is expected is that this Constitution will create a parliamentary form of government in which there is a *balance* between government and parliament. It has been justly said that the Constitutions of 1876 and 1924 provided for 'government *with* parliament',[1] not for parliamentary government.

In the making of the present Constitution the commissions and study groups drew heavily but with discrimination on their knowledge of contemporary democratic states.[2] This fascinating process cannot be studied here; but in the broad it can be said that the present Constitution is as well illuminated by ideas about representative democratic government as enlightened as are to

[1] Ibid., p. 23.
[2] Turkish political scientists are by and large very well informed about other countries' political systems. The Constitution of the West German Republic was one important source for the Constitution makers.

be met with anywhere. In its insistence on patriotism (not an arid nationalism), on laicism, on the legitimacy of power only through elections and on the need for subjecting political power constantly to the inspection of public opinion and the control of political institutions, the Turkish Constitution is as democratic as could be desired.

The third source of inspiration for the Constitution—the present needs of Turkish society—may be summarized under two heads. First, there has been concern that democratic government should be strong—and in particular strong enough to carry through economic and social development in a planned way. (In practice to reconcile democratic with strong government is *the* political problem in Turkey.) Secondly, the realization of social needs of Turkey's populace has led to the inclusion of the many social rights. Among other things, the Constitution is a foundation stone for a democratic welfare state. In this it is very different from the Constitution of 1924.

The Constitutional Court

As we have seen, one of the other major differences between the present and the previous Constitutions is the creation now of a Constitutional Court. Of course, it is politically an institution of very great potential importance and a thorough study of its decisions so far, together with an estimate of its political significance, is very much needed. No more can be attempted here than to give a very brief account of some of the major matters on which it has been called upon to give decisions since it began to function in September 1962.[1]

One of the first results of the setting up of the Court was to attract a host of suits that were rejected because they offended against required procedure or did not fall within the competence of the Court.

One suit not accepted on such grounds was the complaint

---

[1] The delay in opening was partly caused by the need to pass a law regulating the establishment and judicial methods of the Court. This law was passed in April 1962. There was some dispute between the universities and the Grand National Assembly whether members proposed by the university staffs concerned could be from outside the universities. This the universities wanted and managed to persuade the Grand National Assembly to accept. The arrangements for the nominations by university staffs are unavoidably cumbersome and cause delay.

of the deputy Nuri Beşer, that his being kept under arrest was unconstitutional.[1] Another was a suit by former members of the New Turkey Party asking for the closing of that political party. Yet another was a suit from a citizen who wished to prevent the Minister of Monopolies from manufacturing alcoholic drinks on grounds that they were injurious to religion and to the health of the nation!

Much more serious was the suit transferred from the Council of State arising from the suspension of the Chairman of the Inspecting Board of the Ministry of Industry. He had been 'placed at the disposal of the Ministry' in accordance with Law No. 6435, passed before the Revolution and used by the government, for example, to remove university professors from their posts.[2] This law gave no right of appeal, administrative or judicial. The Constitutional Court found Article 34 of this law contrary to the Constitution (Article 114), which says that no act or procedure of the administration may, in any event, be immune from review by the judicial authorities.[3]

In June 1963 the provisions of a law controlling rents were annulled, the Court on this occasion treading on very political ground in deciding whether to restrict property rights, which the Constitution protects, was really in accord with the public welfare, the criterion by which exercise of property rights is to be judged.[4] July 1963 saw decisions of the Court restricting governmental control over the quasi-official chambers of Industry and Commerce.

In August 1963 the Constitutional Court rejected a claim that the law passed in March 1963, to prevent attacks on the revolution, was unconstitutional. It had been alleged that it restricted basic freedoms accorded by the Constitution. Later in the year, in October, a suit from the Justice Party's parliamentary group, that provisions of the Municipalities' Law permitting the Council

---

[1] See above, p. 59, for an account of the arrest of Nuri Beşer.

[2] See above, p. 26.

[3] *Resmi Gazete*, 2 December 1962. See also K. Fikret Arık, 'Anayasa Mahkemesi Usul ve İçtihadı', *Ank. Üniv. S.B.F. Derg*, XVII, nos. 3-4 (1962), pp. 73-83.

[4] *Resmi Gazete*, 31 May 1963. The Court's decision is ably attacked in the socialist journal, *Yön*, by Mümtaz Soysal, *Yön*, 5 June 1963. A good account is by Burhan Gürdoğan, 'Anayasa Mahkemesinin Kiralara Dair Karar Üzerine', *Forum*, 1 July 1962.

of Ministers to dissolve municipality councils were unconstitutional, was upheld.[1]

A matter that had created much bitterness between the Republican People's Party and the Democrat Party in the decade 1950–60 had been the confiscation by the Democrat Government in 1953 of People's Party property on the grounds that it was acquired in the days of the one-party state and was public property. The provisions of the law of 1953 were annulled by the Constitutional Court in October 1963.[2] It was a useful rather minor justification for the revolution.

One of the most important decisions of the Court was not to annul Articles 141 and 142 of the Criminal Law which, in very general terms, forbids class struggle and prescribes severe penalties for those who promote it. The propaganda activities of those on the left are quite considerably restrained by these articles of the Criminal Code. The request for annulment had come from the Workers' Party.

Perhaps the most generally popular of the Court's decisions, though by no means of first political significance, was its decision that increases made to salaries of members of parliament in the summer of 1965[3] were contrary to the Constitution. Members had voted the increases to themselves despite the official opposition of the People's Party, the Justice Party and the Nation Party. It will be recalled that the Court found the increase unconstitutional on technical grounds. The argument of the members of parliament had been that they were not increasing their salaries but bringing them up to those of the highest-paid officials among those in Grade I in the civil service. Members of parliament receive the same salaries as officials in Grade I, but the Constitution does not take cognizance of the fact that some Grade I officials are, by means of special additions, paid more than the usual salary. This decision of the Court was widely acclaimed.

From these few examples of the Court's activities, it is not possible to generalize with confidence. As nearly always in Con-

[1] *Resmi Gazete*, 1 October 1963. The decision to dissolve municipality councils in certain circumstances, viz. if they do not carry out their legal obligations or if they meet outside legally appointed times or places, or discuss political matters, or show political bias, lies now with the Council of State. *Belediye Kanunu*, Article 53

[2] Ibid, 13 October 1963.

[3] See above, pp. 99–100.

stitutional Courts, the trend seems to be in defence of the individual. The Court has not yet been called upon to take decisions in cases of serious attack on the democratic freedoms of the sort seen in the pre-revolutionary period. Perhaps its activity in less dire matters will help prevent any large attacks from ever developing. So far it has been a much-respected institution and at least one distinguished Turkish constitutional lawyer has favourably compared its standing with that of the Grand National Assembly and the government.[1]

[1] İlhan Arsel, 'Giden Meclisin Kazandıkları', *Cumhuriyet*, 6 August 1965.

CHAPTER IX

Political Parties

History

Just before the 1960 revolution, the Democrat Party government had suspended political party activity, a suspension continued by the National Unity Committee. The Democrat Party was closed down on a technical point—that the Party had not held as many periodic meetings as it was obliged by law to do. In July 1960 the N.U.C. took the very important step of dissolving all political party organizations at any level below sub-province (*ilçe*).[1]

Although eleven new parties registered their existence after the National Unity Committee announced, in January 1961, that political parties could be formed, only two were sufficiently serious to contest the general election held that year. These were the Justice Party and the New Turkey Party. The two new parties were out to catch the former Democrat Party vote. This they seemed to do. As we have seen, the Justice Party became the largest party in the Senate and the second largest in the more important National Assembly. In each house the Justice Party and New Turkey Party together outnumbered the People's Party, although this party had the largest representation in the lower house. The People's Party continued in the post-revolutionary period under its veteran—and very firm—leader, İnönü. His direction needed to be firm. One great force to contend with inside the party has for a long time been Kasım Gülek, an educated and talented landowner formerly Secretary General of the party, aggressive, oriented to the needs of the countryside, and critical of the urban outlook of the town-bred party intellectuals. Apart from Gülek, there are others of independent spirit, notably, Nihat Erim, Turhan Feyzioğlu[2] and Bülent Ecevit.

[1] For a good account of political parties during 1960–1, see Weiker, op. cit., pp. 82–104. The abolition of political party organization below sub-provincial level was thought necessary in order to reduce the social disruption that political participation seemed to be creating or encouraging. It was —and still is—a popular notion among the educated urban classes that the peasant is gullible and especially susceptible to propaganda that encourages religion.

[2] He has now left to form the Reliance Party. See below, p. 310.

The other survivor from the pre-revolutionary period, the Republican Peasants Nation Party under its colourful leader Osman Bölükbaşı, obtained a solid representation in both houses, even if it was the smallest. The next largest representation was obtained by the New Turkey Party, under Ekrem Alican, an economist, and said at the time to have the President's ear. The party as a whole was also said to be in particularly good odour with the National Unity Committee, which was surprising considering the party's strong liberal views. Indeed, the party was very critical of the N.U.C.; and one of its leading members, Aydın Yalçın, was sentenced to six months' imprisonment for, among other things, declaring that the Democrat Party era was, despite all, a 'golden age'.[1]

The Justice Party seemed set from the beginning to be the most successful heir to the Democrat Party; and many of its members were soon involved in difficulties with the N.U.C. when they showed sympathy for the fallen Democrat Party and disrespect for the authors of the revolution. Its first leader, General Ragıp Gümüşpula, who died in 1964, was one of the officers retired after the revolution.

In 1961, the Turkish Grand National Assembly was composed of these four parties. With the employment now of a system of proportional representation for election to parliament there were hopes that the smaller parties would gather strength. The Turkish electorate might thus be weaned from its predilection for a two-party system by this reform of electoral machinery. The internal discipline of the two major parties might break down when there were other not-too-distant parties to which to defect. In the event, however, this did not turn out to be so. The battles within the Justice Party between moderates and extremists did not produce defections to the minor parties that seriously altered the balance. The smaller parties anyway lost members during the session as a result of their own internal disputes. The real sign, however, that Turkey was going to maintain a two-party tradition occurred at the end of 1962, when local elections were held and in the summer of 1964 on the occasion of the partial election of the Senate, when the elections clearly showed that the minority parties were on the decline.

The minority parties, nevertheless, increased in number in the

[1] Weiker, op. cit., p. 102.

K

Assembly. In 1962, the R.P.N.P. leader, Bölükbaşı, left the party with twenty-nine parliamentary members to form the Nation Party. This party contested the general election in 1965.

A newcomer to the parliamentary scene in 1965 was the Turkish Workers' Party (*Türkiye İşçi Partisi*), which joined with those above in contesting the 1965 general election.

The Political Parties' Law

The framework of action for the political parties is contained in the Political Parties' Law passed in July 1965. Such a law was required by Article 57 of the Constitution.[1] The law was to be in conformity with democratic principles and should regulate the ways in which political parties were to account to the Constitutional Court for their internal arrangements and activities and the methods of financial control to be exercised by the Court. It is also laid down in the Article that parties are to conform to the principles of a democratic and secular republic and are not to offend against the cardinal doctrine of national unity. Decisions to close political parties belong only to the Constitutional Court. This attempt to control political parties in the interests of democratic government has often been attacked by the 'political' school as a good example of the legalistic mentality. It is so much out of touch with the realities of politics that it does not recognize that political parties are the very stuff of political life and cannot be controlled by artificial means. Certainly the political parties did not rush to bring out the necessary legislation in 1961. They should have done so, for Temporary Article 7 of the Constitution required legislation to be passed within two years. The government did not present a draft bill to the Grand National Assembly until October 1963. It was nearly two years later—and after much discussion and amendment—that the law was passed. The main features of the law are as follows. First, a distinction is made between political parties and associations. To give substance to this distinction was extremely difficult and produced much discussion in parliament. The early intention was to permit to

---

[1] *Siyasî Partiler Kanunu*, no. 648, 13 July 1965. As is the case with many important laws, this law has been published privately, e.g. M. A. Yalçın, *Siyasî Partiler Kanunu ve Seçim Kanunları* (Istanbul, 1965). Article 57 was inspired by Article 21 of the Constitution of the Federal German Republic (according to the Preamble to the Law).

remain as 'associations' those bodies that pursued only limited objectives (like the promotion of re-afforestation) and which did not advocate general policies (like, perhaps, the Society for Socialist Culture)—with exceptions, however, for learned societies.[1] The difficulties of satisfactory delimitation that this would involve are obviously enormous, and it was a serious loss to freedom of political discussion if associations were not to be allowed to express general views on politics. The final version accepted a narrower and more-easily-applied principle, namely, that associations must not support or deliberately oppose any political party, or specific candidates in elections; nor must they seek to promote unity between political parties, or between candidates in elections. In other words, the test is participation in the activities of political parties, or in elections.

Political parties may easily be formed—by only fifteen persons, as long as they possess the not prohibitive qualifications to stand for election as deputies. Their creeds must, however, incorporate republicanism and nationalism. They are also obliged to protect the 1960 revolution as well as the achievements of the Atatürk revolution. They are to be secular and must not exploit religion for political purposes. The titles Communist, Anarchist, Fascist or National Socialist may not be used; and parties are forbidden to exert influence in the armed forces and defence organizations. They are not to disrupt the rule of law nor the multi-party system, which, it is said, 'is tied to the principle of direct elections' (Article 100). Membership of parties is somewhat restricted, however. School pupils and civil servants are not allowed to join them. University teachers may do so, but their party duties are limited to the central organization of the parties. The chief danger the law seeks to avoid is excessive concern with politics in universities.

A large number of detailed provisions is concerned with the internal organization which, it is laid down, must consist at least of a General Congress,[2] the highest organization, a Central Governing Body (of not less than fifteen persons) and a Central

[1] *Yön*, 4 December 1964, for a critique of the then draft law by the Society for Socialist Culture (*Sosyalist Kültür Derneği*).

[2] An upper limit of twice the numbers of elected members of the Grand National Assembly is placed on size of membership. All deputies and senators and members of the government are natural members of their parties'

Disciplinary Organ (of not less than seven persons). The election of the Party Chairman, the Central Governing Body and the Central Disciplinary Committee by the General Congress must now be by secret vote, a practice not previously followed by every party. Under the new law, the Central Governing Body manages the party in between general congresses, but may not change standing orders nor the party programme and may not dissolve the party.

This attempt to make party decisions more democratic changes the previous situation in at least some degree in all the parties. For instance, the People's Party has, in addition to a General Congress, a 'Party Council' of forty members selected by the General Congress. Among the functions of this body used to be 'the determination of the party's general policy'.[1] By contrast, the functions of the party's General Congress were not as closely defined as in the present law. Although the General Congress was described as 'the party's highest authority', its functions were to discuss and decide on national and party affairs only, within the framework of the party's policies. The Justice Party's Central Representative Council is also interposed between its General Congress and the small central executive body, although its determination of general party policy was said to have to be in accord with the directives and general views of the General Congress.[2]

What the law does not do is to abolish bodies like the People's Party's 'Party Council'. Indeed, it specifically gives authority for the setting up of other central organizations in addition to those prescribed (Article 14). It is doubtful if the new legislation will much hinder the operation of the 'iron law of oligarchy'; and the tradition of centralization is long established in Turkish political

---

General Congresses. This changed the previous position in the R.P.N.P. and the N.P. to whose Congresses only one-third of their parliamentary members were admitted. The aim of this provision in the law is to ensure that parliamentary and government party members are subject to control of the party. The equally democratic argument that this device does not so much ensure party control over parliamentary party and government as the reverse was not heeded. This and other aspects of the law are well argued by Cemal Aygen, 'Siyasî Partiler Kanunu', *Forum*, no. 236, 1 February 1964.

[1] *CHP Tüzüğü* (1963) (Standing Orders of the People's Party, 1963).
[2] *Adalet Partisi Tüzüğü* (1963).

parties. It is too early yet to see what differences the new law will make to the realities of party organization, but in a few years' time, it would be a fascinating study to undertake.

Another interesting attempt is made to ensure democracy from the bottom by devices introduced for the nomination by the parties of candidates for general and other elections. Although there are no serious studies of the subject, it is generally held that in the important process of the nomination of candidates for elections, the part played by the central organization of the parties has always been much greater than that of the local party organizations and, above all, of ordinary party members. Candidates for general elections were generally chosen by bodies composed of delegates elected by party congresses and of party officials. The new law introduces important innovations. There now have to be primary elections within the party in which all party members may vote to decide who are to stand as the party's candidates in general, provincial and local elections.

The conduct of the primary elections is regulated in detail (pre-electoral campaigning, for instance, is prohibited); and even these party elections are now controlled by the High Electoral Board, the body which supervises elections proper. Only 5 per cent of a party's candidates for election to the Grand National Assembly may be nominated by the party central organizations unless there is an insufficiency of candidates—a dangerous loophole perhaps.[1] When there are central nominating boards for candidates they have to contain representatives from the provincial organizations.

A very important organizational change from the pre-revolutionary period is that parties may not set up a political organization below the level of sub-province beyond maintaining a single person and an assistant. This perpetuates a law of the N.U.C., and is based on the widely held view that political party rivalry at the village and neighbourhood levels leads to disruption of basic social units. In discussion of this point, the very controversial view usually advanced is the time-worn one that

---

[1] For the 1965 general election, the provisions of the law, which was not passed until July 1965, did not come into effect (see Provisional Article 2 of the Political Parties' Law). Essentially, the only difference between the 1965 primaries and the previous mode of election was that, in 1965, the process was supervised by the High Electoral Board.

political discussion is not possible in places where the most basic needs have not been met. Another interesting development—one that does not accord with a multi-party system using a system of proportional representation—is the designation of the leader of the largest non-government party in the lower house as chief opposition party leader (Article 13).

Other provisions of the law deal with the internal administration of the political parties with the aim of ensuring that their accounts, minutes, etc., are properly kept. There is also a section on party disciplinary matters designed to make discipline less arbitrary. Much more important, however, are the provisions regarding closure of parties and financial control, in both of which matters the Constitutional Court has an important role to play. Suits for the closure of political parties are handled by the Constitutional Court, whose verdict is final. The Court also has a duty of examining the accounts of income and expenditure of political parties to ensure conformity with the law and is empowered to make such enquiries as it finds necessary. This is an odd duty to give to a Constitutional Court; it has been criticized as likely to involve the Court too much in party affairs and thus lower the respect in which it is held.

The need for effective financial control is felt because the new law contains very important financial rules broadly designed to prevent any political party from exploiting the advantage of greater wealth to win votes and influence the electorate. A party entrance fee must not exceed 5 *lira* (£·20), nor a monthly membership contribution 100 *lira* (£4). Public and quasi-public institutions, including trade unions, employers' federations, or, indeed, associations of any sort, may not make contributions to political parties. Private organizations (like commercial firms) may contribute not more than 5,000 *lira* each year (£200). This rather bleak financial prospect is relieved, however, by financial aid from the state, the amount being calculated on the basis of a party's success in the previous general election.[1] The chief drawback in this formula is that it does not provide a means of state financing of new parties.

[1] A party gaining from 5 per cent to 10 per cent of the vote receives annually 500,000 *lira* (£20,000). At the other end of the scale, to have obtained over 50 per cent of the vote would earn an annual state revenue of 3,500,000 *lira* (£140,000). See Article 74.

The Republican People's Party

The People's Party began political life again in 1961 with two legacies it could well have done without. There was the legacy first of the time when it was the sole party in the single-party state. It was distrusted and disliked by many, particularly the peasantry and new entrepreneurs because it had for years up to 1950 been identified with the reformist, heavy-handed state. Atatürk's westernizing and modernizing reforms were not popular with the mass of the populace. The party was deeply implicated in them and its leader Atatürk's lieutenant, İsmet İnönü.

Secondly, the party was undoubtedly identified in the common view with the 1960 revolution. The party leaned over backwards in its attempts not to be so identified, but it was held captive by the situation. After all, those who bore the brunt of the Democrat Party government's policy of curtailment of political freedoms were the members of the People's Party. To the unsophisticated, the military seemed to be going to rescue them, not to rescue a notion called democracy. Even the more sophisticated, when they heard the military proclaiming the virtues of democracy and describing the dangers to which it had recently been subject, could be tempted into thinking they were still listening to the People's Party, by whom the principles of democracy had been given more and more voice as repression had grown. Then again, the inexperience of the soldiers when in power made them rely on those about with some political and administrative experience. They chose the uncommitted as much as possible, but they had to have recourse to a number of able men who belonged to, or stood close to, the party. Consequently, as the popularity of the military regime declined (as quickly happens) so did that of the People's Party.

Yet the party was confident of victory in the promised elections, provided they were not too much delayed; and they consequently did all they could to hurry them along before the new parties could organize themselves effectively. In the 1961 general election they were just successful, in the sense that they were the party with the largest vote; but unsuccessful in the sense that they had a much smaller following than the Justice Party and New Turkey Party together. The party has been strong enough to be the dominant force in government from October 1961 to January

1965. Nevertheless, its history, since October 1961, has been of growing ineffectiveness, culminating in its very poor showing in the 1965 general election.

This failure of the People's Party is not easily ascribable to any single factor. The party entered into post-revolutionary politics as a symbol of stability in a situation where this was a prime qualification for office. It had done less well in the elections of 1961 than had been expected, but the optimists could put this down to the party's passing identification with the military, an identification that might well disappear as time passed by. The party was recognized as the chief author of the Constitution, which incorporated so many of the changes it had long advocated. Its programme in 1961 was not fiercely doctrinaire. As befitted a party composed of many different elements, it sought not to be too rigid. The state was to leave room for private enterprise; foreign capital to serve national economic purposes was welcome, a just taxation system was promised, the landless and land-short peasant were to be given land and social security and social services were to be extended. It was a liberal but progressive programme. The party, it has been said, had become a 'middle-class conservative party'[1] and probably gained some support at that time in consequence. By 1961 it seemed on the way to becoming a middle-class socialist party.

If we follow the party's record since 1961, we find it is full of disturbances. To a certain extent the fact that the party had to form coalitions in order to govern accounts for some of this.[2] The coalition with the other parties meant that the party could not hope, for instance, to push through radical land reform. Nor should it be forgotten that the crucial governmental task in the three years after the revolution was to create political stability.

In this situation, the party leadership was soon attacked by elements within the party. Basically, there were three trends of criticism. First, there were those who thought that by being soft on the former imprisoned Democrats, by tolerating abuse of the

[1] Kemal H. Karpat, *Turkey's Politics, the Transition to a Multi-Party System* (Princeton, 1959), p. 401.

[2] Supporters of proportional representation sometimes forget that by forcing the compromises essential for government in the Assembly instead of in the electorate the system puts members of a party participating in government under a considerable strain. They now have openly to compromise the principles on the basis of which they went to the electorate.

1960 revolution, the party leadership was being untrue to the principles of Atatürk, a dangerous accusation. This could go further—to assertions that the party ought to restore People's Houses in the villages and village institutes, two noted Atatürkist institutions designed to carry the revolution to the people. This criticism could easily slip into a second stream of broadly socialist criticism, which maintained that too much opportunity was given to private enterprise, that the party would not take a stand against the large landholders, particularly the landlords (*ağas*) of the eastern provinces. These sorts of criticisms emanated from the intellectuals and the youth organizations. Eminent members of the party could also give them voice.[1]

A third line of criticism emanating, it seems, from the party's provincial organization was that whatever the government had to do, it should do it with energy and determination. This was not so much dissatisfaction with compromise, but with the vacillation that compromise was producing. This general criticism gave strength to the numerous attacks on particular ministers for incompetence.

Underlying much of this criticism of the leadership was a great deal of ambivalence in attitude about the respected leader, İnönü. He was—and still is—in many ways indispensable. Resentment in the party about excessive centralism is difficult to disentangle from resentment a minority strongly feels against İnönü himself.

A combination of these dissatisfactions produced in 1962 and 1963 very disagreeable signs of party disunity that must have seriously upset the general image of the People's Party as a symbol of real stability. In 1962 Kasım Gülek, Nihat Erim and Avni Doğan, three leading members of the party, were expelled for one year.[2] In the following year party unity was strained still further when it emerged that a small number of distinguished party members had been in touch with the author of the attempted

---

[1] Notably Nihat Erim and Kasım Gülek. The latter, who is a large landowner, declared that he was prepared to pay heavier taxes and give up land‘ One senior and prominent member of the party, Yakup Kadri Karaosmanoğlu, resigned on the grounds that the party had compromised the reforms of Atatürk. *Cumhuriyet*, 15 October 1962.

[2] They were suspended just before the XVIth Annual Congress of the party which they were, in consequence, not able to attend. This, no doubt, helped the party to maintain its unity at this critical time; the party leadership did not have to cope with serious opposition at the Congress.

coup of 20–21 May 1963, with members of the 'fourteen' expelled from the military Junta and with those involved in the attempted coup of February 1962, on the subject of forming a new political party.[1] In December 1963, Kasım Gülek and Avni Doğan were expelled.

The effect of these criticisms was to force the party to move slowly towards the left. In March 1962 the Party Council began to look again at the programme in the light of the force of the Atatürkist and socialist criticisms. What was really happening was that the party was being increasingly forced to locate itself somewhere along the line from extreme left to extreme right. By 1965 the party's stance as somewhere left of centre was becoming apparent. The momentous decision came when, for the elections of 1965, the party declared itself as 'left of centre'.

This shift to the left had both internal and external effects. First, it increased the distance between the party and its colleagues in the second coalition government (the Y.T.P. and the R.P.N.P.) and was undoubtedly one of the underlying causes for the break up of that coalition. Secondly, the move to the left alienated the centre group within the party of which Turhan Feyzioğlu was a prominent member and which basically favoured a coalition with the Justice Party. Feyzioğlu, in fact, declined appointment in İnönü's third government and apparently refused later invitations to join. So did other experienced politicians like Aksal and Erim (when returned to favour). This in turn aggravated the difficulties İnönü experienced in his last period of government in finding a sufficient number of really competent ministers.

Yet the most insignificant results of the party's taking up a position 'left of centre' lie in its relations with other parties and its partial relinquishing of the Atatürk tradition.

First, it is quite clear that for a broad-based party like the People's Party to adopt so definite a position on a left–right continuum is to invite the emergence of a really left-wing party (in this case the Turkish Worker's Party) and to make many of the middle-of-the-road supporters realize that they are, perhaps, really right of centre—and right of centre seems the most appropriate position for newly emerging middle classes. Secondly, and

---

[1] The party members concerned were not accused of complicity in the 20–21 May attempted coup. The party's concern was with their fidelity to the party. For the historical context see above, p. 81.

perhaps even more important, the party has not maybe fully appreciated how its implicit acceptance of a definition of political differences in simple, basically Marxist, terms of left and right undermined its claim to represent more faithfully than any other party the Atatürk political tradition.

The relevant Kemalist tradition here is populism,[1] an expression of the idea of social harmony among individuals forming occupational groups that basically rejects the Marxist socio-economic class struggle. In adopting the label 'left of centre' the People's Party is not, of course, going so far as to say that it is a class party, but it does seem basically to be compromising its populism (still a principle in its programme) by accepting socio-economic class conflict between left and right as the basic political fact of Turkish society.

The manifesto with which the party entered the 1965 general election revealed the influence of the four years of internal party reaction against the compromises that the party had made with its coalition colleagues and with itself. The position officially occupied of 'left of centre' did not make it intransigent in the crucial question of state enterprise. Its position was not different from 1961; private enterprise was to be given a place alongside state enterprise. Moreover, the manifesto makes it clear that the party envisages a programme of economic development to benefit all classes and this was to be done within a democratic system.

[1] Populism (*halkçilik*) was a doctrine developed in the early years of the Atatürk Republic as one of the three basic principles of the Republic, of which the other two were nationalism and secularism. Since those days, both nationalism and secularism have come to be more liberally defined, but not to the point of disrupting national unity or of permitting any religious voice in state affairs. Populism expressed the idea that society is made up of individuals in occupational groups whose economic interests do not clash. It was denied that there were socio-economic classes in Turkey. Political parties were regarded as based on socio-economic class; therefore, there was no need for a multi-party system in Turkey! There was also the illogical but realistic *arrière pensée* that, if they were permitted, parties would promote the class struggle that populism rejected as divisive of national and social unity. The early notion of the close connection between political parties and socio-economic classes had to be amended when multi-party politics became possible in 1946, or else populism would have had to be jettisoned. The political parties hastened to dissociate themselves from any particular socio-economic classes; and it was any way in their practical interest to broaden their appeal. This analysis derives from K. Karpat, *Turkey's Politics*, pp. 51–3 and 308–14.

Freedom was not to be sacrificed for bread, yet the party recognized the uselessness of freedom without bread—a most succinct expression of the difficulty of being 'left of centre' in an economically underdeveloped society.

In particular policies the party was now able, however, to give a much firmer notion of what it intended. Land reform was to be on the basis set out in the Land Reform Law that the party had just failed to get through before its coalition Government with Independents was overthrown in February 1965. The law on oil exploration and exploitation would be changed to remove certain limits on exploitation by Turkish enterprise; and to prevent the profits foreign companies exported from the petrol they produced in Turkey from exceeding half the value of the petrol on the world market. There was also a harder attitude evident about the importation of foreign capital, particularly the need to see that it did not hinder local development or exhaust local resources or create balance-of-payments difficulties. Economic aid from foreign countries, it was categorically stated, would be without strings. The emphasis on Turkish independence was to be carried into defence. Without putting aside the system of western alliances, Turkey was, above all, to direct foreign policy with regard to national aims. (Many Turks feel they have been obliged to sacrifice national interests over Cyprus to the needs of the western alliance.)

The Justice Party

The Justice Party was founded in February 1961, under the leadership of a retired General Ragıp Gümüşpala. He had been retired in August 1961, one of the 5,000 then retired, but he had held high command for a period after the 1960 revolution. He was not, therefore, overtly anti-revolutionary.

It was incumbent on the Justice Party, if it wished to participate in the elections of 1961 at all, to make a show of accepting the revolution and not posing as heir to the fallen Democrat Party. This the party just about managed to do; it was generally circumspect enough to persuade the military that democratic politics might work, although sharp warnings were necessary from Gürsel from time to time, particularly during the election campaign of 1961 when electoral fever made some Justice Party orators overstep the line. Yet it was quite obvious that the Justice Party programme in 1961 was very little different from that of the Democrats and, more ominous, that the new party had inherited a very large part of the Democrat Party's extensive and experienced local organization.

The party's 1961 election manifesto places the party just right of centre, though it does not say so. Its rightist inclination stems not from authoritarianism, but from liberalism, which is freedom basically for the new commercial and industrial middle classes and for 'traditional', landowning and religious interests. Almost everyone, however, is promised an increase in freedom from something. That increased freedom for some may mean increased restriction for others does not, of course, enter into the picture.

Briefly, there is to be encouragement for private enterprise, whilst it is recognized that state enterprise is necessary in some spheres. In this connection, the de-nationalization of some state monopolies was also envisaged, whilst for others the control of the export of their products would be turned over to private enterprise. The taxation programme declares against land, property and animal taxes and expresses serious doubts about the advisability of agricultural income tax for an underdeveloped country like Turkey. Taxes on small traders and the like would also be reduced, whilst obligatory savings bonds, which particularly affect officials and employees of all sorts, would also be removed. It is difficult to see from the programme who would finance the state.

On land reform, the party recognizes the need to provide land for the landless peasant (the amount to vary according to regional agricultural differences); and intends to leave existing landowners with medium-sized farms. For economic reasons, it is said, land must not be divided into too small plots. The accent generally in its agricultural policies is on economic efficiency, for which large-scale private ownership is deemed to be a necessity; and agricultural workers (presumably on someone else's land) are a necessary part of the agricultural scene.

The manifesto includes the right to strike given to all workers in the new Constitution. It also gives a large place to the needs of public health and social assistance. 'Socialized' health is accepted, with a place here, too, for private enterprise. Social security is also stressed; security against unemployment and old age are envisaged as part of social security schemes.

Education the party wishes to see expanded to fit ability and inclination and provided for all on an equal basis, girls included. The two principal evils, it seems, are sheer lack of any education for many and inadequate provision for diverse talents and abilities. The need is stressed, however, for much more diversified education in different types of schools; and education is to encourage democratic attitudes that will prevent the perpetuation of the hierarchical single-party type of mentality.

One of the most liberal sentiments is the party's desire for greater autonomy in local government. The bare bones of an interesting but not very clear scheme appear in which local government is to be based on those villages and towns that are economically and geographically important. The accent is on integrating the village into the national culture and on a greater amount of decision-making in the locality. This is in effect an attack on the existing rather authoritarian system which the Justice Party sees as a powerful relic from the days of the one-party state and imbued with its mentality. In this connection, the manifesto stresses the need for more humane and imaginative handling of the people by the administration.

It is, perhaps, needless to add that the manifesto stresses economic development as *the* policy for Turkey. All parties do so, but the Justice Party in its manifesto makes less mention of planning, which in principle it was obliged to accept, since it is in the Constitution.

A comparison of this important foundation manifesto of 1961 with the party's declared aims in 1965 shows certain changes. These show the party to have moved a few degrees to what is generally understood somewhat ambiguously as the 'right'.

As we have seen, in 1961 land reform (in the sense of redistribution of land to the landless) was very guardedly mentioned; the peasant was to be made 'owner of a parcel of land' (amount unspecified). In 1965 the wording is even less definite; and despite the discussion during the period that resulted in 1964 in a draft law, there is no discussion of detail at all.

In planning, which the 1961 manifesto does not mention, the party takes the view that its purpose is to see better the relations between the different sectors of the economy, to prevent disagreements and to provide a means of profiting from informed analyses based on sound statistics. Planning is not a 'strait-jacket'; and there is no necessary connection between planning and state economic enterprise. There must be a positive approach to private enterprise; the planning organization is not an authoritative organ, save for the public sector. The party believes in close participation of the private sector workers' representatives in planning for the private sector. The party could not formally abolish planning without changing the Constitution. Significantly, perhaps, there is no real mention of positive developments in planning, by contrast with the People's Party manifesto, which talks of setting up a 'Social and Economic Research Board' and 'planning units' in ministries for the better execution of the plan. Whilst both major parties profess belief in planning and private enterprise, and do not see them as incompatible, they differ considerably in emphasis.

The Justice Party position in the matter of foreign capital differs from that in 1961. Then it spoke very cautiously about the need of low interest rates and long periods of repayment. In 1965 the party's manifesto goes to some lengths to explain the need for foreign capital and criticizes those opposed to it. Its use is, however, to be restricted or directed to those fields most relevant to Turkish economic development. As compared with the People's Party, it is not so much a difference of view as a difference of emphasis. The Justice Party in its manifesto is more positive, more confident. In the closely connected oil question, which did not appear with full force in 1961, the Justice Party, whilst mindful of the national interest, does not suggest anything like the quite extensive legal controls suggested by the People's Party.

In social matters, the Party gives a more pronounced place in 1965 to social justice and social security than in 1961. There is to be equality of opportunity and social security schemes are to be extended. Unemployment is the greatest injustice and inequality; it can only be removed by creating new opportunities for work. Unemployment insurance must be started. In all this, the party is vying with the People's Party which, as a party 'left of centre', naturally has very extensive schemes for social justice and social security. The Justice Party stresses the individual rather more than does its chief rival; and relates social justice and social security to economic development (through private enterprise) more positively than the People's Party. Individual effort is everywhere stressed more.

In education, much more place is given to university education in 1965 than in 1961. The party includes in its policies an amelioration of the general working living conditions of students including, significantly, the intention to increase the value they obtain from their spare time. There is a promise of new universities; and the value of academic advice in governmental problems is stressed. The party is, obviously, out to get the universities on its side.

A new feature in the 1965 manifesto is the party's concern for national unity. This is a case of attack being the best form of defence. Since 1961 the Justice Party has been accused, not without injustice, of ruining the chances of stability by insistence on, and fostering enmities by, their amnesty demands. To ensure social peace—and to solve Turkey's many problems effectively—stable government is seen to be necessary. To obtain this, the electoral system must be changed. The usual arguments against proportional representation are seductively presented. Shrewdly enough, it is claimed that since, under the 1961 Constitution, power is divided among so many institutions, there is more than ever a need for stable majority party government. Public opinion is said to be sufficiently alert to prevent a majority party government from establishing a dictatorship. There were some who believed this in the 1950's.

The fortunes of the Justice Party from 1961 are full of interest. The party began its political life in coalition with its principal opponents, the People's Party. This is usually described as a 'shot-gun marriage', but there was a certain amount of common ground between the parties, particularly between the moderates on both sides who were responsible for creating and working the coalition. The coalition began to falter when more extreme groups in both parties rejected further compromise of their principles.

In the Justice Party, the chief principle that agitated the minds of the extreme elements was the necessity for a pardon for those imprisoned in Yassıada; but this was allied to a keen dislike of İnönü, a detestation of what was seen as the People's Party's authoritarian and self-righteous style of ruling—allegedly an inheritance from the days, now long past, when it was the sole party. This was laced with some normal dissatisfaction that ministerial posts had gone to moderates.

During the early part of 1962 'rightist' criticism within the Justice Party was given more and more voice. It began to come to a head in February over the case of the Justice Party deputy, Nuri Beşer, who made insulting remarks about the Army.[1] Speeches made by other deputies were also causing offence to the military. The unsuccessful coup of 21–22 February underlined the danger. In this dangerous situation, the Justice Party cleansed itself of some of its extremists and others resigned. Even in early April, in response to complaints by the People's Party that its extremists were causing trouble by inflammatory speeches in their constituencies, the Justice Party was taking disciplinary measures against its malcontents; but then quite suddenly the tail began to wag the dog.

In early April 1962 the party's Executive Council resigned, to be replaced by one that was supposed more fairly to represent all provincial regional organizations.[2] This may have been a sop to the extremists, who still insisted that recent expulsions from the party should be reviewed before the meeting of the Great Congress to be held at the end of the year. Gümüşpala was forced by this pressure into both praising those expelled and yet still refusing to discuss their re-entry into the party. More important, he now had to take a firm stand in favour of an amnesty by trying to trade an amnesty for the soldiers who had participated in the abortive February coup for an amnesty for those in Yassıada.[3]

When at the end of May 1962 the coalition fell—on just this amnesty question—the moderates were furious and tried to bring about the downfall of Gümüşpala. At first they seemed to be in the ascendant—there were more resignations of extremists—but another new Executive Council formed in early June contained a majority of their opponents. The moderates staged a counter attack, some sixty-five deputies and senators presenting a demand for a Great Congress, the resignation of the Executive Council and the party's parliamentary group's executive committee.

[1] See above, p. 59, for further details.

[2] A new Executive Council was appointed by the small group of persons who founded the Justice Party. This was the procedure to be followed until the first meeting of the party's 'Great Congress' (*Büyük Kongre*) of which there had not, as yet, been a meeting. The Executive Committee would then be elected by the Congress. It seems that the party founders largely left the nomination of the Executive Committee to Gümüşpala, the party's leader. (*Cumhuriyet*, 4 April 1962).

[3] This was in contradiction to his participation in an all-party agreement at the time of the attempted February coup to pardon those responsible.

Instead, however, a meeting was called of the chairmen of the provincial organizations, who could be expected to support the extremists. Moreover, the moderates were badly outmanœuvred, being prevented from presenting their case effectively. The 'extremists' were confirmed in their position. Resignations of moderates now began, though not in as large numbers as might have been expected.

Undoubtedly, once over its immediate fright, the party began to realize that the affair of 21–22 February showed that military intervention was less likely to re-occur than they had thought. Consequently, the party as a whole became bolder and more intransigent. It is also clear that the parliamentary group, in which extremists were strong, could impose policy on the party's Executive Council, partly, perhaps, because the Executive Council at this time lacked the legitimacy of election by the Great Congress. Another factor in the parliamentary group's supremacy was that its chairman, the Deputy Party Chairman, Saadettin Bilgiç, was very influential in the party's provincial organization. As was shown, the chairmen of the provincial organizations could be brought in to support the 'extremists'.

The party's first 'Great Congress' met in December 1962, after a summer of fiery provincial party congresses which saw a certain amount of gross anti-intellectualism and many claims that the party, not the army nor the intellectuals, was the true representative of the national will. Although there were signs that the moderates/extremists' battle was on the wane, it is still meaningful to say at that time that influence lay with the extremists. Expelled moderates were not allowed to be heard at the Congress; Gümüşpala was elected chairman and the now-elected Executive Council was largely in extremists' hands. One straw in the wind, however, was the election to the Executive Council from the moderates' list of one, Süleyman Demirel.

It is pertinent, at this point, to enquire a little further into the meaning of the epithets 'moderate' and 'extremist' as applied by the not-too-friendly press to the two wings of the party. By 'extremist' was largely meant those who clamoured for an immediate pardon for the Yassıada prisoners and who, by extension, were supposed to be basically in opposition to the 1960 revolution, in sympathy with the fallen Democrat Party and out of sympathy with the military. All this was, of course, emotional and backward-looking and perhaps only disguised other more substantial underlying differences within the party. It might, perhaps, better be said that, at this time, the party contained three basic groups. First, there were the real reactionaries, very sympathetic to religion, very conservative and anti-Atatürkist; they had reached the parliamentary level, often for the first time, in the general confusion attending the birth of the Justice Party. Secondly, there were those emotionally attached to the former Democrat Party, some liberal, some authoritarian. Thirdly, came the moderates, men closer to the state than the rest, often in state employ, more responsible, better educated and more inclined to compromise.[1]

The first Great Congress did not allay the Justice Party's discontents. When in April 1963 the former President Celal Bayar was temporarily released, the Justice Party was seen to be implicated in the general disturbances that occurred. After some wavering, the party took a firm line, was unrepentant and watched the exit of more of its moderates of whom, by now, some forty had left the party. In the meantime, legal enquiries continued, accelerated by the second attempted coup of May 1963 into allegedly anti-revolutionary speeches by Justice Party and other deputies.

Yet now the tumult in the party began to subside—no doubt because releases of political prisoners were getting under way; and for a long period comparatively little was heard of the Party. In speeches in the provinces, Gümüşpala seemed to be striving to create a new image for the party as a party of law and order, friendly to the military.[2] He did not believe the military would prevent the party from assuming power. When, following Justice Party successes in the local elections at the end of 1963—and the collapse of the second coalition—Gümüşpala was asked to form a government, he failed, not because of potential military opposition, but because the Y.T.P. and the R.P.N.P. were afraid of their big brother.

The party was now very confident and became more so after its success in the partial Senate elections in June 1964. The sudden death of its leader, Gümüşpala, soon after the elections, now caused, however, a new struggle within the party between,

---

[1] These views are based on general opinions current at the time, not on detailed studies of the backgrounds and careers of Turkish politicians, which need to be made.

[2] E.g. speeches in Yozgat, November 1963, reported in the press.

principally, two contenders for the leadership, the deputy leader, Saadettin Bilgiç, and Süleyman Demirel. Both first entered politics after 1960; both are relatively young, born in 1921 and 1925 respectively. They have both practised professions, Bilgiç as a doctor and Demirel as an engineer. They do not come from the ranks of the military or administrative elite, but both have worked in a professional capacity for governmental institutions. Demirel, under the Menderes regime, was General Director of State Water Undertakings, in which he acquired a reputation for administrative as well as professional competence. He has risen from humble village origins and has prospered materially, through private enterprise, which it is, therefore, natural for him to view as a blessing. He does not impress as an orator, but has some knowledge of economics. Bilgiç knows very little economics and speaks even less well than Demirel.[1] His strength lies in his hold over the party's organization and his political sang-froid; but he is not as well regarded as Demirel by the party's intellectuals. Most important, perhaps, Demirel has the support of most former Menderes supporters in the party.

The election of the new leader took place at the party's second Great Congress in December 1964. The conflict between the chief two contenders was not on policies, as the party published a draft policy before the Congress—a document in which both Bilgiç and Demirel had presumably concurred since they were both members of the Executive Council. This largely precluded any argument between the two candidates on policy, which would, no doubt, have redounded to the credit of Demirel. Nevertheless, Demirel was elected leader by a very convincing majority (1,072 to 552 for Bilgiç). In addition, over half the members of the Executive Council were changed at the Congress, producing a council of men of more moderate inclinations. What was, perhaps, most significant about Demirel's election was that his opponent's acknowledged control of the party organization did not bring him to victory. One of the problems created by Demirel's election was that he would not be able directly to control (or co-ordinate) the parliamentary group since he was not a member of parliament. Yet the friction between the parliamentary group and Executive

---

[1] A speech he delivered (very badly) in a general discussion in the National Assembly on Cyprus, 7 September 1964, was considered a great misfortune for his chances of election to leadership.

Council was much reduced by the greater legitimacy that election by the Congress gave to the Executive Council.

The role of the party in the overthrow of İnönü's government in February 1965 has already been explained.[1] The party now seemed to go from strength to strength, except that one nasty and indicative little storm blew up in April 1965, when a small group of deputies accused the party of having become an employers' and businessmen's club, to the neglect of the interests of the small traders, peasants and workers. This attack was, to some extent, justified by the increased emphasis given to private enterprise. What the authors of this attack had in mind was a half-materialistic, half-idealistic national socialism, akin to the currents running in the R.P.N.P. under its new leader, Türkeş. This could not, however, prevent the Justice Party from romping home in the General Election of 1965.

The minor parties

The Turkish Workers' Party. This party lies furthest to the left. It was formed in February 1961 by a group of trade-union leaders in Istanbul, one of eleven new parties which were formed at that time.

The history of the development of the party has now become much clearer.[2] It seems that it was intended at first as little more than a political means of furthering the interests of industrial workers by seeking their representation in parliament. It did not begin with a socialist doctrine; and did not seek to address any other sections of the society but the 'workers'. In early 1962 the party reduced the size of its executive committee from twenty to seven. During 1962 the party was in close contact with socialist groups in Ankara.[3] As a result a noted socialist, Mehmet Ali Aybar, became its leader—a turning-point in the party's history.

The party's first publication appeared in 1963.[4] Its appeal was

---

[1] Above, pp. 94–5.

[2] Thanks to an excellent article by Kemal H. Karpat, 'Socialism and the Labor Party of Turkey', *Middle East Journal*, vol. 21, No. 2, 1967, pp. 157–72. Previous attempts to form socialist parties were frustrated by the unwillingness of the trade unions.

[3] See *Yön* 27 December 1961, 4 April 1962, 5 May 1962, 12 September 1962 and 26 September 1962 for interesting, but not complete, information about these contacts.

[4] Türkiye İşçi Partisi, *Amacimiz, Yolumuz, Yönelimiz* (Ankara, 1963).

to the working class and was based on socialist doctrine, though the language was more guarded than in later publications. The party began slowly to establish a provincial organization and competed, but with hardly any success, in the 1963 local elections. It had held an open meeting in Istanbul in November 1962, which became violent. An attack by the party's leader, Mehmet Ali Aybar, on *inter alia* those who in the past had neglected the working class, on landlords, speculators and capitalists was quieted with 'death to the Communists' and general uproar. On the whole the party's approach was too ideological and dogmatic. In February 1964 the party held its first Congress in Izmir. The delegates were hand-picked for their ideological firmness. The leader, whose position was confirmed by the Congress, declared his disbelief in the government's intention with regard to land reform and saw the Constitution exploited by reactionaries, those intent on revenge and by traditional wielders of power over the people. Some trade unions were described as serving capitalists, an important point which underlines the fact that not all trade unionists are with the Workers' Party. Indeed, in industrial disputes in the Zonguldak coalfield in 1965, the Turkish trade-union movement refused to be pushed into lending its support to the party's views on the necessity of class conflict. The Turkish unions, for the most part, prefer to be above politics; and retain both their bargaining power —and their unity—on which their power to bargain depends. The future for the Turkish Workers' Party may lie as much with the landless peasants as with the industrial and other workers.

The party's manifesto for the 1965 elections is normal enough for a very left-wing political party that accepts the democratic system. Yet what it has to say is new for Turkish politics, and therefore seems fresh and dynamic. Its literature is also written in simple, direct, sometimes quite stirring language that some of the other parties would do well to study.[1]

The manifesto begins with a slashing attack on American imperialism and Turkey's subservience to this foreign influence. Agreements with the United States that give privileges to the Americans would be dissolved, it is said.[2] This is a good start in a

---

[1] A very succinct and forceful election publication (a shortened manifesto) is *Türkiye İşçi Partisini Tanıyalım* (Istanbul, 1965).

[2] The attack on the Americans is quite vicious. 'They first came', it is claimed, 'to our capital as aid missions. Now they have experts in every

way since it excites national feeling; it also, however, suggests that the party is pro-Russian—which it actually is careful not to say—and thus no doubt created a bad impression in this respect among the majority to whom Moscow is still as evil as ever it was.

A telling point—to judge from the reactions of other parties—was the claim that the Workers' Party was the only party whose candidates were in any large numbers themselves manual workers. 'By voting for us, you are electing yourselves' was the message the party tried to get across. The third of its candidates who were not manual workers were described as brain workers, whose lives were devoted to the cause, and included lawyers and engineers. Members of these professions in other parties were capitalist lawyers and engineers in the employ of merchants and landowners.

The party preaches then a completely independent foreign policy (the Americans were not to be replaced by any other power) but advocates a return to the allegedly Atatürk tradition of friendly relations with neighbouring states, of which the Soviet Union is mentioned first.

Despite the pride of first place to relations with other states, the manifesto declares that the party's chief concern is with accelerated economic and social development. This is not possible through capitalism, as the experience of the past forty years is adduced to show. Although under the necessary etatism heavy industry and large units of production will be in state hands, there is a place for private enterprise for some time. It will, however, gradually become less important and perform a subsidiary function. It is not stated that private enterprise will completely disappear; nor is it said that it will not. In such an uncertain and menacing situation, it would anyway probably die of its own accord. It almost goes without saying that foreign capital would be nationalized and so too would foreign trade. The exploitation of oil and other mineral resources would also be completely in state hands, as too would banking and insurance.

In the shorter, even more popular, manifesto referred to above,[1]

---

ministry. They are agents of the American government working under the title of "experts". No state secrets remain. The Americans know all our business. But they are not content with knowing, they exert pressure if necessary to direct us along the road they want.' *T.I.P. Seçim Bildirisi* (1965), p. 3.

[1] See footnote 1 p. 150.

the party gives land reform first place as the principal measure to develop Turkey. It comes out with the definite policy of restricting all land holdings to a maximum of 500 *dönüms* (125 acres) and does not pull any punches in its attack on landowners to whom the peasants, it is bluntly said, are slaves. Middle-sized peasant landowners are reassured, however. Their land will not be touched: and nowhere is there any mention of collective farming. The execution of land reform laws would be in the hands of locally elected bodies.

All parties now promise much for the worker in social security, but none proposes, with the Workers' Party, a five-day, forty-hour week. Nor does any other party condemn the employers' right to lock out the workers.

As to be expected of so left-wing a party, there is to be accent on education, including adult education. To this end, People's Houses would be re-established. Youth would be organized and labour exalted. Property rights and inheritance are recognized; but not if they lead to exploitation.

All this is pretty much to pattern, but one aspect of the party's policies where original thought is necessary is its relationship with democratic institutions. Here, the party proclaims its adherence to political democracy. It would respect minority parties and, if defeated at the polls, would withdraw. There would be respect for the basic freedoms, including freedom of religious belief. However, the party is not satisfied with a democracy that amounts to little more than elections every four years.[1] Beginning with their places of work, the people would actively participate in administering their own affairs in villages, town wards, municipalities, provincial councils and, of course, the Grand National Assembly. Much of the party's apparent respect for representative democracy seems to evaporate, however, when it attacks those who, under the guise of representing the national will, do not really wish to see the people wake from their sleep and who use political institutions to perpetuate their form of economic and social regime.

If Turkish democracy is not representative, then, apparently, it will not be retained. It is a harsh condition. Representative democracy is nowhere perfect. In less-developed countries,

---

[1] It could be argued that there are now many, perhaps too many, elections in Turkey, especially as one-third of the Senate is elected every two years.

particularly, small groups of classes can often obtain the vote and use its alleged 'legitimacy' to bolster up their own positions of power. It is tempting to replace it with a regime led by disinterested intellectuals that really concentrates on basic economic and social reforms for the workless and homeless. The Workers' Party is vitally concerned with solving the basic problems; it is difficult to see how, despite the intentions of many of its leaders, it could really prevent itself from seriously curtailing democratic freedoms if it came to power. Less drastic solutions are possible if the other parties address the shirtless and pantsless with the same honest realism as the Workers' Party. Some of them could profit from emulating the directness of the Workers' Party's appeal.

The New Turkey Party. The party that makes the least appeal to the masses is, probably, the New Turkey Party. This is not because it is right wing in the sense that an aristocratic or monarchist party is right wing. It does not despise or look down upon the people; it just does not seem to make contact with them.

The party is the most liberal of the parties and, like many essentially liberal parties, is somewhat too intellectual, too idealistic, too devoted to leaving people to be free to be able to make real contact. It earns respect but not support.

The party began its career in February 1961. Most important amongst its founders was a group of former members of the Freedom Party founded in 1957, a splinter party from the Democrat Party. The party began with chances that seemed as good, if not better, than those of the new Justice Party, its chief rival for former Democrat Party votes. It made some remarkable *faux pas* in its relations with the National Unity Committee with whom the party was at first on good terms; yet bad relations with the military Junta would only increase its appeal for former Democrat Party votes.

As it turned out, the Party did attract former Democrat Party supporters in quite large measure in 1961. Its basic problem was to reconcile these supporters to the leadership of more moderate elements, many of whom, like the leader Ekrem Alican, had belonged to the Freedom Party. Of the former Democrat Party supporters, it seems that some really wanted the party to join the Justice Party, to climb on the bandwagon, in fact, before it was too late. Others wanted to oppose the Justice Party in a vigorous competition for the former Democrat vote, to establish themselves as heirs to the Democrat Party in fact. Many of these former Democrat Party supporters were to an extent palmed off with posts in the New Turkey Party organization and could not easily move to the Justice Party without losing something. There was no sudden exodus, therefore, when, in 1962, the party, by participating in a coalition with the People's Party, handed over the role of opposing the People's Party to the Justice Party.

This participation in government with the People's Party probably did more than anything, however, to weaken popular support for the party which, in 1961, was the third largest. Those in the party whose origin lay with the Freedom Party actually disliked the People's Party less than they did the Justice Party, especially the Justice Party in its less moderate periods, when it clamoured for an amnesty and showed its sympathies for the Democrat Party. Unlike the Justice Party, the New Turkey Party did not waver in its generally moderate tone; the leadership stood up and fought against its more extreme elements better than the Justice Party leadership. This permitted it to participate in government, but the party was, in consequence, wracked with argument, disrupted by indiscipline (the parliamentary group was especially independent of the party executive) and ruined at the polls. The failure in the local elections at the end of 1963, when the party's vote was cut by half, surprised no-one. An extraordinary Congress in May 1964 before the Senate partial elections gave a measure of unity to the unhappy party, but did not save it from further failure. A rather empty declaration following this Congress dwelt on the important role of the party without exactly saying what it was though it seems the party could not envisage anything more hopeful than a balancing role between the two major parties.[1] In January 1965, when the party joined in a four-party coalition, with the People's Party in opposition, Alican declared that now the possibility of a government without the People's Party had been established there was now no need to fear splitting the opposition vote—a Justice Party plea to the electorate. This sophisticated argumentation ignored the other now fully apparent argument for not splitting the vote—namely, that coalition government had been shown in Turkey to be very troubled government. Ironically, the New Turkey Party leadership was of all the least

[1] Text in *Cumhuriyet*, 11 May 1964.

responsible for this situation. The party paid the penalty of virtue.

The party's programme in 1965 does not call for much comment. The party strongly supported private enterprise and stressed the need for foreign capital. In tune with recently aroused national passions, the party saw fit, nevertheless, to state that oil should be in national hands, though foreign help was still considered necessary. In amending the laws concerning foreign enterprise, international law should not be disregarded. On land reform, the party's view was hardly distinguishable from that of the Justice Party. Provided agricultural production was not upset, state land was to be divided among the landless. State planning was not a device to put every centre of production under state control, but rather to provide co-ordination and harmony between economic units that were unknown to one another. In true liberal vein, the party declares itself in foreign policy friend to all, and includes 'our neighbours' and those recently free. The programme is not so markedly more liberal now than that of the Justice Party, whose manifesto seems more to miss no opportunity to base itself on the freedom of the individual. The party describes itself as middle of the road and for Turkey's development sees no need for any ideological or rigid system.

The Nation Party. Of the minor parties contesting the 1965 election, this party did best; and better than most expected. It is easy to see that its policy, as revealed by its manifesto, must have some very attractive features for the Turkish voters. There is a strong element of realism and restraint running through the Turkish character, a practical moral and social conscience to which the party makes appeal.

Like the Justice Party, the Nation Party stresses the value of private enterprise (but does not forget private responsibility) and advocates flexible planning. Nor should economic competition, which is much stressed as desirable, lead to the extinction of small firms, another concern of the party.

The party's image becomes clearer when it states its views on 'extremists'. Fascism and communism are rejected; Communism gets particular censure. Communism is described as painting the Devil's portrait on the wall.[1] For Turkey the greatest danger is

[1] Anybody's portrait is abhorrent to the strict Muslim.

indeed 'godless communism'. By comparison, extremists of the traditionalist sort are very lightly dealt with. Only by its enemies is religion presented as reaction. In contrast with a quite moderate attitude on foreign capital, the party is nationalist in its foreign policy. Turkey should cease trying to please her allies. It is regretted, for instance, that Turkey remained a spectator during the Anglo-French attack in Egypt in 1956, or again has been too weak and vacillating in the Cyprus affair. The party's chief foreign bogey is, nevertheless, the Soviet Union. It is claimed with pride that, during the coalition government under Ürgüplü, the Nation Party ministers prevented the promulgation of a decree containing the Russian Turkish cultural agreement made by the İnönü government.

The party has built up a coherent programme around what appear—in the absence of opinion polls—a number of widely held views. Respect for religion is combined with private enterprise. The old enemy Russia is still the familiar old enemy and the West is still imperialist, particularly the European West; and there is an appeal to morality. The Americans are not criticized so much as they are by the Workers' Party. What chiefly distinguishes the party from the Justice Party is its less sanguine attitude to Turkey's problems and its greater emphasis on religion and morality. Its manifesto suggests it is a more serious, less ebullient party than the Justice Party; but it is very conservative and obnoxious to the Atatürkists.

The party's history goes back to 1948, when a party was formed under the title Nation Party from dissident conservative members of the Democrat Party. The party was dissolved in 1953 on the grounds that it was opposed to Kemalist principles. It later re-emerged and, after absorbing a small peasants' party, became known as the Republican Peasants' Nation Party. Its leader was now Osman Bölükbaşı, an able and very colourful politician who, not without bitter strife, came to dominate the party. Despite this very positive leadership, the R.P.N.P. did not do very well in the elections until 1961, when its share of the vote became 14 per cent, twice that in 1957. The R.P.N.P. always drew its chief support in the 1950–60 era from a conservative area of the country east of Ankara.

In June 1962, Bölükbaşı led twenty-nine parliamentary members of the R.P.N.P. out of that party and formed the Nation

Party. Bölükbaşı had previously resigned from the party leadership. The collapse of the People's/Justice Party coalition government provided an opportunity for him to leave the R.P.N.P. with a group of supporters. Neither Bölükbaşı nor those who resigned with him were, apparently, prepared to enter into a coalition government with İnönü. The reasons were partly personal, partly tactical and in part reflected the fact that those who left the R.P.N.P. to form the new Nation Party were further to the right than those they left behind.

The new party did not come to the forefront of affairs until the formation of the fourth coalition, under Ürgüplü, in February 1965. The Nation Party joined in that coalition, but hardly had it done so than it began to proclaim its dissatisfaction with the coalition and certain important aspects of its policy. The party made a great deal of fuss over the alleged partiality of the state broadcasting service and sought to bring it under closer ministerial control—which would have been a reversion to the position under the Democrat Party governments, when misuse of radio for political purposes was a prime political question. Then the party attacked Ürgüplü's visit to Moscow and generally deplored the new friendship with Russia. An attack was made, too, on allegedly partisan civil service appointments. Bölükbaşı and his party intended to show how independent they were—and that they were not responsible for governmental policy. These were unblushingly political tactics; they seem to have succeeded. Apart from replaying of these themes the party's national Congress held in July 1965 was largely given over to expressions of religious piety, attacks on the People's Party (chiefly for its lack of religion) and adulation of Bölükbaşı, in whose honour many delegates had composed enthusiastic if not very good poems. They were appreciated for their sentiment if not for their art.

The Republican Peasants' Nation Party. Those who were left in this party after the departure of Bölükbaşı and his supporters settled down to a quieter life. The party participated in the second coalition in June 1962 with the People's Party and the N.T.P. Like the N.T.P., its morale was affected by its lack of success in the local elections of 1963 and the partial Senate elections of 1964.[1]

[1] During 1964 there was talk of the emergence of a 'third group' made up of the minor parties. This came to nothing. Personalities count for much in

The party joined the fourth coalition with the Justice Party and the other minor parties in February 1965. It was about this time that some very exciting things began to happen to the party.

Towards the end of March 1965 there were rumours that the party was to gain a new member, none other than Alparslan Türkeş, the leader of the 'fourteen' expelled from the Junta in 1960. Was that hero to find a role in party politics? There had indeed been previous indications that the 'fourteen' were contemplating a move into politics. In August 1964 they were reported as having decided to set up a new party.[1] At the end of March, Türkeş and four other members of the 'fourteen' joined the party. This injection was soon to show its effects.

At the end of May the leader of the party, Ahmet Oğuz, visited the former President Celal Bayar without first consulting the party's executive committee. Apparently, Bayar congratulated the party on its firm opposition to the People's Party and for participating with the Justice Party in İnönü's overthrow.[2] If the point of the visit was to demonstrate the party's continuing loyalty to those (probably many) of its supporters who did not approve of the 1960 revolution—and Türkeş—or to show defiance to Türkeş, the immediate result was to encourage Türkeş and his supporters to demand an early general congress. At the end of May, three Justice Party deputies joined the party, complaining that the Justice Party was becoming a capitalists' club. In mid-June the party's leader Oğuz succumbed to the new pressures and resigned. The event was generally interpreted as a victory for Türkeş; it was rumoured that this victory by Türkeş prevented the older members of the party from saving it by establishing close relations with the Justice Party. By the end of June, ten of the 'fourteen' had become members of the party.

The real test of strength between the old cadre and the new Türkeş group was to come at the July General Congress when a

---

the minor parties, which, by virtue of their small size, are not so subject to forces from outside as are the large parties.

[1] *Cumhuriyet*, 22 August 1964. The report suggests also that the 'fourteen' had reached agreement with the R.P.N.P. and the N.T.P. but does not say in respect of what. The new party was expected to attract members from the Justice Party and People's Party deputies and senators and from the natural senators.

[2] Ibid., 25 June 1965.

new leader would be chosen. Before this should take place, there was a determined attempt by members of the executive to turn Türkeş out; but this only resulted in a protest resignation by the pro-Türkeş Secretary-General—a resignation which did not, however, upset the Türkeş majority on the executive committee. What is most important—and not clear—is how the Türkeş group obtained the support of a majority of the executive committee, especially as they were for the most part long-standing members of the party. They might justly have feared they were beginning to give pride of place to the Nation Party as *the* right-wing party. Previously accustomed to strong, colourful leadership under Bölükbaşı, they perhaps could not feel safe and prosperous without another strong leader. However this may be, skill in military politics is obviously transferable to the larger political field. There is some evidence to suggest that Türkeş was astute enough to take care that the party's local organizations would return pro-Türkeş delegates to the Congress. As the party's 'general inspector'[1] he had ready access to and influence over local party organizations.

The party was anyway in the doldrums. It had become little more than a limited company of politicians with a formless programme that well-nigh defied any change. Abandoned by Bölükbaşı, who at least provided action, if not political inspiration, the party seemed to have lost its *raison d'être*. At the General Congress Türkeş was hailed as a saviour, his lieutenants were acclaimed; the old guard hardly found any places for themselves in the crowded cinema. More important, they lost chairmanship of the Congress to the principal recent recruit from the Justice Party, Gökhan Evliyaoğlu. They wisely put up only one candidate to contest the election for the party leadership with Türkeş, but even so they lost, Türkeş being elected by 698 out of the 1,214 delegates' votes! His speech contrasted Turkey's poverty with the high qualities of her people, the need for unity and reforms. A few days later, eight deputies and senators who did not wish to be united under the Türkeş banner left the party. They included two ministers, one former minister, one National Assembly deputy-chairman and the previous party leader Ahmet Oğuz. When Türkeş declared he would especially try to ensure to those defeated

[1] It seems that he bargained for this position before entering the Party. See *Forum*, 1 August 1965.

at the Congress success in the forthcoming Assembly elections, one of the old guard retorted he had always understood the nation chose its deputies, but that henceforth this presumably was to be done by Türkeş. He was more prescient than he knew. At the 1965 Assembly election when the party obtained most of its few seats under the national remainder rule, the appointment of the one-third to be chosen by the party's central organization was left by the party to Türkeş. The departure of the old guard, mainly to the Justice Party, was a moral boost for that party; but those of the electorate who voted for them, it was generally thought, would transfer their votes to Bölükbaşı's new Nation Party. However able Türkeş was in manipulating a political party, he did not succeed in attracting the electorate—the failing of the old-guard politicians he replaced. The party only won eleven seats and 2·24 per cent of the votes. Perhaps it was a case of new wine in old wineskins, or, worse, old and new wine mixed, but not blended.

What, then, is this new wine? The party's programme explains it, but often in a very general way.[1]

The first point that ought to be made is that the party does not claim to be revolutionary. By default almost, it may be taken to accept modern representative democracy; but does not openly avow its democratic beliefs. The basic principle underlying the programme is social solidarity, but this is not expressed in extreme terms. The basis is the individual. Then again, although social security and participation in management in industry is promised to the workers, the right to strike is accepted, though without laying the usual stress on its importance. Class or group exploitation is denounced (and, of course, class conflict), but the existence of different classes created by the division of labour is accepted as natural and necessary. The partisan mentality of political parties is rejected and morality is said to govern politics; but parties that seek broadly to influence the social and political order, after consulting the electorate, are provided for. Youth is called to serve the state; but disciplined organizations for this purpose do not appear to be envisaged. Private economic enterprise is encouraged—so, too, is the development of a general

---

[1] Bahri Savcı examines the political beliefs of the Türkeş group in 'Bir Otoriter İdeoloji Denemesi Üzerine Mütalâalar', *Ank. Üniv. S.B.F. Derg.*, XVIII, nos. 3–4, pp. 71–103.

spirit of initiative, but the party is against large profits obtained from tricks of trade and capitalist exploitation. Planning is necessary. Indeed, there is the most pronounced concern for the ordering of society. The party sees that the majority of people are helpless in the struggle for life and proposes to do something about it. There is considerable emphasis on equality of opportunity; and full employment is one of the chief elements in the extensive social security measures envisaged.

Perhaps the chief concern of the party is with education and culture. It is regarded as far too important a subject for merely one ministry. The whole emphasis is really to be on preparing the people for participation in the life of an economically developed nation state and, as ever, on unity. The people are to be educated from cradle to grave. For instance, the cinema is to be regarded as a place of education rather than for entertainment.

Not unexpectedly, the programme devotes much space to the development of educational institutions at all levels. There is emphasis on the community life in the residential halls or hostels that are promised. Teachers are to be re-educated. Religious instruction is also to be greatly developed. The pupils of religious schools who will fill religious offices are to be allowed entry to the universities. As long as public order and general morality is not harmed, there is to be a wide freedom for religious practices and for religious teaching. Only religion is not to be exploited for other ends.

On land reform and village life, the party presents some fresh views. 'Production' is the key principle and the land would be divided region by region into units of a size giving the most economic production. In the process, large estates, it seems, would be broken up, the land being divided into the appropriate production units and redistributed. The party eschews the idea of distributing the land to all the landless, as there is not, it is claimed, enough to go round. Agricultural land is regarded as a social heritage as much as a matter of private property. There is, however, no threat in principle to private property. The basis of agricultural production is that there should be a modern agricultural production unit worked and owned by a family.

It is basically an authoritarian philosophy that does not pay much attention to democratic devices, whilst not opposing them outright. It harks back to Atatürkism in its emphasis on

M

social solidarity; but joins forces with religion in this regard, as Atatürkism could not. It could be a powerful blend if most Turkish intellectuals were deeply religious, but they are not. How far the party would limit freedom if given the chance would largely depend on the nature and content, which is not precisely stated, of the cultural education intended. One delegate at the Party Congress in 1965 voiced his misgivings. 'The programme', he complained, 'made the party more étatist than the People's Party; and the political education of youth rested on principles found only in Leninist Russia, Mussolini's Italy, Hitler's Germany, Mao's China and Franco's Spain.'[1] It is a dangerous doctrine and one encouraged by unstable and irresolute coalition government. The massive electoral victory of the Justice Party in 1965 will remove that evil for a while.

General characteristics

The particular is often more instructive than the general, but what may generally be said about Turkish political parties?

In the first place, they are not a sham. They are not the tools of a narrow elite group. The political parties are not mere factions. Universal adult franchise, real competition for nomination and election to party electoral lists, well-developed local party organizations—these are characteristics of a viable political system. In brief, Turkish society is deeply permeated by political organization.

To say this does not imply, however, that all major institutions in Turkish society are deeply affected by politics. It would hardly be desirable if they were. The civil service is not politicized, for instance, and neither are the trade unions. On the whole political forces express themselves through the political institutions, including the political parties.

Yet equally this does not mean that the Turkish peasant necessarily makes political choices by comparing rival policies, or even rival images. (Of course, in this respect they differ only in degree from citizens of developed democracies.) To discover more about the motivation of Turkish electors is really important if only because students of Turkish politics sometimes assume that the participation of the masses is soon going to make a massive difference to politics in Turkey. Once properly roused from his

[1] Zonguldak delegate, Müfit Duru, *Cumhuriyet*, 1 August 1965.

deep Anatolian sleep, the Turkish peasant will, it is said, make far-reaching demands on the political system.

What is important is the likely nature of these demands. At present the peasantry is conservative. New leaders are almost certainly rising from a village background through the political party organizations, but they must remain conservative in their policies if they are to retain support. At present there does not seem much danger that the political mobilization of the masses is going quickly to produce radical change. They are being led into politics by political parties that are already part of the system.

This leads us to underline the significant fact that there is in Turkey as yet no important element that is opposed outright to the existing political system. There are minor elements on the extreme left and right who would no doubt abandon it for a Communist regime or an Islamic theocracy—and there is an increasing number of socialist intellectuals as authoritarian minded as Atatürk—but there is no entrenched aristocracy or proletariat organization determined to overthrow the system. Nor do the new industrialists and businessmen really spurn politics, even though their prestige is now perhaps higher than that of politicians and civil servants.

The Turkish political system is usually described as multi-party, but a more than superficial look at how it has operated in the recent past reveals what is essentially a two-party struggle. The multi-party system of 1946-50 gave way to a struggle between the Democrat Party and the People's Party and a similar two-party struggle began to emerge soon after 1961. To go further back, the Young Turks were composed of authoritarian modernizers and liberals.

Given this bi-polarity in politics, is it merely a reflection of a basic division in Turkish society? It does seem to be the case (lacking real evidence) that urban-educated groups support the more secularist People's Party—a beginning of a significant division—and that businessmen and industrialists support their opponents. Yet for the most part the two parties seem to share support from the same groups or classes. So landowners here will support the one party, there the other. One village will be for the People's Party, its neighbour for the other side. Or again a village will itself be divided, but on no basis that can be generalized for the country as a whole. It is a puzzling situation.

One explanation must for the time being suffice. It is suggested that in middle eastern societies there is a tendency to two-way splits (moieties), even though the nature of the division may differ in different places. If one group votes for Demirel, the opposing one automatically votes for İnönü. Further research on the nature of allegiance to political parties is urgently needed.[1]

Whilst it is generally true to say that Turkey has a two-party system, it is possible to be more precise. Election figures since the war certainly show that two major parties have emerged. Yet the two-party pattern is not quite like that, say, of the United States or Britain. It is true that the two major Turkish parties do obtain almost the same very high proportion of votes between them as do their American or British counterparts, but there are two significant differences.

In the first place—and excepting 1961—the gap between the votes garnered by each party has always been fairly wide: and secondly, there has never been any swing of the pendulum—the People's Party has never won an election against its principal opponent if again we exclude 1961. In fact the system has really been one in which one party has been predominant over a considerable period of time.

In this connection it is surely significant that the 1960 military revolution occurred during the period following the 1957 election when the Democrat Party gained only 7 per cent more of the vote than the People's Party. Taken in conjunction with the partial fudging of the 1957 election by the Democrats, the election suggested to the military that the Democrats were no longer the rightful rulers. The error of the Democrats was to maintain a predominant party style of politics in a situation which was more nearly two-party than it ever had been. A military intervention between 1954 and 1957 would have been much more difficult than it was in 1960.

That Turkish party politics essentially results in a predominant party regime is underlined in a cyclical theory of Turkish political development advanced by one Turkish scholar.[2] The cycle begins

[1] For a very informative article see J. S. Szyliowicz, 'The Political Dynamics of Rural Turkey', *Middle East Journal*, XVI, no. 4 (1962), pp. 430–2.

[2] Arif Payaslıoğlu, 'Political Leadership and Political Parties', in R. E. Ward and D. A. Rustow, *Political Modernization in Japan and Turkey* (Princeton, 1964), pp. 427–8.

with a period of (i) political freedom (when political opinions are freely expressed and political organizations established) and leads to (ii) the victory of one of the competing political groups and (iii) the establishment of its dominance. This is followed by a second period in which the dominant group rules in an authoritarian or dictatorial style. After a period opposition groups unite and succeed in overthrowing the regime, when they then in turn establish a period of freedom.

The theory fits the facts very well. Abdul Hamid's despotism is followed by the 1908 liberal revolution. The Committee of Union and Progress emerges and establishes an authoritarian regime. The first world war rather disrupts the process, but after the liberation struggle—a period of free political expression—the People's Party establishes its dominance. The regime disintegrated between 1946 and 1950 and the Democrat Party then established its hegemony. The 1960 revolution falls into place neatly and presumably now, if the pattern is to be repeated, the Justice Party is becoming authoritarian in character. It is a dangerously predictive theory which invites intervention in the historical process. Man has rarely been able to leave history alone. It is too tempting to speed-up or by-pass this or the other aspect of the process.

There is, however, perhaps some justification for hoping that Turkish politics will not necessarily continue this wearisome round. After knowing *what* has happened—and making a theory out of it for the sake of intelligibility—it is then necessary to know *why*. When we do this we see that predominant party regimes in Turkey have not arisen every time in recent history for the same reasons. The reasons for the emergence of the single People's Party regime under Atatürk were very different from those which gave birth to Democrat Party hegemony in the 1950's and the regimes were authoritarian in different ways and with regard to different elements in society. Society itself was different in important respects in the two periods.

There are certainly similarities between, for instance, the rule of the Democrat Party and that of the Justice Party, or between even the revolutions of 1908 and 1960. Yet at each stage in recent Turkish political history the factors at work have varied so greatly, the general climate of each period has been so different, that valuable though the general pattern is, it does not carry too much conviction.

CHAPTER X

Pressure Groups

As the most casual students of politics is aware, politics is more than a matter of electors, political parties, and parliaments. Groups that exert pressures for their own ends are a common phenomenon in politics and difficult to absorb into democratic theory. Organized groups are naturally less likely to exist in an underdeveloped than a developed society; but pressures are exerted in underdeveloped countries by such organized groups as have come into existence. These include such bodies as chambers of commerce, professional organizations, rent payers' associations, red cross (or crescent) societies, and sports and culture societies, examples of all of which—and many others—may be found in Turkey.

Many of these groups exert pressures from time to time in matters of lesser and greater magnitude. Sometimes they operate through members of parliament and sometimes—probably more often—through the administration.[1] This study is not concerned with listing all these groups and tracing, if this were possible in an introductory study, their effects on particular policies. It is only feasible to consider those groups whose effect on politics appears, from following the course of political history, to have been most important in determining the general flow of politics. To this observer, the important groups outside the normal political boundaries are the military, the students and the trade unions.[2] They will now be briefly considered in turn.

[1] Turkish officials are very cautious about admitting the influence of pressure groups on policy. This is understandable. Pressure-group influence on the administration requires, if it is to be accepted, a well-entrenched and generally accepted tradition of civil service impartiality and incorruptibility, or a vigorous and well-informed public opinion, or, better, both. Pressure-group influence may not be at all corrupting, but in a developing country it can easily be represented as such.

[2] It could be argued that Turkish farmers constitute the greatest single pressure (for good prices for agricultural produce and the minimum of taxation). This is pressure from an unorganized pressure group and readily finds outlet into politics via deputies and senators. For introductory in-

The military

We have examined above the main reasons for the intervention of the military in 1960 and have seen how they handed back power to the political parties. However, when, in October 1961, the military was formally removed from the scene this did not mean that they suddenly became mute. No doubt they hoped to slide silently into the background; and this could most easily be achieved if the 1961 elections returned a workable People's Party majority in the Grand National Assembly. The military trusted İsmet İnönü to shield them from their enemies among the former Democrat Party supporters; and of the political parties, the People's Party was generally acknowledged as the real heir to the Atatürk tradition. However, so easy a passage was not to be; and the military knew, if only by the narrow vote by which the referendum on the new Constitution was carried, that it might well not be. Before the elections even, they took up a proposal for a meeting of the leaders of the political parties to agree to certain limitations on political debate. A round-table meeting presided over by the military produced agreement by the parties to abandon the Democrat Party mentality, not to discuss the court decisions on the members of the former regime, not to exploit religious feeling, not to claim that the revolution was in the interest of any section or class, to oppose extremes of right and left and, finally, to accept the legitimacy of the forthcoming elections.

When in these elections the People's Party did not succeed well enough to form a government on its own, for the military things had gone wrong; they had to watch very closely indeed.

In our account of the political history of the period after 1961 we have seen that the military did watch carefully. During the period unrest in the military manifested itself in various ways. There were two attempted coups, the first more important than the second; there were sudden resignations or retirements of small numbers of officers; there were numerous rumours of collusion between politicians and officers in high places; and there were prosecutions of small numbers of officers who set up or joined

formation on pressure groups and other aspects of Turkish politics see Yavuz Abadan, 'Türkiyede Siyasî Partiler ve Tazyik Grupları', *Yüzüncü Yıl Armağanı* (Ank. Üniv. Yayınları, 15) (Ankara, 1959), pp. 77–118.

groups inside the military to urge the defence by the military of the betrayed revolution.[1]

These movements occurred when the revolution (and the military) seemed to be in danger from politicians intent on revenge and when the military's honour was impugned. One valuable feature of the situation was certainly that the military did not refrain from saying plainly when they considered they, or the revolution, had been slighted. For instance, in November 1964, the then Chief of the General Staff, Cevdet Sunay, wrote a warning letter to the President of the Grand National Assembly and the party leaders, in which it was stated that military intervention would be necessary if steps were not taken against those attacking the military and the revolution.[2] The Minister of Justice promptly requested the removal of parliamentary immunity from a number of deputies to permit their prosecution. This action by the military was occasioned by the attacks on the revolution made in provincial party congresses, notoriously overheated affairs, during the previous summer and autumn.

On the whole, during the period since the revolution, the military command seems to have consolidated its hold over its dissident elements. This it has been able to do by acting as a channel for, and by giving official voice to, military resentment against attacks on the military and the revolution; and by obtaining retribution. It was a difficult situation for the military command to handle. It was eased considerably, however, when, in December 1964, the moderates won ascendancy at the Justice Party Congress. Thereafter, matters wonderfully improved—to the extent that the military made no objection to a Justice Party plus minor parties' coalition in February 1965 and a Justice Party government after the general election of October 1965.

It is clear from this that the military's chief motive in exerting considerable influence over politics from 1961 to 1965 was a fear of revenge and a determination not to let its enemies undermine its work and prestige. Underlying this basic requirement, two others are, however, discernible. One is impatience with political

[1] For example, as late as 21 October 1964 five officers were dismissed for spreading manifestos in the name of the Army of Young Kemalists (*Gen. Kemalistler Ordusu*).

[2] The text is not available save in newspaper reports, e.g. *Cumhuriyet*, 18 September 1964.

wrangling in the face of the dire economic and social problems to be tackled. The military have frequently been outspoken on this and have helped İnönü in this respect to press on with various schemes of economic and social reform. The military does not, however, appear to have put forward any definite ideas. It has left the content of legislation in, for instance, taxation, land reform, political parties very much to the İnönü governments, which could not for political reasons do anything very drastic. Moreover, there was no outcry from the military when, in 1965, the new government (dominated by the Justice Party) shelved the previous government's modest enough land reform proposals. The military wants action in economic and social development. It wants a bigger cake; it is not, as yet, deeply concerned about the distribution of slices. This is another way of saying that it is not deeply politically divided and this has made its exit from politics easier. It is not easy to imagine the exit of the military in a situation of competitive politics if it is itself deeply divided along the lines of conflict between the political parties.

Secondly, another motive underlying the military's exodus—and, in part, stemming from its dominant concern to protect the revolution and itself—is the desire to see multi-party politics properly disciplined. The military's immediate and whole-hearted acceptance of ideas for the reorganization of political institutions is evidence of this. In addition to requiring a senate, a constitutional court and a new electoral law incorporating proportional representation, the N.U.C., it will be recalled, abolished political party organization below sub-province level. Politics had to be disciplined. The military—as evidenced by its spokesman—the natural senators—always supports measures like the Political Parties Law; they try to keep politics as democratic and as restrained as possible. They want—as do many others—to prevent, by these means, the emergence of a powerful party that will be tempted to authoritarianism, as were the democrats they overthrew.

How singular is the Turkish experience? Essentially, it is a case of the transfer of power from a military regime that for the most part really respects democracy (provided it really gets on with the job of modernization) to a competitive political system. This, one suspects, is not too difficult if the political party likely to come to power itself respects democracy. The military can slide out gracefully. The politicians it removed by force, because they had corrupted the democratic system, are in a minority and once the system is back on its feet again, will not matter much. The Turkish military ran into difficulties because the Democrats were more popular than they had imagined. They took a chance in returning to democratic politics. From their point of view, they were a little incautious. They allowed political activity to develop in the early days of their regime. They knew they were less popular than they thought after the referendum on the new Constitution in 1961. Yet they still went ahead. Although the People's Party might only just get into power its leader was İsmet İnönü, whom, by and large, they trusted to protect them and bridge the gap. It was, nevertheless, a near-run thing.

The Turkish experience of demilitarization straightway to competitive politics suggests certain conditions that have to be met if in any such situation the operation is to be successful. They are: (i) (obviously) the military must eliminate its anti-democratic element; (ii) it must maintain unity between the Junta and the military command; (iii) it must not be politically divided along the lines of cleavage between the political parties; (iv) there should be one party or combination of parties likely to succeed in forming a government in which the military can trust—it is obviously a great help if the leader of such a party is a former respected military leader; (v) the party to which it expects to turn over power should believe firmly in planning economic and social development and possess a cadre that can be expected to carry it out efficiently; (vi) political competition must be disciplined in order not to disrupt national unity (otherwise, the anti-democrats in the military increase their influence) and, as a corollary, no party is to deny the principle of the modern secular state, which it can do by exploiting—and perhaps being exploited by—traditionalist (including religious) elements in society.

All these conditions assume the military does not wish to continue to rule; and do not answer the basic question why the Turkish military wanted to get out of politics. This is, of course, very difficult. Only a few suggestions may be made.

First, there is the tradition at the back of the minds of the military, that the Turkish military is prepared to make its voice heard but shies at overturning the basic structure. The accepted basic ideal structure is democratic politics; and it is important that it is still regarded (in the Western example) as economically and socially efficient.

Secondly, although the Turkish military is big and could quite easily take over the government with some civilian support, it is big for a purpose, namely, the defence of the state against the traditional and powerful enemy from the north. The military has more than enough to do.

Thirdly, the present and recent provenance of military aid and instruction, the U.S.A., should not be overlooked. Ideas of military elitism do not occupy the minds of American military instructors. The emphasis is all in a contrary direction. Moreover, over the past fifteen years, the Turkish military has to a large extent been humanized. The rights of individual private soldiers have been much developed. (In theory, he may not now be kicked.) The tone has changed. Individuals matter more. It is not democratic, of course, but it is an influence in the inculcation of values that lowly persons matter and should have their say. Perhaps it helps the military look more favourably on democratic politics.

Students in politics

Two students' organizations embrace the bulk of Turkey's student population of 80,000. They are the National Turkish Students' Union (founded in 1916) and the National Turkish Students' Federation (1948).[1] As by law any student has the right to be a member of these organizations, no lists of membership have been drawn up. It is not known what proportion of the student body participates in elections of officers of these organizations—this normal measure of their representativeness is not therefore available. The presidency of these organizations has been held when students by a number of prominent politicians and not exclusively of any one political party. The Federation and the Union combine with other organizations (e.g. 'The Union of Turkish Women' and the 'Turkish Agricultural Society') to form the 'National Youth Organization of Turkey',[2]

---

[1] Since 1960 these associations have been financed by the state. The annual subventions are, National Youth Organization of Turkey, T.L. 200,000 (£8,000 approx.), National Turkish Students' Federation, T.L. 180,000 (£7,200), the National Turkish Students' Union, T.L. 120,000 (£4,800).

[2] The source of this information and for much else in this section is Nermin Abadan 'Türk Gençliğin Siyasî Davranışı', Ank. Üniv. S.B.F. Derg., xx, no. 1 (1965), pp. 199–221.

but this attempt at unification has not as yet produced positive results.

The political activities of Turkish students include statements in the press, meetings, demonstrations, silent processions and the boycotting of university classes. They have also made formal public protests about certain political acts; they have also run campaigns (e.g. in support of the referendum on the new Constitution) and have sent telegrams to the government on aspects of its policy. Statements in the press, meetings and demonstrations have been the chief modes of pressure.

Do Turkish students constitute a political pressure group? It depends, according to the president of the National Turkish Students' Federation on the definition of politics.

Politics is the struggle of the various social classes to improve their circumstances by means of political parties within a democratic system. [However] youth and student organizations do not act in the name of any party, or as the agents of any party . . . As Atatürk did not in any complete sense believe in any social struggle, he entrusted the Turkish Nation to Turkish youth. He did this because youth had not been soiled by the effects of any social relationships. Those whose attitudes and decisions are most objective are youth.[1]

This is a very good statement which sets out the dilemma in which the Turkish student finds himself. Party politics is seen largely as a socio-economic class struggle, which is abhorrent to the disciples of Atatürk. Therefore students are not to participate in party politics, nor, presumably, to act as agents in any other way of a socio-economic class struggle. Yet another feature of Atatürkism is a belief in the possibility of liberal democracy, which requires party politics.

We can obtain a further picture of student attitudes than that suggested by the students' president if we look at the result of some surveys that have been undertaken in this field.[2]

---

[1] *Cumhuriyet*, 23 April 1965, from an article by the President in 1965, A. G. Ketenci.

[2] The results of a survey of *lise* (*lycée*) pupils in 1959 is available in F. W. Frey, 'Education', *Political Modernization in Japan and Turkey*, ed. R. E. Ward and D. A. Rustow (Princeton, 1964), pp. 205–35. For the survey of university students see H. H. Hyman, A. Payaslıoğlu and F. W. Frey, 'The Values of Turkish College Youth', *Public Opinion Quarterly*, xxii (1959), pp. 275–91. See too B. Daver, 'Youth and Politics in Turkey', *Ank. Üniv. S.B.F. Derg.*,

A survey of *lycée* pupils in 1959 showed that they were strongly in favour of government 'by the people' as distinct from 'for the people' and particularly advocated the participation of all their compatriots in general elections. They were very democratic in their attitudes, but their beliefs stem from Atatürkism. They held Mustafa Kemal in particular esteem, and strongly advocated modernization along Kemalist lines. Religion did not enter into their view much, except that they thought some sort of spiritual understanding necessary in order to comprehend life in its entirety. A survey of university students made in 1958 showed that although they too were strongly attached to the nation, for which many showed themselves prepared to sacrifice time and money, yet on the question of political forms it seems that over half of the students favoured a multi-party system (more than two parties) and about one-fifth a two-party system. Nearly three-quarters of the students, that is to say, express a belief in liberal democratic politics. They did not, however, appear to be quite so starry eyed as the *lycée* pupils about government 'by the people' (78 per cent of the *lycée* pupils supported this ideal).[1] Finally, the university students accorded more importance to national than to international questions, while believing Turkey's role in international organizations should be an active one.

Further information is available on students' views in a content analysis of statements by the student organizations in the press over the years 1950–64 inclusive. This shows that 41 per cent of the total of 143 statements (ten a year on average) are concerned with problems of internal politics. Statements on Cyprus accounted for 17 per cent, as did pronouncements on Atatürk and his reforms. Ideological matters amount to 15 per cent—protests against reactionary movements and against communism. On internal politics there are many statements on the 1960 revolution (14 per cent of all statements), whilst those that might be regarded as concerned with democracy, including basic democratic freedoms, amounted to some 17 per cent.

The 1960 revolution has been much defended. The revolution

---

xix, no. 3–4 (1964), pp. 47–57. These and other sources, including an unpublished study by the Public Opinion Research group of the Faculty of Political Science, Ankara, are used in Nermin Abadan, 'Türk Gençliğin Siyasî Davranışı'.

[1] Nermin Abadan, op. cit., pp. 207–8.

and the events preceding it, when police opened fire on the students, are commemorated and there have been statements protesting against counter-revolutionary demonstrations and amnesty for those condemned of crimes under the Democrat Party regime. The students have also defended the basic democratic freedoms when these have been threatened, including academic freedom and university autonomy. Nor do all these protests occur before 1960. The students protested when in the year of the coup the military regime summarily dismissed the 147 university teachers.

It has been noticed that while statements before 1960 tended to be informative, since 1960 they have become more dynamic, demanding that something should be done. This is due, no doubt, to the students' increased sense of their own significance after their part in the 1960 revolution and to the more liberal atmosphere since 1960 as compared with that of the latter half of the previous decade. They also appear to be much less patient with democracy since 1960, as when in 1962 the Istanbul University Law Faculty Students' Society announced 'We know our duty; if necessary we shall not listen to the police, nor to the judicial authorities, nor even to parliament.'[1]

Do these student attitudes add up to a coherent philosophy? By and large they show that the rising generation is still deeply influenced by Atatürkism—by, in particular, nationalism, secularism and the desire to modernize and reform. They are not markedly socialist—at least they are not doctrinaire. To some extent they are inoculated against acceptance of ideas of social class conflict by the Atatürk tradition with its stress on Turkish social solidarity. They stress social welfare as a part of the process of economic and social development, something the state will achieve without social disruption. In their emphasis on modernization they are now inclined to impatience with democratic modes of government. Yet this clashes with their rather personal liberalism which they value partly, perhaps, because they are among the first to be affected by curtailment of the democratic freedoms and partly, perhaps, because they are at an age of self-assertion in a society where authority weighs heavy.

Their intervention in politics is not in everyday party politics. They are not political in this sense. This is in one way a blessing,

[1] Nermin Abadan, op. cit., 212.

but it reveals a dangerous degree of arrogance. They seem to be in favour of a liberal-democratic political system as long as it is seen to work without disrupting society and without creating marked social and economic irregularities. If it does not work, the authoritarian strains in their Atatürkism could lead to authoritarian solutions. Should Atatürkism be replaced by socialism as the most relevant philosophy, a fairly authoritarian version could well be favoured.

The reasons why Turkish students involve themselves in politics are not all peculiar to Turkey, however. The phenomenon of student participation in politics is pronounced in many of the less developed countries. That Turkish youth does hold itself in high regard as guardians of Atatürkism is reinforced in a society where literacy gives respect and education great esteem.

This more general factor is buttressed by others of a similarly general kind. Turkish students' organizations do not have to share with other social groups to any great degree the exercise of influence over politics. They have a large part of the field to themselves. In this wise, they have a representative character that extends beyond their own members; they express general demands that might otherwise go unvoiced.

The student organizations derive strength too from their representing students who all seem to have a sincere interest in national politics. Few other student organizations exist to draw attention away from the political scene. The Turkish student has little money for other pursuits but cinema going; and it is still difficult even for relations between the sexes to be established on a non-critical basis.

The universities are overcrowded. Classes are generally large and informal contact between teacher and student difficult. Added to this students are usually accommodated in overcrowded 'dormitories' (Turkish families do not take in students as lodgers), with the result that the political debater—or haranguer—finds a ready-made audience. Politics is the most interesting and—in an underdeveloped country—the most vital pursuit in Turkey; student involvement in national politics is just one political aspect of economic and social underdevelopment.

Trade unions

One developing force that seems likely increasingly to offset the influence of both students and military are the trade unions.[1]

As might be expected in a country only recently developed industrially, Turkey does not have a long history of trade unionism.[2] Although there are beginnings in the late nineteenth century, Turkish trade unionism did not really get under way until 1909. After a brief burst of freedom at the beginning of the Young Turk era, when there was considerable freedom to set up societies and professional organizations, the right to establish such organizations came to be increasingly limited. The high point in restriction of trade union activity was reached in 1938 with the passing of the Societies Law of that year. After the war restrictions were loosened somewhat and the unions began to look forward to being granted the use of the weapon that really would tell, the right to strike. Despite the promises made, this essential right was not granted during the Democrat Party regime. It was, however, granted in the 1961 Constitution and spelt out in detail in the subsequent new Trade Unions Law and the Law on Collective Bargaining, Strikes and Lock-outs passed in July 1963.[3]

One achievement of the 1946–60 period, however, was the creation of the Confederation of Turkish Workers' Unions (*Türk İş*) in 1952. At its first meeting held in Izmir, the Minister

---

[1] The evidence suggests that the trade-union movement is not regarded with complete sympathy by the military, which might be expected if the military were generally socialist in conviction, as is sometimes suggested. This is clear from a book by the Commander of the Army, Cemal Tural, *Kara Orduları ve Hedefleri* (Ankara, 1964). For comments on the book see *Yön*, 5 February 1965 and 10 December 1965.

[2] For much of the substance of this section I must acknowledge a particular debt to the writings of Prof. Dr Cahit Talas, the authority on Turkish trade unionism. For a brief introduction to the subject see particularly his article 'Türk Sendikacılığı', *Yüzüncü Yıl Armağanı* (Ank.: Ank. Üniv., S.B. Fak, 1959), pp. 223–44 and 'Grev Hakkı Üzerine Düşünceler', *S.B.F. Derg.*, xx, no. 2 (1965), pp. 39–42. See also his 'Türk-İş Hakkında,' *Forum*, no. 236, 1 February 1964—and on political aspects of trade unionism Alparslan Işıklı, 'Sendikalar, Politika ve Türk İş', *Forum*, no. 278, 1 November 1965.

[3] *Sendikalar Kanunu*, no. 274, 15 July 1963 and *Toplu İş, Sözleşmesi, Grev ve Lokavt Kanunu*, no. 276, 15 July 1963.

of Labour welcomed its appearance, but this did not, however, prove to be an indication that the Democrat Party government would thenceforth promote trade-union activities. In fact, by the end of the decade *Türk İş* was firmly under governmental influence.

The potential political significance of the trade unions is apparent when it is realized that Turkey has nearly a million manual workers divided between the private and public sectors in the proportion of about two to one.

One of the basic Turkish doctrines about trade unions is that they should concern themselves with social and economic, not political matters. This was made clear in the first Trade Union Law of 1947; and, during the following period up to 1960, the definition of what was political was kept wide. When, for instance, in 1953, the Istanbul Textile and Clothing Workers' Union advocated that Turks should use only Turkish-made goods, their action was defined as political. This insistence on separation from politics still appears in the present Trade Unions Law, which states (Article 16) that unions, whether of employees or employers, 'may not receive in any form material aid from political parties, nor from organizations attached to political parties, nor may they give aid to such bodies. Nor may unions take any place within their organization; and no union (or professional organization) may be set up under the name of any party.' There would still seem to be room for quite a deal of political activity, but it has to be remembered that, as they are defined as 'societies', unions are also subject to the provisions of the Political Parties Law, which forbid societies to support any political party or to support particular candidates in elections.[1]

For all these restrictions preventing direct participation in party politics, it is difficult to prevent the unions from exerting influence. The line between influence and participation is thinly drawn. The threat of industrial disruption through strikes[2] and the union members' vote in general and local elections are increasingly important. The unions' influence on politics since 1961 has ranged from demands for information about the financing of the five-year plan to offering advice on proposed legislation affecting

[1] See above, p. 134.
[2] There were ninety strikes between July 1963 and August 1965 (only one of which was in the public sector).

N

industrial matters. Some occasions when unions have exerted pressure have caught the public eye. For example, in April 1963, when the new law governing trade unions was still in commission in the Grand National Assembly, a meeting took place in Ankara of 320 leaders of trade unions affiliated to *Türk İş*.[1] As they agreed with the basic provisions of the draft laws, no great difference appeared between themselves and the government—they did not, for instance, believe with the Turkish Workers' Party that the employers' right of lock-out should be removed. They did, however, object to the extent of the government's discretion in obliging strikes to be postponed in the national interest and certain modifications in this respect were made.

Again, in August 1965, *Türk İş* asked political parties to include certain candidates who would support working-class interests among those to be put forward by the parties' central organizations. This was a first step along a slippery path. The next was the publication by *Türk İş* of a 'black list' of nine deputies for whom workers were advised not to vote in the forthcoming primary elections.[2] This raised a storm. The publication was confiscated by the authorities and the Federation's headquarters searched. It was held that *Türk İş* had offended against the Political Parties Law, which forbade to political parties during the primary election period any propaganda by publications, or public meetings, for or against candidates. *Türk İş* was not a political party, but it was held, against the appeal made by *Türk İş* that 'this right which was not given to political parties could not then be granted to (other) associations'.

The position of the trade unions in politics is, therefore, very delicate. The theory is, basically, that they should concern them-

[1] Relations between *Türk İş* and the Turkish Workers' Party (T.I.P.) were very strained at this time. The party was accused by *Türk İş* of revolutionary socialism as a result of the nature of its alleged participation in a strike in the coalfield in Zonguldak.

[2] Two of the nine had spoken against the new trade-union laws in the Assembly, five had opposed, in the interests of pharmacists, the distribution of medicines in health centres organized by the Workers' Insurance Society. (It seems that inclusion in the list had some effect in persuading some deputies not to be candidates and in ensuring places at the lower end of the party primary election lists for others. See *Yön*, 3 September 1965. In the end result, only three out of the nine were re-elected to the new National Assembly in October 1965.

selves only with economic and social matters; but political decisions seem to them to be necessary to secure their ends. They support land reform, tax reform, equitable distribution of income, planned development and the nationalization of oil resources. Save in conditions of economic scarcity, it seems unlikely that trade unions will continue to be political or take up a stance anywhere further left than left of centre. Except in a general way, they are, however, as we have seen, legally prohibited from involvement in politics.

There is something to be said for the basic idea justifying this arrangement, namely that Turkey should be spared political division along the lines of socio-economic class interest and the social bitterness that this can create. If this is the problem, it is doubtful if, in the long run, the legal barriers will hold back the flood. If this is not the problem, if, that is to say, the unions will be content to remain somewhere left of centre and will continue not to want to support any one party, the restrictions on political activity seem pointless. One effect of these restrictions is to encourage the unions to adumbrate a political programme which they describe as 'above party'.[1] This has its dangers because it implies a reduction of the importance of political parties and by consequence of the democratic system itself. The relationship between the trade unions and the political parties merits close study over the next few years. At present, their relations are in a very fluid state.

[1] Which the General Council of *Türk İş* did in 1964. See A. Işıklı, *Forum*, 1 November 1965.

CHAPTER XI

Elections

The electoral system

We have seen how the Turkish electoral system developed between 1946 and 1960. Indirect election was replaced in 1946 by direct election, and provision was made for secret voting and a public count. In 1950 the Judiciary was made responsible for the fair management of the elections, after pressure from the newly emerged Democrat Party. This did not, however, after 1950, prevent the People's Party from claiming injustices in the application of judicial control—in the use of radio time during elections, for example. There were also allegations that the government was gerrymandering in redrawing certain constituency boundaries. Most important, the People's Party, now in much reduced strength in the National Assembly, began to advocate proportional representation. The Democrat Party would have none of it.

A system of proportional representation was one of the first announced desiderata of the military in 1960 when the Onar Commission was given the task of drafting a constitution. After some hesitation, the system of election of the Grand National Assembly by proportional representation was not included in the Constitution as it finally emerged in July 1961. The requirement was, however, included in the new Electoral Laws previously passed by the Constituent Assembly in April and May, 1961,[1] but only for the National Assembly, not for the Senate. The Senate has 150 elected members, one-third of whom retire every two years.[2] The National Assembly has 450 members elected for a four-year period.

The electoral laws give expression to the electoral principles that normally form part of democratic representative govern-

---

[1] *Seçimlerin Temel Hükümleri ve Seçmen Kütükleri Hakkında Kanun*, no. 298, 26 April 1961. *Cumhuriyet Senatosu Üyelerinin Seçimi Kanunu*, no. 304, 24 May 1961 and *Milletvekili Seçimi Kanunu*, no. 306, 25 May 1961.

[2] In view of the situation created by the attempted coup of 21–22 May 1963, the Senate elections were postponed by the Grand National Assembly (29 May 1963) for one year.

ment. Voting is secret, counting is public. Every Turk twenty-one years and over may vote; competition for votes by individuals and political parties is permitted and elections are direct. The elections are supervised by electoral councils at the levels of sub-province and province and the High Electoral Council is the final court of appeal for all complaints concerning the administration of the elections. It is composed of four members of the Supreme Court of Appeal and three members of the Council of State. They are elected by secret vote by each of these two bodies. The electoral councils at the lower levels include representatives of the political parties, this representation being more pronounced in the sub-provincial electoral councils. In addition to numerous administrative functions that are required by the holding of an election, the High Electoral Commission has to arrange with the political parties an equitable distribution of radio time for political broadcasts.

Candidates for election to the Senate have to be forty years old; for the National Assembly, thirty. For both houses the political parties may, of course, put forward candidates, but to do so they have to have held at least one general congress, and to have maintained an organization for at least six months in at least fifteen of the sixty-seven provinces. A list of as many candidates as there are seats to be filled in each province contested has to be put forward. The parties have to establish their lists of candidates by democratic methods of election over a month before election day.[1] The candidates put up by any party's central organization must not exceed 10 per cent of all candidates put forward by the party.[2]

The principal difference between the present and the previous system is, of course, the introduction of proportional representation for the lower house, subsequently extended to the Senate as well. The new requirement that a party intending to contest the election must possess an organization in at least fifteen provinces is intended to prevent the emergence of splinter parties.

[1] Detailed prescription of the required primary elections is given in the *Political Parties Law*. See above, p. 133.

[2] In draft, the law provided for the nomination of 20 per cent of candidates by the parties' central organizations, a step which the leadership of the People's Party (the majority party in the Constituent Assembly) had tried unsuccessfully to persuade the party's Congress to accept for a number of years. To include it in the new electoral laws also proved unsuccessful. See Cemal Aygen, 'Seçim Kanunu Tasarısı ve Parti Merkez Adayları', *Forum*, 15 April 1961.

There is an important innovation in the introduction of primary elections as a device to make the presentation of candidates by the political parties more democratic. Another new development is the inclusion of representatives of the political parties in the supervisory machinery, a reflection of the fact that, in the 1950-60 decade, supervision by members of the Judiciary alone was not seen by the opposition parties to be completely impartial. The new laws also attempt to plug holes apparent in the previous structure, as, for example, in the detailed laws on preparation of electoral registers. It was often alleged in the previous decade that voters had been deliberately excluded from the lists by the authorities.

The 1961 general election was held under the new laws. That experience and the experience of the local elections held in November 1963 gave much food for thought. It was not long before amendments to the electoral laws were brought forward.

The first of these was the extension to the Senate partial re-election, due in 1964, of the system of proportional representation. It was abundantly clear to the People's Party and to the minor parties after the local election of 1963 that the Justice Party was prospering and would greatly increase its hold on the Senate if the majority system of election was kept in force. The law was, therefore, changed despite Justice Party opposition.

The second change that has taken place has been the amendment of the system of proportional representation to provide for what is known as 'national remainder'.[1] The system adopted in 1961 was based on the 'highest average' rule invented as a means of proportional representation by a Belgian, named d'Hondt. The chief effect of this list system of proportional representation is to bias the result slightly in favour of the larger parties, a situation to which the People's Party was not averse in 1961. By 1964, however, it was apparent that the trend against the minor parties, as revealed by the local elections of 1963 and the Senate elections of 1964, was in favour of the Justice Party. Both the minor parties and the People's party, therefore, developed an interest in any modification of the electoral system that would be likely to increase the representation of the minor parties. The system was consequently changed to another list system of proportional

---

[1] This and the other principal changes in the electoral system are contained in the law. *Seçimlerle Kanunların Bazı Hükümlerinin Değiştirilmesi Hakkında Kanun*, no. 533, 13 February 1965.

representation, usually known as 'greatest remainder'. Under this system, the votes cast in each constituency are divided by the number of seats. The resulting quotient is then used to divide the votes cast for each party list or independent candidate. A party list with 4,500 votes when the quotient was 2,000 would, therefore, gain two seats. Thus, so far, the system actually has the effect of helping the smaller vote-winning lists (usually those of the minor political parties). It assists this movement still further when the remaining votes—500 in the example given above—are then transferred to a national pool, as they now are in Turkey. This, in effect, constitutes another, this time national, constituency. The seats available are those left unfilled in the constituencies by the working of the system.[1] They are divided among the parties by the same method used for each constituency. The problem then arises of which candidates will be chosen as deputies. The solution used is to make a list of constituencies for each party showing the proportion that its remainder vote formed of each total constituency vote. From those constituencies where a party did best its candidates are chosen in list order, except that one-third of a party's places from the national pool may be filled by each party's central organization from its total list of all constituency candidates.

Another change introduced in 1965 was the substitution of an official voting paper, containing all parties' lists, for voting papers printed separately by the political parties (under prescribed rules). This was intended to prevent abuses by those who were tempted to supply voters with completed papers before they entered the polling booth. The new system was more complex and undoubtedly more confusing for inexperienced voters.

Electoral campaigns

Electoral campaigns are subject to some regulation by law. The principal provisions are, first, that after the beginning of a general election period (some two months before the election date) public offices must refrain from any publicity of governmental achievements, ministers and deputies must not be accompanied on any provincial tours, nor must they use any public vehicles. The aim of these provisions, which appear for the first time in the

[1] For those interested in this important subject, there can be no better introduction than W. J. M. Mackenzie, *Free Elections* (London, 1957).

new electoral laws, is to prevent the party in power from exploiting its governmental powers for party propaganda purposes.
The governments of the Democrat Party were notorious offenders
in this respect. On the eve of the 1957 general election the Democrat Party government, for instance, gave much publicity to the
opening of new roads, factories and housing estates.[1] Secondly,
the Constitution provides for the replacement, just before the
beginning of the general election period, of the Ministers of
Justice, the Interior and of Communications by ministers selected
by the President from among independent senators or deputies.
This is, of course, a device to secure impartiality in the three
ministries most able to influence elections. The lack of impartiality
of the administration in elections has frequently been a cause of
complaint.

The electoral campaign begins officially some two months
before election day, but the campaign does not really get under
way before the party primary elections held six weeks before the
election. The primaries are keenly contested.[2] Given that there
turns out to be real substance in the provision for all parties'
members to vote in primaries, there may well come to be much
more change than in the past in the party lists. In the 1965 primaries, in which, as a temporary measure, all party members were
not given the vote, the influence of the local party organizations
was supreme. This meant that chairmen of local party organizations and the like were very successful. This affected, too, the
composition of candidates in terms of their professions. Lawyers,
in particular, showed up strongly in the lists of candidates and
they were more or less proportionately successful in the primary
elections. The professionally qualified in other fields, like finance
and technology, did not figure so prominently. In the Nation
Party, however, candidates in agricultural, commercial and industrial professions were numerically most conspicuous. There

---

[1] K. Karpat, 'The Turkish Elections of 1957', *Western Political Quarterly*,
XIV (1961), pp. 436–59.

[2] For the 1965 primaries, the numbers of candidates for the Justice Party
were 954 and for the People's Party, 685. Both parties were contesting all
constituencies. Numbers of candidates in the other parties were Workers'
Party, 507 (fifty-four constituencies), New Turkey Party, 334, R.P.N.P., 371
(both parties contesting forty-eight constituencies), Nation Party, 232
(thirty-four constituencies). Five per cent of candidatures for seats are, however, at the disposal of the central organizations of each political party.

were few manual workers as candidates, except in the Worker's Party.

When we look at the fortunes of deputies in the primary election, an interesting discovery is that 20 per cent of the People's Party's deputies did not put up for re-election, compared with only 4 per cent of Justice Party deputies. The People's Party position was like that of the small parties in this respect. It suggested a lack of confidence in, or dissatisfaction with, the party. Of those People's Party deputies who did stand, a large proportion were successful in the primaries (88 per cent), as compared with 77 per cent for the Justice Party, where the competition was rather keener.[1]

In the 1957 election campaign, the chief issue was, probably, economic development, but religion was a close second. This was not a contest between minaret and factory chimney, however. Both the major parties wanted to build both. The Democrat Party was really the first to realize that a mixture of more religion and more food and goods was what the peasant really wanted. The People's Party had to follow this line—if it was to increase its vote. It could certainly claim that economic development was its own distinguishing mark; but it could not claim the same for unplanned economic development, and it could not match the enthusiasm which some Democrat Party quarters showed for individual economic enterprise and the importation of foreign capital. Moreover, the People's Party had long lived by the light of the doctrine that Islam and material improvement did not mix, that unless the dead hand of religion were removed nothing would prosper materially. Secularism was partly justified by the need for economic development. The Democrat Party's philosophy was different. The party did not believe first that it was necessary to curtail religious practices in order to prevent the re-emergence of an Islamic State; in this they were undoubtedly right; the process of economic and social development seems to entail everywhere a weakening of religious ties. Then again, the Democrat Party did not accept that *Muslim* peasants would

[1] These figures are from N. Abadan, *Anayasa Hukuku ve Siyasî Bilimler Açısından 1965 Seçim Tahlili* (Ankara, 1965). For much of the information on the election of 1965 I owe a debt to this study. I rely otherwise on my own less extensive use of newspapers and other similar material during a visit to Turkey during the election period.

not want to be better off materially. In this they were right too.

Although by 1957 the People's Party was, still timidly, recognizing private enterprise and the desire for more religion, its own chief preoccupation was with the defence of the basic freedoms against Democratic Party authoritarianism. These were particularly important to the middle classes who understood them and were affected by them—and the workers appreciated the party's demand for the right to strike—but to many voters proper safeguards for the judicial review of executive acts, a double legislative chamber, or university autonomy seemed rather less than matters of first importance, even if they understood them.

In the new Constitution of 1961, these demands of the People's Party found their place. The 1961 election turned then really on the record of the Democrats, but by that time the Justice Party had not stood forth as in effect the sole heir to the Democrats. In the local elections of 1963 they showed, however, that they were the rightful heir. The writing was on the wall for the minor parties. As if to rebut the stridency of its own noisy extremists, the Justice Party presented itself to the electorate at the end of 1963 as a respectable party which respected law and order—and believed in national unity, which, it was claimed, its political opponents were intent on breaking with their cry of danger from rightist extremists. The Justice Party also made out that they trusted the military to allow the party to come to power. The People's Party appeal was based on planned development; but its speakers did not neglect to point out that many mosques had been built and that many had gone on the pilgrimage to Mecca.

The 1963 elections were local and gave much place to local affairs. The Senate partial elections of June 1964 were more national in character. The People's Party stressed security, domestic peace and development based on justice. They—and the minor parties—attacked the calibre of the Justice Party leaders, likened by one prominent People's Party deputy to 'backward hojas'.[1]

The minor parties frequently attacked the People's Party leadership, but, in particular, İsmet İnönü, who is a bogeyman for the minor parties. In fact, the preoccupation of the minor parties in this election was with opposition to the People's Party, not the Justice Party. The minor parties seemed unable to get over the

[1] T. Feyzioğlu, *Cumhuriyet*, 23 May 1964.

fact that at the beginning of the period of multi-party politics, opposition meant opposition to the People's Party, which has run everything single-handed for so long and they needed to assert their independence of their senior coalition partner; so they criticized the People's Party mentality (of authoritarian high-handedness). They accused the Justice Party of heading in the same direction; but the essential minor parties' criticism of the Justice Party in the 1964 campaign was simply of their leaders' alleged incapacity and dishonesty.

The Justice Party in 1964 again stressed national unity, their opposition to governmental restrictions on freedom, including the large doses of martial law to which the country had been subject. The Party made some play out of 'Balkan socialism' which they claimed land reform of the wrong sort would produce. Justice Party spokesmen, however, were anything but negative in their electoral promises. They also made the point—to reappear in 1965 more strongly—that the lack of decisive government produced by the working of the electoral system was driving the country to communism and dictatorship. This was to express crudely the serious disquiet among thoughtful Turks that proportional representation was giving too much of a say to extremists and might well open a road in the Turkish environment to national disunity, the bogey of so many Turks. Whilst Justice Party speakers began to slip easily into pointing out the dangers of the left their indication of the dangers from the right was not so noticeable.

The 1965 campaign preceding the election of a new National Assembly was naturally much more extensive than those in 1963 and 1964.

Perhaps the most significant feature of the 1965 campaign was that the People's Party took up a definite position, on the left-right axis by declaring itself as 'left of centre'. This gave direction to its campaign, but there were signs that some of its spokesmen were losing confidence half-way through when they suspected the slogan was doing injury to the party's chances. Towards the end, İnönü and other top leaders stepped in to reaffirm the party's new stand. The principal reasoning behind the party's new stand was that votes on the left would tend now to go to the Turkish Workers' Party in the absence of a moderate leftist party. To go left was also less dangerous when there was a more leftist party in existence; accusations of communism or of Russian sympathies would be more appropriate to the buffer Workers' Party.

The 'left of centre' stand by the People's Party made it seem that the Justice Party must be right of centre. Some of its supporters made the claim, but the party generally preferred a more eclectic approach. It seemed to have something for everyone, peasant, worker, landowner, businessman—and even for academics with its promise of more new universities. Yet by implication the party began to look right of centre; and this siting in the political landscape may well come to do it harm in time. Similarly, the People's Party 'left of centre' stand may just have been mistimed for 1965. In 1969 it may find a wider response if, as is likely, economic and social development breaks more people away from their old moorings and changes their ideas.

During the campaign, the minor parties attacked the two large parties; the two major parties, however, were almost exclusively concerned with each other. The People's Party saw the Justice Party as wanting to re-live Democrat Party times. There would be a return, it was claimed, to insecurity for higher civil servants, radio partisanship and the persecution of the intellectuals. The workers, it was claimed, would get short shrift.[1] The merits of planned development were stressed; and it was not forgotten to claim that foreign experts approved of the plan. Their opponents, it was said, approved of planning in theory, but not in practice (a shrewd point). They should come out in the open, in fact, and say whether they were really in favour of the revolution of 27 May. (This is on the way to becoming a sacred cow.) The People's Party also pointed to the dangers of the importation of foreign capital not properly controlled in the national interest. This is an important, emotional point because Turks have long memories for the 'capitulations' imposed on the Ottoman Empire in the interests of foreign firms. The Justice Party was also challenged on its attitude to tax reform. The rumpus over foreign oil concessions had also not died down. The favourite jibe was that, whilst those who earned salaries of 250 Turkish lira (£10) a month paid tax, those who made 25,000 lira a month in agriculture paid nothing. Allegations of irreligion and communism were of course vigorously refuted. The main trouble in the party's appeal was

---

[1] İnönü used the Ürgüplü government's rather severe treatment of the strikers in the Zonguldak coalfield in 1965 as evidence for his views.

that it looked so much like a party for intellectuals and officials. It was not yet convincing in its turn to the left; it tried hard to explain its worthy aims to the uninstructed, but it is, perhaps, necessary to be partially uninstructed (or else specially gifted) to do so. Then again, the party had suffered from so many internal troubles and had a leader whose style was not charismatic, but just old-fashioned.

The Justice Party made considerable play of the importance of the national will, in order to make the point that legitimacy lay with the political party that got out the vote. This seems to have been more a defiance of the military than of the People's Party; but the conviction lies deep in the Justice Party that İnönü was in some way responsible for the 1960 military intervention. To give proper expression to the people's vote in the form of stable, effective government, the Justice Party declared it would return to a simple majority electoral system, an intention that upset the minor parties rather more than its principal opponents. As if to drive home its attachment to the ways of the past, the Justice Party called for a revival of the 1946 spirit of opposition to the People's Party. That such a call was considered necessary may indicate, what this observer feels, that the basic antagonism between Justice and People's Party leaders is not now anything like as deep seated as the antagonisms of the 1950's. The Justice Party leaders, however, and particularly the leader, Süleyman Demirel, showed himself too sensitive to personal attacks, rather reminiscent of the Democrat Party leaders' lack of tolerance in this respect. Demirel resented, in particular, being called Johnson's satellite or an American imperialist agent.

Like their principal opponents, the Justice Party called for national unity whilst more extreme elements in both camps were labelling each other as communists, reactionaries and American agents.[1] Even the leaders could get excited. When one heckler told Demirel that İnönü would send him to join Menderes he replied it was nothing to go to the gallows for the sake of Turkey, even to go to hell (an unfortunate choice of destination in the

---

[1] The Justice Party symbol was a grey horse, the iron-grey horse (*demir kır at*). The merit of this was that it was more or less the common pronunciation of 'democrat'. One particularly biting cartoon—*Cumhuriyet*, 6 October 1965—showed a Trojan grey horse being led by Demirel into Turkey.

circumstances).[1] Bölükbaşı observed that those who became excited before a crowd usually expressed a wish either for the gallows or for hell. To an extent, both the major parties got carried away. They certainly developed a tendency to promise everyone everything. In the swell, the Justice Party also got carried away further to the right than probably in more sober moments it would have wished. In a speech on the eve of elections, Demirel declared it was not possible to give land to everyone, a clear response to the Workers' Party's claims in this respect.[2]

It was, in fact, the Workers' Party that astonished almost everyone in the campaign. They started off rather badly, particularly in broadcast speeches by being too blunt. They seemed by this to lose sympathy in a society where outspokenness is regarded as hardly civilized. The party was, of course, particularly liable to be dubbed communist and pro-Russian. It had to contend with vicious attacks from all the parties; and became the veritable *bête noire* of the election. Obviously it was much feared. One of its successes was to claim that land could be given to all the landless and that it would restrict holdings of land to 500 *dönüms*. This was, no doubt, an unworkable gross simplification of a complex problem; but it was a concrete proposal and therefore had electoral merit. The party leader was once taunted about loyalty to the Turkish flag. The party strove to make it very clear that it was not anyone's satellite and believed in a fully independent Turkey. One of its most telling appeals was for representation of the peasants and workers in the National Assembly by peasants and workers. By voting for us, the party said, you will *yourselves* get into the Assembly. It claimed that of its 382 candidates 216 were peasants, workers or lesser tradesmen.

The Nation Party, which won third place in the Assembly, was similarly successful in its campaign, but without much attention to policy. A great deal was made of Bölükbaşı's refusal to allow Nation Party ministers in the Ürgüplü coalition to sign a Cultural Agreement with Soviet Russia; and there were the usual attacks on İnönü. Apart from these attacks on the other parties—a technique in which the party leader excels—the main emphasis lay on the role of arbiter that Bölükbaşı saw for the party. It was argued that history was repeating itself, that there must be a

[1] *Cumhuriyet*, 5 October 1965.
[2] Ibid., 8 October 1965.

powerful third party to stop the war of the giants whose quarrels would flow into the streets. The success of the Nation Party was probably due to the personality of its leader and his ability to attract attention. Bölükbaşı would at least have the courage to be an arbiter.

The role of arbiter could better have been assumed, however, by the New Turkey Party; its leader, Ekrem Alican, is a statesman more than an effective party leader. The party's campaign was not very exciting. Its organization was weak, its confidence lacking, its slogans dull. Its attacks were mainly directed against the People's Party—and the problems of planning were insisted upon. One commentator summed it up by saying it was a party everyone approved of but no one voted for.

The campaign of the last of the five parties, now under Alparslan Türkeş, was awaited with some eagerness. Was there room for his brand of right-wing doctrine in Turkey? The party started well, but lost momentum; its rather involved message was difficult to get across. Its tirades on behalf of Turkish nationalism and national unity, particularly directed against the Workers' Party, did no more than repeat the cries of the other parties. In a country where every political party fervently preaches nationalism and national unity, it is difficult to seize upon these ideals, develop and refine them and then make an electoral appeal out of the result. The party did much less well in the elections than was expected. Was it just another indication that the 1960 revolution and its authors were just not wanted by the Turkish electorate?

To sum up the issues in the campaign of 1965, the features that were perhaps most important were the Justice Party's emphasis on strong government, and on accelerated economic development with the accent on individual enterprise and without too much respect for planning. Demirel often made the point that, full of learning though the plan was, what the Justice Party really believed in was in getting things done. By 1965 the Justice Party had fully developed as the sole heir to the Democrat Party. Religion seems to have remained in second, or even third, place in importance to economic betterment. So too did the appeal for the social welfare state made by the People's Party. It was so moderate and, in the present Turkish environment, so colourless. By comparison, the blunt, concrete, if not practical, solutions to Turkish problems advocated by the Workers' Party did much to arouse the electorate. The Workers' Party seems able to talk to the Justice Party in its own down to earth terms when its speakers are not carried away by Marxist logic and jargon (a bad point in electoral speeches). The People's Party seems too sophisticated for its environment. The question that seems most to confound Justice Party deputies is the sort a villager asked Demirel. Holding up a crust of stale bread, the peasant told the Justice Party leader—'This is what we eat'[1] and then asked 'What do you eat?' This sort of question the Workers' Party is prepared to ask— and has yet to answer. The emergence of a hard-hitting opposition to the Justice Party was, perhaps, the most significant feature of the electoral campaign. No wonder the Justice Party tried hard to get the Workers' Party disqualified on technical grounds from participating in the election.

As to the general character of the electoral campaigns, a few points are worth noting. First, there seems to be a decline in the popularity of open-air meetings; the parties certainly did not take advantage of the number of open-air meetings they were allowed. By contrast, radio speeches were listened to with more attention; and the radio was particularly important to attractive speakers like Bölükbaşı. A study of the subjects of wireless talks shows that the Nation Party and the Justice Party devoted rather more time than the other parties to attacks on other parties and their leaders. On economic and social matters, the Workers' Party and the People's Party were most prominent. The Justice Party spent a lot of time on the dangers from the left. The R.P.N.P., as might be expected, was much given to self-adulation. It turned out to be a case of self-praise being no real recommendation. Religion was always most approved by R.P.N.P. speakers, with the Justice Party not far behind.

The role of the press in the electoral campaign seems to have been greater than in 1961.[2] The newspapers took trouble to cover various areas of the country with special electoral teams of reporters; and they enlivened their reports with photographs, voting speculations and so on. The papers also entered into comparisons

---

[1] *Cumhuriyet*, 28 September 1965.

[2] Turkish newspapers circulate chiefly in Istanbul, Ankara and Izmir. The total daily circulation is 1·5 million. If, as suggested by Nermin Abadan, *1965, Seçimlerinin Tahlili*, ten persons use one newspaper, then over one-third of the population receives some impact.

with elections in 1961 and 1963 and they developed political caricature to a new degree. They developed a new interest too in the candidates' personal lives, not omitting their wives! It was altogether a more versatile and lively coverage than in the past. Most of the newspapers supported the Justice Party.

Finally, although the 1965 election was important and was regarded as such, paradoxically, the impression gained was that the tone was less serious than in, say, 1961, or even 1957. This may be due to what appeared to be lessening interest in or even indifference to political principle and political argumentation. It was a gayer than normal election. Politics does not seem to bite so deep.

Electoral trends

The creation of a Senate in 1961, especially the requirement that one-third of its membership should be elected every two years, has meant that the Turkish electorate has been given much more opportunity to participate in national politics (by voting) than in the past. Moreover, local elections are a guide to the electorate's views on national politics.[1]

Participation in Turkish elections shows some decline since 1961, when 81 per cent of the electorate voted in the National Assembly and Senate elections. By 1965 this had dropped to just under 70 per cent. Participation in the local elections in November 1963 was quite high at 77 per cent, but the partial Senate elections in 1964 and 1966 brought only 60 per cent and 56 per cent of the electorate to the polls respectively.

The division of the valid vote among the parties in elections since 1957 to 1966 is as shown in Table 7.

Although much more detailed analysis of Turkish voting statistics is needed it is clear that the Justice Party has been

[1] The local elections on 17 November 1963 were for every elected organization of local government, namely, the Provincial General Council, the Presidency of the Municipality, the Municipality Council, the Village Headman, the Village Council of Elders, the Ward (or Precinct) Headman and the Ward Council of Elders. The Provincial General Council and the Municipality Council were both to be elected, for the first time, by a system of proportional representation. The remainder continued to be elected by simple majority vote. For the first time, however, the Municipality President was to be directly elected. The figures used in the voting percentages given in the text are those for Provincial General Councils only.

o

TABLE 7

Grand National Assembly Elections, 1957–66
(Percentages of Valid Votes Obtained)

Year	Election	Justice Party	People's Party	Republican Peasants Nation Party	New Turkey Party	Turkish Workers' Party	Nation Party	Inde-pendents	Democrat Party	Freedom Party
1957	National Assembly	—	40·9	7·2	—	—	—	—	47·7	3·8
1961	Senate	34·5	36·1	12·5	13·0	—	—	3·9	—	—
1961	National Assembly	34·8	36·7	14·0	13·7	—	—	0·8	—	—
1963	Provincial General Councils	45·9	37	2·8	6·5	0·4	3·1	4·3	—	—
1964	One-third of Senate	50·3	40·8	3·0	3·45		—	2·3	—	—
1965	National Assembly	52·7	28·75	2·2	3·7	3·0	6·3	3·3	—	—
1966	One-third of Senate	56·9	29·6	1·9	2·4	3·9	5·3	0·5	—	—

Sources: Publications of the State Statistics Institute, nos. 434, 474 and 483, for statistics for elections in 1961, 1963 and 1964. The 1957 figures are from Weiker, *The Turkish Revolution, 1960–61*, p. 113; for 1965 from *Cumhuriyet*, 15 October 1965; and for 1966 from *News from Turkey*, vol. III, no. 11, London: Turkish Embassy, 1966.

steadily increasing its share of the vote. A new trend since 1965 which will be of crucial importance to Turkish politics if it continues is the sharp decline in the vote for the People's Party. The relative success of the splinter Nation Party in 1965 probably owed much to the leadership of Bölükbaşı and the party may be joining in the decline of the two post-revolutionary parties that contested the 1961 elections. The one minor party that seems to be making steady progress is the Workers' Party, but the 1966 elections were held in only twenty-two of the sixty-seven provinces and the percentage of the electorate who voted, was very low, at 56·2 per cent. In these latest Senate elections it is, perhaps, significant that, while the Workers' Party's proportion of the votes in the western Turkish provinces declined, it increased in the east, where landlordism is particularly strong.

CHAPTER XII

Parliament

In our discussion so far of political institutions we have considered organizations (like the military, the students' organizations and the political parties) that exert pressures on the political machinery in order to influence policy. Political parties do not completely fit into this category because a political party, especially if it is in power, both takes and exerts influence over decisions.

In dealing with the Grand National Assembly (and later the Council of Ministers and the President) we are considering institutions whose task is primarily to take decisions, although the business of influencing the decisions to be taken is never absent. Parliament is taken first because it is as much, if not more, a decision-influencing than a decision-taking body. The main features of the Council of Ministers and the Presidency are explained in the next chapter, where an attempt will be made to put in perspective the relations of these two institutions that with parliament lie at the hub of Turkish government.

General organization

The Grand National Assembly is empowered to meet of its own accord on the first day of November each year and sits for seven months. There are also provisions for parliament to be called to meet during vacation time, by the President directly or on the recommendation of the Council of Ministers. Both the Senate and the National Assembly may also call meetings on their own initiative for special sessions. Turkey need never be deprived of the presence of her elected representatives.

At the first meeting of a new parliament the first task is for each house to choose its president and members of the presidential council (*divan*). The president of each assembly is elected for a period of two years. Party groups may not nominate candidates for the presidency of either Chamber; presidents are elected by each house for two years, by a two-thirds majority of all members. The superiority of the National Assembly is emphasized by making its president the president also, when the houses meet together as the Grand National Assembly. The posts of deputy president and the other positions in the presidents' councils are filled in proportion to party strengths. Nevertheless, like the presidents, the deputy presidents are forbidden to participate in political party activities, inside or outside parliament, except that, unlike the presidents, the deputy presidents may vote.

The functions of the presidents' councils include the preparation of agenda and the arrangement of times of meetings. Under the 1924 Constitution, which left the formation of the president's council completely to the discretion of the Assembly, governments were much criticized for packing the councils in their favour. In order to avoid this the 1961 Constitution (Article 84) required that presidents' councils should reflect the strength of political party groups in each house, and that political party groups should not be permitted to nominate candidates for the position of president. These new provisions have, however, caused quite a deal of trouble, so much so that the Constitutional and Judicial Commission of the Senate requested a study on the subject from the Institute of Administrative Sciences of the Faculty of Political Science, Ankara University. The particularly thorny problems were whether independent M.P.'s could also be council members and whether the president should be treated as part of the quota on the president's council of the political party to which he belonged. That he could not be nominated by any party seemed to raise him above party and made it difficult to decide whether by virtue of his election his party was then represented on the council by him. However, it was argued that it was not necessary for a member elected president to leave his party and it was recognized that however much the Constitution prevented direct nomination of candidates for the presidency by the parties, nothing could stop the parties from exerting influence. It seemed wiser on the whole to recognize necessity. The other problem of participation in the council by independent members also shows up a shortcoming in the Constitution. The original draft wording, which permitted 'political groups' to participate in the presidents' councils had been changed to 'political party groups' in order to prevent possible domination by pressure groups. The aim was not to exclude independents, and it has been agreed to allow them to be members.[1]

[1] For a thorough discussion of these problems see the report of the

Each Assembly possesses a number of standing commissions about whose work in detail and the influence to which they are subject little is known.[1] Some of the commissions are concerned with the examination of draft laws and other proposals affecting governmental work generally, such as the Commission on Constitutional and Judicial Affairs and the Commission on Budget and Planning, whilst others deal with major but rather more separate fields of governmental activity. The divisions of governmental work used for commissions of the Senate are broader than those employed by the National Assembly. The commissions may invite ministers, for whom a civil servant may deputize, and also experts. Ministers do seem to attend quite often. *Ad hoc* commissions are set up from time to time and some commissions are joint between the two Houses. Appointment to commissions is by reference to party strength. To overcome the problem of representation of independents they are permitted to organize themselves into groups, which have to be of not less than ten members in order to obtain representation on commissions.

Each house has adopted a set of procedural rules, though a catalogue of procedural rules is not so important as the general attitude that underlies them. The French Fourth Republic had rules that sought for the most part to prevent parliament from easily over-throwing government or delaying its legislative work. The problem there was an acute one of relations between government and parliament. The Turkish situation is different. In Turkey the problem has been to prevent a government that disposes of a large majority from reducing parliament to insigni-

---

Commission set up by the Institute of the Administrative Sciences referred to above. Ank. Üniv. S.B.F. İdari İlimler Enstitüsü (S.B.F. Yayınları, no. 152–34. Ankara, 1963).

[1] There are very few studies of the working of Turkish parliamentary institutions as distinct from some excellent discussions of constitutional and legal problems that arise from time to time. The reports of the parliamentary commissions form part of the printed record of the proceedings of each House. The reports are brief and usually not very informative. More substantial reports of the work of each commission appear in the Official Gazette, twice yearly in the case of the National Assembly and for the Senate every quarter. The most valuable source of information probably is the collection of summary minutes (and on occasion verbatim accounts) of each commission's meetings and the documents prepared, filed in the Grand National Assembly's archives.

ficance, relatively easy to do in a society where to the great majority, it seems, parliament is not much understood let alone revered. From 1950 to 1960 the Democrat Party dominated the Grand National Assembly through its disciplined majorities; but their government did not completely prevent the opposition from functioning as an opposition *inside parliament*. At the time of the revolution rules of parliamentary procedure were not generally called into question. The Turkish parliament, now as in the past, recognizes the need for effective government. The rules recognize the government's need to press on through the timetable but also the need to allow the opposition (including independents) to have their say. The reformers really based their hopes for a less executive dominated parliament on permitting deputies and senators to participate in all Assembly activities on the basis of party strength (Article 85 of the Constitution). The system of proportional representation in the new electoral system was also expected to prevent the emergence of any one very powerful party. As we have seen, this turned out to be the case between 1961 and 1965; but not after the election of October 1965.

Legislation

The new Constitution provides that legislation may be initiated by the Council of Ministers or by members of the Grand National Assembly.[1] The Constitution also requires that the first discussion of all legislative proposals take place in the National Assembly, an important limitation on the power of the Senate. Any legislative proposals rejected by the lower house must, however, be discussed by the Senate, so senators' legislative proposals do not in fact run the risk of never being heard of again should the National Assembly turn them down.

The lower house, then, possesses the initiative in discussion; it also possesses the final authority in case of disputes between the two houses. There are three circumstances in which dispute can occur. First, the Senate may amend a proposal from the National Assembly in ways which are unacceptable to it. In this event the proposal is referred to a mixed commission, composed of equal numbers of senators and deputies. The joint commission's

---

[1] The nature of private members' legislative proposals and how influential they are is another subject that merits detailed study.

proposals are then submitted to the National Assembly, which now has either to insist upon its own original proposal, or accept that of the Senate or that of the joint commission. Secondly, the Senate may reject the National Assembly's proposal outright. If this rejection is by an absolute majority of all members of the Senate, the National Assembly has to show a similar absolute majority of all members for the measure to pass. If the Senate rejects with a two-thirds majority, then a similar majority must be found by the National Assembly. If the two houses are elected under different electoral systems, as was the case until 1964, before which time the Senate was elected by the simple majority vote, then the situation might arise of markedly different party strengths in each house.[1] If this does not happen, then the chance of serious dispute between the two houses leading to a Senate victory is slim. The third possibility is that the Senate will independently approve a proposal rejected by the National Assembly. In this case the National Assembly has to discuss the proposal again, although rejection once more by the lower house finally kills the proposal. Real power in fact rests with the National Assembly. Given a similar electoral system now for both houses, it is very unlikely that the Senate will take a different line from the National Assembly on any matter of real importance.[2]

[1] The re-election of one-third of the Senate elected members every two years can also give rise to differences in composition.

[2] The Senate, however, has not been slow to assert itself. At one time it was urged that the Senate's obligation to return draft bills to the National Assembly within a month could be interpreted to mean that they should not be returned before the month. Similarly it was held that bills labelled urgent should wait the full fifteen days allotted to the Senate in which to discuss them. There has been considerable legal dispute over Article 92 of the Constitution which seems to prohibit the Senate from returning draft bills in less than a month (or those labelled urgent in less than fifteen days). This conflicts with another part of the same article which states that the Senate should come to its decision in a period of time not longer than that spent on the matter by the National Assembly. In the upshot the Senate's Constitution and Justice Commission advised that it was the *discussion period* that should not be less than the month (or fifteen days for urgent bills), not the decision period, which could be less. The Senate during 1961 to 1965, it should be remembered, had far greater proportion of Justice Party and New Turkey Party members than had the National Assembly. The constitutional and legal issues are discussed at length by Muammer Aksoy,

Legislative procedure is otherwise simple enough. The discussion stage is divided into two parts. The first discussion occurs in the National Assembly on report from the commission concerned. This is first a discussion of the proposal as a whole. It is then decided by vote whether the house should pass on to a discussion of the individual articles of the bill or legislative proposal. If the verdict is negative the measure is lost; if affirmative discussion of, and voting on, the article then proceeds. The house then votes on whether to accept the proposal as a whole.

The second discussion does not normally take place until at least five days after the first and is devoted to a consideration of amendments. At this stage no discussion of the proposal generally is intended; but in practice the right of deputies to express views on the bill or proposal before the final vote leads again to some discussion of principle.

Not all bills and legislative proposals need to be discussed twice, however. The procedure for normal legislation may be reduced to one discussion on grounds of emergency, if the house agrees—and this seems to occur quite often. Moreover, the single discussion procedure is always used for the budget and connected proposals. Budget procedure also differs from normal legislation in that the government's proposals are submitted to a joint committee of the Senate and National Assembly. The Commission is weighted in membership on the side of the National Assembly, thirty-five deputies to fifteen senators. More important, thirty of the forty-five members belong to the party groups sustaining the government. The Commission's version of the proposals is first discussed by the Senate, after which it goes back to the Commission, who now submit its version (altered now perhaps) to the National Assembly for discussion and decision. In their houses members are not permitted to discuss separate articles or amendments, which are simply voted upon. The discussion becomes in fact a useful debate on the work and problems of each major department of government.

Control

The Constitution lays down five methods of parliamentary control of government. They are questions, general discussion, censure,

'İkinci Meclisin Kanunlar Görüşme Süresi ve Benzer Sürelerle Karşılaştırma', *Ank. Univ. S.B.F. Dergisi* XVII, no. 2 (1962), pp. 393–481.

assembly enquiry and assembly investigation. Of these methods of control, censure belongs only to the National Assembly, whilst assembly investigation is undertaken when the two houses meet as the Grand National Assembly. The other methods of control may be used by either house.

The Constitution does no more than state that questions in parliament constitute one of the means of parliamentary control of government. The elaboration of this control is contained in the Standing Orders of each house. The object of the questions is said to be to obtain information. They are submitted in writing with the request for oral or written answer. The written answer has to be given within fifteen days. Questions and answers are printed with the record of proceedings. The procedure for oral reply to questions is a little more elaborate. Space for the reply has to be found in the agenda of the third sitting after the submission of the question by the president's council to the minister. On that day the minister is supposed to read out the reply. Often the minister is absent and postponements occur. Sometimes the member putting the question objects, but postponement is in fact permitted by Standing Orders—and unfortunately no limit is placed on the number of times postponements can occur. It also seems to happen quite often that the member who asked the question is not there to receive the reply.[1] After the minister has delivered his reply the member asking the question may state his

---

[1] This is only an impression gained from reading the record of proceedings of the two houses. It is not based on a count over a period of time. Questions are another aspect of the Turkish parliament that merit attention. A random survey I have made of some 100 questions which are recorded in the proceedings of the National Assembly at the end of 1962 (*Millet Meclisi Tutanak Dergisi*, Cilt 9, 1 November 1962 to 10 December 1962) shows that almost a third of the questions are about administrative problems—for example, a very revealing question asked how many chemists there actually were in state hospitals. The questions on administration relate to both inefficiency and alleged corruption (e.g. How much was paid to a certain official for travelling expenses?). Questions relating to specific economic interests come next (about one-fifth). For example, why was there no Turkish representative at an international conference on butter production, or again, why have regulations been changed in favour of producers of poppies for opium manufacture? Many questions are about local needs—a road here, a sewer there—and a number are political in character. For example, what is being done about Communist and other leftist publications? Others relate to individual rights. Why was so-and-so beaten up by the Gendarmerie?

views and the minister may speak again too. Very little time is allowed for this, however, and there is no chance of a general debate developing; a tendency towards this was stopped by the government in 1957. It is not the practice to ask supplementary questions. The parliamentary question is not so powerful a device as it might be.

At the time the present Constitution was drafted it was generally held that the means of parliamentary control needed strengthening. Interpellation (the principal device of the 1924 Constitution) was an unsatisfactory form of control because it was too severe a measure to be employed by those who, while generally supporting a government, wished nevertheless to have some light shed on some aspect of governmental policy or activity. The device of general discussion has therefore been introduced. Although it is called 'general', it is intended as a means of obtaining with a minister or ministers, or with the government as a whole, a discussion on some specified subject. Once a motion for a general discussion is carried by the Assembly (Senate or National Assembly) the government or the minister or ministers concerned specify the day. There is provision for the automatic inclusion of the general discussion in the agenda should a day not be specified. General discussion is a new and milder form of interpellation— an invitation to the government or its members to come to the Assembly to explain policy. Characteristically there is provision for a general discussion when a new government presents its programme.

Another innovation—assembly enquiry—which permits each house to set up a temporary research commission with the object of obtaining information on any specified subject, is also followed by a general discussion. These enquiries or research commissions could be very effective as they are empowered to obtain information from anyone, including ministers. The final means of control open to both Assemblies, though on this occasion conjointly as the Grand National Assembly, is that of investigation into alleged illegal doings of members of the government.

The device of censure may be used only by the National Assembly. It is a development of the former device of interpellation, which in its milder form has become, as we have seen, general discussion. Censure is handled with considerable caution. A motion for censure is only discussed at the sitting following the one in which it is moved. It is then decided whether it shall be placed on the agenda. Only the spokesman of each party group and of the government may speak (together with the mover, or spokesman for the movers). If the motion is accepted for the agenda, the date must also be fixed; it is laid down that at least two, and not more than seven, days must elapse before discussion takes place. When on the discussion of the motion itself a vote of no confidence or confidence is moved, it may not be voted upon for twenty-four hours. Censure has been used very little in Turkish parliamentary history.

Members

We now turn to ask who are the members of parliament who through that institution support and criticize government and from whose ranks the government is so largely recruited. Thanks to Professor Frey[1] we now possess detailed information on the background of Turkish members of parliament over the period 1920 to 1957 and this we can compare with information about the parliaments of 1961 and 1965.

From Frey's work the following conclusions are of particular interest for this study. First, one constant factor in the members' background ever since 1920 has been their high level of education. Between 70 per cent and 80 per cent of all deputies have enjoyed higher education at university level. Secondly, and in contrast with this consistency in educational attainment, the occupational composition of the deputies has shown considerable change. The largest single occupational group has come to be that of the legal profession—and in this it has come to resemble western parliaments. The professional element has also increased, though not as much as that of the lawyers. (The professional group includes doctors, dentists, chemists, engineers and the like.) By contrast, the once dominant official group has declined very considerably, a group composed of deputies with civil service and military backgrounds. The economic group of deputies in trades of various sorts and agriculture has also increased. The occupational backgrounds of deputies in the fifth Assembly (1935–9)— the high-water mark of Kemalism—and in the tenth Assembly (1954–7) are given below, abstracted from Table 7.5 of Professor Frey's work.

[1] F. W. Frey, *The Turkish Political Elite.*

TABLE 8

Occupations of Deputies, by Assembly,
1935–9, 1954–7

Occupation	Fifth Assembly 1935–9	Tenth Assembly 1954–7
	%	%
Law	12	27
Medicine	9	11
Dentistry, Pharmacy and Vet. Medicine	2	2
Engineering	1	4
Government	19	9
Military	18	4
Education	11	8
Trade	10	17
Agriculture	8	10
Banking	1	2
Religion	3	1
Journalism	5	4
Other	—	1

Another point of considerable interest from Professor Frey's study is the trend since Kemalist days towards localism. That is to say, Turkish deputies have come more and more to be natives of (i.e. born in) the constituency for which they were returned. In the eleventh Assembly localism had reached 66 per cent as compared with 34 per cent between 1935 and 1939. The importance of the old national elite of Atatürk times in parliament has declined. New social elements have entered, notably since the introduction of multi-party politics. Professor Frey concludes from this study that '. . . the deputies have changed from being primarily a national elite group, oriented toward the tutelary development of the country, to being primarily an assemblage of local politicians oriented to more immediate local and political advantages'.[1]

The question is whether this trend has continued in the parliaments of 1961 and 1965. An examination of the two important

[1] Frey, op. cit., p. 196. The key conflict of Turkish politics, according to Frey, is 'the conflict between the residual "national elite", basically found within or in support of the People's Party (perhaps until recently) and the new breed of local politicians basically found in the Democrat Party and its successor' (p. 197).

characteristics of the occupational background and the degree of localism of members of the parliaments elected in 1961 and 1965 reveals the following situation.

TABLE 9

Occupations of Members of Grand National Assembly 1961 and 1965
(in percentages)

| | 1961 | | 1965 |
Occupation	National Assembly	Senate	National Assembly
Law	32·5	29·5	32·0
Medicine	9·0	11·5	7·5
Dentistry, Pharmacy and Vet. Medicine	2·0	5·0	1·5
Engineering	1·5	1·0	3·0
Government	8·5	15·0	10·0
Military	6·0	22·5	8·0
Education	5·0	7·0	8·5
Trade	17·0	4·5	12·0
Agriculture	9·5	·5	7·0
Banking	1·0	1·0	1·0
Religion	—	—	—
Journalism	6·5	1·5	5·5
Other	1·5	1·0	3·5

Source: Albums of the Grand National Assembly (1962 and 1966).

TABLE 10

Degree of Localism of Members of Parliament
(in percentages)[a]

1961 National Assembly	Senate	1965 National Assembly
63	48	57

Source: Albums of the Grand National Assembly (1962 and 1966).

[a] Percentages of total for whom birthplaces were identifiable. A small number proved unidentifiable. (1961 National Assembly, 2; 1961 Senate, 1; 1965 National Assembly, 4).

From these tables we may observe for the National Assembly that the trend in the direction of selecting lawyers continued in 1961 but has now levelled off a little. There was not generally much change between 1957 and 1961 in the representation of groups and it is interesting that the military did not increase its numerical influence at all significantly in the 1961 National Assembly. On the other hand, the 1965 Assembly shows a slight increase in members with a governmental and military background; and there is a small decline in the proportion of members from trade and agriculture. There is not much suggestion here of new elements forcing themselves into the political arena. The information on localism too suggests a levelling out, if not the beginning of a reversal, of the trend noted by Frey.[1] With this later evidence it is not quite so clear that the official and military political elite is continuing to be replaced by an elite more legal and commercial in origin.

When we compare the Senate with the National Assembly we can observe a greater 'government' and 'military' element, but this is partly accounted for by the inclusion of the life members who were formerly members of the N.U.C. and who are included under 'military'.

Another important feature of any parliament is the previous parliamentary experience of its members. A large influx of new members may well be a sign of the responsiveness of parliament to change. To the National Assembly of 1954 and 1957 48 per cent and 54 per cent, respectively, of members of the immediately previous assemblies were re-elected, whereas in the time of single party rule about 74 per cent were re-elected.[2] The situation in regard to the parliaments elected in 1961 and 1965 shows a few expected differences. In the 1961 National Assembly only 26 per cent of the deputies had any previous parliamentary experience, the People's Party being the highest with 43 per cent, the Justice Party the lowest with 8 per cent. (Former Democrat Party deputies were of course banned.) In the 1965 general election the overall re-election rate was 46 per cent, not very different from the figures in 1954 and 1957 given above.[3] The highest re-election rate was that of the Justice Party (73 per cent) followed by the National Party (57 per cent). The People's Party came next with 43 per cent. When we look at previous parliamentary experience

[1] So far as possible—and with guidance in this respect from Professor Frey—the analysis of occupations has been made in accordance with the principles adopted by him.

[2] Frey, Table 7.1, p. 164.

[3] Re-election rates are based on figures that exclude an *estimated* number of deaths, calculated on a 6·5 per cent death rate on the basis of the death rate in Assemblies 1 to 7 studied by Frey.

we find that the Justice Party is rather low (48 per cent) compared with the People's Party (62 per cent). Overall about half the 1965 deputies had served in parliaments previously.

The accession of new blood is not, however, restricted to the Justice Party. In this respect the People's Party is anything but static. Considering its losses in the election it is surprising that so many new men obtained seats.

To sum up the nature of Turkish parliament in the virtual absence of any really thorough analysis of the functions of the institution is not really possible; and the broad question of relation of parliament to government will be discussed in the next chapter. At this point only some of the general criticisms that have been made of parliament since 1961 will be mentioned.

One of the criticisms of the 1961–5 parliament is of the ill-becoming behaviour of its members. Their stridency—their coarseness of speech even—their 'greed' (for higher salaries), the unseemly wrangles and even fights in parliament, all these have, so the press says, earned parliament a general contempt, and members' quick resentment of criticism has also been noted. All this is usually ascribed to a generally low level of culture among Turkish M.P.'s (which the facts do not support) and to their concern with local and sectional interests—to their inability, in other words, to represent the nation as a whole with a fitting dignity and decorum.

The press also points to the failure of this first parliament of the present Republic to give firm expression to the constitutional description of Turkey as a social welfare state. There have been no real reforms, for instance, it is alleged with some justice in land tenure, taxation, or the ownership of oil installations.

Explanations of the 'failure' of parliament vary. One very convincing line is that parliament is unrepresentative of the population as a whole. This can be all too easily demonstrated. The representation in this sense of the peasant, the worker or the minor tradesman is practically negligible. It is contended that however much members may be supposed to represent the nation in an underdeveloped country, personal or sectional demands are too urgent to permit of much thought for others. Unless the workers are represented in parliament in goodly numbers by themselves they will not get a fair deal. This approach is usually allied with the view that in Turkey political parties do not provide for the uneducated electorate any really meaningful choice either of programmes or persons. To these critics political institutions must recruit their members from society in a properly balanced way. If this were to occur the educational standard of members might not, however, be increased.

Another popular but rather more sophisticated criticism admits that whilst the present government and parliament may be from and by the people, it is not *for* them. It does not satisfy their *real* interests. It does not always seem to be realized that this is dangerous doctrine because it involves someone (or some elite) saying what is good for the people, as the Atatürk elite did. The probability is that left alone the Turkish peasant immediately wants mosques, consumer goods and entertainment—and a parliament that mirrored Turkish society would not be different. Only after some education does the peasant see the need for public health measures, investment for the future and so on. To many of the intelligentsia the 1961–5 parliament seemed to provide a new opportunity for a resurgence of state tutelage for the eventual good of the people. The People's Party was expected to provide the impetus and has been much criticized for not providing the type of leadership required. Certainly in parliament there seems to have been little evidence of any urge to go crusading among the populace on behalf of the new welfare state.

There is something to be said, however, for politics as the art of the possible. The People's Party did not possess an absolute majority in parliament; they had to compromise if *parliamentary* government was to be made to work. Turkey was dangerously divided in 1961. The 1961–5 parliament brought all the conflicts out into the open. By 1965 they had declined and undoubtedly parliament played an important part in the resolution of the conflicts left by the revolution. By bringing them out into the open, by demanding immediate solutions parliament played an important part in healing the deep divisions that might otherwise have embittered Turkish politics for many years. A deeply divided and agitated parliament has been an aid to political stability.

In the upshot there was not much of a move in any definite political direction until 1965 showed very definitely whom the electors supported, but there is some point in postponing new political debates until old political battles have died down. Otherwise the new is contaminated by the old.

P

CHAPTER XIII

The Council of Ministers and the President

The Council of Ministers

The Council of Ministers, or Cabinet, is composed of the Prime Minister and all the ministers. Most of the ministers are departmental, but there is also a small number of Ministers of State and one or more Assistant Prime Ministers. The number of ministries varies from time to time but not drastically; and coalition government since 1961 has not resulted in a splitting of existing ministries in order to satisfy coalition partners. The numbers of Ministers of State and Assistant Prime Ministers have varied somewhat with the requirements of coalition governments, but the overall size of the Cabinet has hardly altered.[1]

The burden on ministers is everywhere heavy. In Turkey it seems unnecessarily the more so because there are no political assistants (e.g. parliamentary under-secretaries) to give relief to the minister. Since 1961 it seems that the ministerial burden has increased—chiefly due to the creation of the Senate (not forgetting its commissions, which the minister must often attend) and partly to the complexities that planning has introduced. There must also have been an increase in the sheer volume of work.

Why then does Turkey not appoint political assistants to ministers?[2] In fact, such political under-secretaries were appointed in 1937, but the innovation lasted only nine months and it has become one of the myths almost of Turkish politics that in Turkey the system of political under-secretaries just does not work. It seems that the expected quarrels between ministers and their new under-secretaries soon broke out. A deplorable situation in the

---

[1] All but two (of the five) cabinets from 1961 up to and including that of October 1965 have had twenty-three members. The June 1962 and December 1963 cabinets each had twenty-two members. There have usually been three Ministers of State and one Assistant Prime Minister. The June 1962 coalition had two Assistant Prime Ministers; on the formation of his government in October 1965, Mr Demirel did not appoint any.

[2] A very useful article on the subject is by Adnan Guriz, 'Bakan Yardımcılıkları Kurulmalı Mı?', *Forum*, 15 July 1963.

Ministry of the Interior more or less paralysed the work of the Ministry and led to the abandonment of the experiment. The chief difficulty seems to have been that the under-secretaries were allowed to be too independent of their ministers and were not easily dismissible. To say this does not explain much, but suggests that a more restrictive set of rules was necessary. More careful regulation of their position would, perhaps, have helped, but the reasons for the failure of the innovation are probably to be looked for elsewhere. There does not still appear to be much of a natural hierarchy in Turkish political parties—there was probably hardly any in 1937 when Atatürk was alive. There was just the leader or at most a very small group—and then the rest, none of whom with any particular pull.

The question of political under-secretaries was mooted again in 1963 and it was firmly expected that the government would do something. It was, however, all quietly dropped. One great drawback to the present system is that there is no way of training future ministers; and that many need the training seems to be generally agreed.

The appointment of the Council of Ministers begins with the selection of the Prime Minister by the President. The remaining ministers are then chosen by the Prime Minister and confirmed by the President. Ministers need not now be members of parliament, but the Prime Minister must. Appointment of persons outside parliament has been restricted to an average of about two in each cabinet. The Justice Party government of October 1965 has only made one such appointment. The appointments have been of persons of particular technical proficiency. The ministries to which appointments have been made include Foreign Affairs, Finance, Public Works and Energy and Natural Resources. One unexpected use of the new provisions was that it enabled Mr Demirel, not then a member of parliament, to become Assistant Prime Minister in the Ürgüplü Cabinet in February 1965.

The Council of Ministers is collectively responsible for carrying out the government's general policy, whilst each minister is also individually responsible for matters under his own authority. In practice, there is the usual problem of deciding what is government and what is ministerial policy. Governments have sometimes extended their protection to individual ministers in trouble (as the Ürgüplü government supported the Minister of Energy and

National Resources in 1965); sometimes a minister is abandoned and is forced to resign. There is nothing very unusual in this situation. What has been a novel (and exhausting) experience for the coalition governments of 1961–5 has been to maintain unity both inside and outside parliament. There was, of course, first the tremendous problem of unity between the People's Party and Justice Party wing of the first coalition. The coalition broke up because of pressures from the wings. The remaining coalitions experienced trouble with the minor parties. The second coalition was rent by strife between the People's Party and the New Turkey Party—a circumstance that led to odd devices like setting up a committee of coalition partners to iron out differences. The coalition minor parties also could not always be relied upon to vote with the government in parliament. As we have seen, the minor parties were also for the most part in the government for what political capital they could make out of it. In the fourth (Ürgüplü) coalition the Nation Party under Bölükbaşı acted more like an opposition party, running some 'fine hares', like the attack on the state radio authorities as pre-election stunts.

In this period of coalition governments, too, the two major parties had to manage a great deal of internal criticism. The discipline of neither party really broke down but the strains were considerable. It is, of course, of the essence of responsibility that government should be subject to real pressures and have to frame policies accordingly. But if the pressures are too diverse and capricious, it becomes a madhouse. Turkish government did not quite become like this during 1961 to 1965, but at a time it looked rather close to it. The government was too responsive—and yet, paradoxically had to be, or there might have been no government save a military one.

In these sorts of conditions of unstable coalitions, it becomes almost meaningless to ask the classic questions like 'Are all ministers equal?' and 'What is the position of the Prime Minister *vis-à-vis* his colleagues?' In theory, the Prime Minister is now rather more powerful than under the 1924 Constitution. 'He . . . ensures co-ordination among the Ministries and oversees the implementation of government policy . . .' (Article 105 of the Constitution). The Constitution gets the situation exactly right, but a prime minister is more powerful if he does not, in fact, have to act as co-ordinator. The probability is that, given even non-coalition government, the Turkish Prime Minister is going to be less powerful than he was. The old domination over the party expressed by Atatürk, İnönü, Bayar, or even Menderes, seems to be on the wane. In the Justice Party there is apprehension now of the dangers of unbridled leadership of the Menderes' sort. In the People's Party, the mystique of the old liberators of the nation diminishes and their authoritarianism is resented by the liberal and left-wing elements. Under the conditions of modern society, a rebirth of the power of the Prime Minister may occur in line with developments in democracies in developed societies, but before this can happen, there will probably have to be in Turkey a quite massive development of the mass media of communication. There is as yet, for instance, no television at all.

As to relations among ministers, they are legally equal, but a certain primacy is accorded to the Minister of Finance in practice, though it seems that this influence was reduced during the 1961–5 period by that of the State Planning Organization. There does not appear to be any small group of ministers with more than normal influence derived from the importance or prestige of their departments. Assistant Prime Ministers perform largely co-ordinating functions and not a lot of the authority of the Prime Minister rubs off onto them. Ministers of State are concerned not with co-ordinating functions as among ministries, but very largely with the supervision of the work of offices attached to the Prime Minister's Office. This is one of the problems of the organization of the work of the Council of Ministers which is discussed below (Chapter XIV) in the context of administrative functions and organization.

The President

In 1923, when the Republic was proclaimed, a Presidency was established; and by this step, Turkey began to turn from the convention system then in operation towards a parliamentary form of government.[1]

From the beginning, the problem of how to fit the executive arm of government into the convention pattern was not easy. It was simply said at first that there should be a Council of Ministers elected by the National Assembly but without any head, any disagreements between ministers being solved by the Assembly.

[1] See Chapter III for a discussion of these changes in their historical context.

Difficulties of election led to the ominous requirement that candidates for election as ministers were to be nominated by the President of the Assembly (Mustafa Kemal).[1]

The Law of Fundamental Organization (1921)[2] still maintained that the Grand National Assembly represented both the executive and legislative power and that the government was the 'Government of the Grand National Assembly' (Article 3), but another step away from direct assembly control was discernible. The Council of Ministers now elected one of their number as chairman, but the President of the Assembly was authorized to confirm the decisions of the Council of Ministers and was said to be also the Council's natural chairman.

This rather awkward arrangement was carried over into the next stage of constitutional development beginning in 1923, which very seriously modified the convention system.[3] There was now to be a President of the Republic who, as Head of the State, could in this capacity chair both the Assembly and the Council of Ministers. He also chose the Prime Minister (who chose the other ministers) and then presented the Council of Ministers to the Assembly.

The 1924 Constitution broadly reaffirmed this position, except that the President was not now to preside over the National Assembly save on ceremonial occasions. It was also stated that he was not to participate in Assembly discussion, nor was he to vote. He was given a delaying power over legislation, but this was about the summit of his powers. He was still elected by and from the Assembly for a period to coincide with the Assembly's term. He had no power to dissolve the Assembly and all his decisions had to be countersigned by the Prime Minister and the minister concerned. Although the situation was very different from that obtaining before 1923, the Presidency was not in theory an office endowed with very significant attributes of independent power; whether there was constitutionally speaking a separation of powers is a moot point.[4]

[1] *Icra Vekilleri Kanununun Ikinci Maddesini Muaddil Kanun*, Law no. 47, 4 November 1920.

[2] *Teşkilâtı Esasiye Kanunu*, Law no. 85, 20 January 1921.

[3] *Teşkilâtı Esasiye Kanununun Bazı Mevaddının Tavzihan Tadiline Dair Kanun*, Law no. 364, 29 October 1923.

[4] There are interesting discussions of the constitutional position which do not ignore practical politics, in *Ank. Üniv. S.B.F. Derg*, XVIII, nos. 3–4

Nevertheless, despite the constitutional position, Kemal Atatürk, the first President, was in fact a very powerful figure. This was not only because he drew strength from the office of President as head of state, but also because he dominated the single authoritarian People's Party, which in turn dominated the Assembly. Politically speaking, there was no separation of powers.

During the period 1924–60, the *institution* of the Presidency was not strengthened; consequently, it is not surprising to find that the real power of the Presidency declined after the death of Atatürk. After the change to a multi-party system in 1946, the position of President came to be seriously questioned. Elected by the Assembly for the term of an Assembly, he could hardly but reflect the political colouring of its majority; and more particularly so as he had to be a member of the Assembly, which meant being supported in elections by a political party.

The 1961 Constitution seeks to change the situation by creating a politically impartial Presidency. Under the new provisions, the President is elected for seven years, so that he overlaps the period of office of the National Assembly.[1] Although elected from among members of the Grand National Assembly, in which, of course, he might well have been an appointed member, the President must resign after his election both from his party and from membership of parliament.

The President may still preside over the Council of Ministers if he wishes; but he is not responsible except for treachery and personal crimes—the same position basically as under the 1924 Constitution. Nor are his powers over legislation altered. He may return laws to the Grand National Assembly once; if they are insisted upon, he has to promulgate them—and, as before, he may not return laws on constitutional and financial matters. Where he does gain influence in comparison with the previous situation is that, in the event of a third prospective change of government within eighteen months, he may authorize new elections, but only on the request of the Prime Minister. He is also

(1963) pp. 319–40; XIX, no. 2 (1964) pp. 175–92; XX, no. 3 (1965) pp. 141–52, by Professors Bahri Savcı and Turan Güneş, in which opposing views are argued.

[1] It will be recalled that one-third of the Senate elected membership is subject to re-election every two years.

chairman of the National Security Council, chooses fifteen members of the Senate, has two appointments to the Constitutional Court, and is one of the authorities which may open suits of annulment there. He also appoints all members to the Military Court. He also appoints the Chief of the General Staff, but on the recommendation of the Prime Minister, to whom the Chief of the General Staff is responsible.

Altogether, the aim is to make the President impartial but not to invest him with substantial independent powers.

The first President to be elected under the new scheme was the late General Gürsel, the leader of the 1960 revolution and chairman of the National Unity Committee.[1]

The question then arises—'What has the President made of his position?'—a question that may be treated under a number of headings.

First, there is an example of the use of the delaying veto over legislation that also existed in the 1924 Constitution but of which no use was made. In 1963 the President vetoed a law that (i) allowed deputies (of the 1958 parliament) to pay back debts contracted with the Agricultural Bank over an extended period without payment of interest and (ii) permitted deputies of the 1957 parliament not to refund to the state payments of salaries and expenses made in advance and relating to the period after May 1960, when, of course, the 1957 parliament came to an end. There were strong legal and moral arguments against the law and particularly against treating deputies differently from other citizens, who were not excused payment of interest on loans. The deputies in question, it might be added, were of a parliament not held in high regard by those who carried out the 1960 revolution. By many it was considered important to demonstrate that the revolution *rightly* put an end to the 1957 parliament in 1960. To admit deputies' rights to their salaries after the termination of the 1957 parliament could be interpreted as meaning that it was illegal to bring the 1957 parliament to an end. The President took a hard decision in an important matter. The delaying veto was not without effect; the legislation was amended in the ways desired by the President.[2]

[1] When Gürsel became seriously ill, the Chief of the General Staff, Cevdet Sunay, was elected in his place in 1966.

[2] A second use of the presidential veto occurred in 1964 when the Presi-

Secondly, there is the role of the President in the choice of a Prime Minister. In theory, the matter is simple. The President appoints the Prime Minister and the government is submitted to the National Assembly for approval. It seems, therefore, inescapable that the President should ask the leader of the party with the largest following in the lower house to form a government. If the party cannot form a government, then logically the next largest party must be invited to form a government and so on, as far as practically possible. However, in conditions where coalition is necessary, the situation becomes more complex and it is very difficult for a President not to become very deeply involved. There is little point in asking the leader of a party to form a government unless there is a reasonable chance of one being formed. General Gürsel acted in fact very much like a broker. The fall of every government was a sign for numerous discussions not only among party leaders, but between the President and the party leaders. In helping to solve difficulties between likely partners in a coalition, the President played a positive—and very responsible—role. Without the President's paternal help, it would probably have been much more difficult to get coalitions into being. As it was, it was difficult enough, but the process was assisted by Gürsel's awareness of urgent national problems and the need of a government to solve them.

This active concern with the national situation was of great value but, of course, it had its disadvantages. The view could be and often was taken that the President should leave all discussions to be held between the parties without his participation. He should simply have asked the leader of each party by size and in turn to form a government. For instance, during the attempts to form a government in June 1962 the President stated that when İnönü informed him that he was unable to form a government he then consulted the leaders of the other parties, and it became clear that it was necessary, in view of the country's situation, to continue discussions and reach some conclusion. He then urged İnönü to continue in his attempts to form a coalition, which

---

dent objected to provisions in the Land Titles Law that opened the way to the spoliation of the state lands and would, therefore, reduce the amount of state land for distribution to landless peasants.

were then successful.[1] Why, it might be asked, did Gürsel persuade İnönü to change his mind instead of merely turning straightway and openly to the Justice Party? This might have led to a crisis and new elections but, democratically speaking, that was what the situation indicated.

Again, in the formation of the fourth Ürgüplü coalition, the President played a very positive role. He had clearly come to the conclusion that an independent Prime Minister was necessary. With the fall of the İnönü government a reasonable course seemed to be to request the Justice Party leader (now Süleyman Demirel) to form a government. This was not done. Instead, an independent senator (Ürgüplü) was asked to form a government, a government in which Demirel agreed to be Deputy Prime Minister. There were good reasons why this should be done. The elections were close, so that a holding government was all that was necessary; Demirel was inexperienced and he was not a member of parliament, though he could have been made senator as part of the quota of senators appointed by the President.

There is also another aspect to this appointment of Ürgüplü as Prime Minister. Although it would have been reasonable to ask the Justice Party to form a government, it would still have been more correct to request İnönü, whose party was still the majority party. It was rumoured that at this time there was a basic disagreement between the İnönü government and the Presidency on foreign policy and other matters.[2] However this may be, it is clear that the President exerted a great deal of influence in the formation of governments. Given a large majority for any one party in the National Assembly, as in October 1965, this influence is, of course, difficult to sustain.

The President's general comments on the political situation during the period also merit some discussion. Gürsel did not refrain from expressing his views in public. For instance, before the break up of the first coalition in 1962, he criticized the insistence on an amnesty and pointed to the need for attention to other more serious matters. For comments of this sort he was attacked and was accused of preparing the way for a dictatorial

---

[1] This is an abridged translation of the President's communiqué of 21 June 1962: from the text given in *Cumhuriyet*, 22 June 1962.

[2] See *Yön*, 19 February 1965.

regime.[1] This was exaggerated criticism, but obviously if Gürsel expressed dissatisfaction with the run of politics, it was an encouragement to dissatisfied military elements to intervene again. Moreover, the President had also said, on 21 May 1963, that, should the present government fall, another would be found. This sounded ominous.

The President's pronouncements did not, in fact, amount to any special view of politics, nor did he normally advocate solutions of any particular political problem. Gürsel adopted a paternalistic attitude, regarding himself as the upholder of the 1961 Constitution and the system of democratic politics. He was in favour of democracy and moderation in all things and said so pretty firmly. He was very much a father figure. He has been described too as a political Chief Mufti. In the 1962 governmental crisis he was accused by Bölükbaşı in his attack on the President in the National Assembly as giving a political *fetva*[2] to those who wanted to destroy the existing regime.

Whether he could give a political *fetva* depended in the last analysis probably on whether he was thought to be a power still with the military. He was certainly frequently in contact with military leaders; and he did not refrain from saying in a very authoritative way what the attitude of the military was. For instance, in July 1962, he announced in a press interview that the military were intent to keep to their own sphere, and realized that interference in politics meant a loss of public respect.[3] It seems that latterly Gürsel's spokesmanship for the military was replaced by that of Cevdet Sunay, the Chief of the General Staff. With Sunay's election to the Presidency, the military influence was renewed—perhaps only temporarily—at the presidential level. It may be rather useful to have the military voice heard in the political system and by means of an otherwise not very powerful President. An indication of how powerful a President might not be under conditions of firm majority government was shown in October 1965. The new Justice Party government decided to transfer to other posts some half-dozen senior officials in the state economic enterprises and similar economic institutions. The President declared he would examine the decrees (which he has

---

[1] Notably by Osman Bölükbaşı in the National Assembly, 21 May 1962.
[2] A political ruling given by the Chief Mufti in Ottoman times.
[3] *Cumhuriyet*, 21 July 1962.

to sign) very carefully, and that he would look for a way that would not allow injustice. 'Injustices will not pass through my hands,' he declared.[1] A week later he signed all the decrees, despite, it seems, pressures from various groups, including student organizations. This incident illustrates in a pointed way the general character of the Presidency in times of firm political control. There may be a large bark, but not much of a bite.

[1] *Cumhuriyet*, 18 October 1965.

PART IV

Administration

CHAPTER XIV

Organization and Central Functions

The organizational framework

It is not difficult to comprehend the overall pattern of Turkish administration thanks to its being based on a clear French model. Some 60 per cent of Turkish public servants are employed in the central administration which chiefly comprises what are known as 'general budget', 'annexed budget' and 'revolving capital organizations'.[1] The general budget organizations are largely ministries and are subject to direct financial and administrative control. 'Annexed budget' organizations are attached to ministries, but have a degree of financial and administrative autonomy. Examples of these are four of the universities and the General Directorate of Forestry. 'Revolving capital' organizations mostly engage in industrial, commercial or educational and cultural activities, and enjoy a degree more financial autonomy. Examples of this type of organization are trade schools, agricultural institutes and prisons. They approach in type, but not in scale of function, the state economic enterprises, which, with local government and certain other special institutions, account for the remaining two-fifths of public servants. In connection with local government, it should be borne in mind that the central administration includes employees of the ministries or other organizations of the central administration who work in the provinces. The most important of these central officials in the provinces are the governors of the sixty-seven provinces (*valis*) and the sub-provincial governors (*kaymakams*) who are on the staff of the Ministry of the Interior. Officials of other ministries work closely with and for the governors and sub-governors in the provinces. In addition, some ministries have developed regional organizations overlapping provincial boundaries.

Under the Turkish Constitution the executive function is said to be performed by the President and the Council of Ministers,

[1] There is also a number of small organizations administering special funds.

but the Council is the real executive organ. It is composed of all the ministers with departmental duties together with Assistant Prime Ministers[1] and Ministers of State, whose numbers vary, as they must in conditions of coalition government.

What we shall loosely term for present purposes the Prime Minister's Office consists on the one part of what in a literal translation would be the 'Prime Ministry', namely the Prime Minister, the Ministers of State, the Permanent Secretary and a small number of other officials. The other part would be what is strictly meant in Turkey by the 'Prime Minister's Office', namely a small number of departments known as 'directorates', which are directly under the Prime Minister and among which is included the directorate responsible for assisting the Council of Ministers in its work on laws and decrees. Attached to the 'Prime Ministry' are nine offices, among which are included the State Planning Organization, the Institute for Public Administration for Turkey and the Middle East and the State Personnel Office.

Turkish ministries are normally organized into 'general directorates' and subordinate 'directorates'; below these are usually 'branches', 'offices', and, very occasionally, 'tables'. However, there is a wide variety of usage, 'office', in particular, being used for organizations at many different levels. Every ministry has an organization to perform: personnel, supply, filing and essential common functions. Nearly every ministry has a legal section and an inspectorate. About two-thirds are shown as having organizations for study and research, and about one-third have advisory bodies attached to them.

Below the minister and his Private Office is the *müsteşar*, who is a career civil servant and whose title is usually translated into English as permanent secretary. He is not in fact quite as powerful as a British permanent secretary, but the general directors in a ministry are formally responsible to him.

As to relations between the ministries, they appear to be on as equal a footing as the shifting course of politics allows. In particular, it should be said that the Ministry of Finance has never exercised the degree of control over the other ministries that is associated with the Treasury in Britain; and, more recently, its

[1] The position of a Turkish Minister of State is broadly equivalent to that of a British Secretary of State—without departmental responsibilities. The position is not similar to that of a British Minister of State.

influence has been decreased by the participation of the State Planning Organization in budget preparation and the State Personnel Office in personnel matters.

Apart from the Ministry of Foreign Affairs, all the ministries and a number of other central government organs possess provincial organizations, though not all are represented in every province. There are sixty-seven provinces, each province (*il*) being divided into subordinate units, namely the *ilçe*, *bucak*, and *köy* (village). The system by which central authority is reconciled with local democracy owes much to French example. Elected councils are related in various ways to the centrally appointed officials of the Ministry of the Interior, of whom the governor of the *il* (the *vali*) and of the *ilçe* (the *kaymakam*) are the most important. Over half of the *valis* and 80 per cent of the *kaymakams* are graduates of the Faculty of Political Science of Ankara University, almost all the remainder being graduates in law. The officials of all the ministries which are represented in the provinces are responsible to the *vali*, or *kaymakam*, in the first instance, again after the French pattern. Recently, however, some ministries and other central bodies have begun to make use of a legal loophole to establish regional organizations cutting across provincial boundaries and free from the control of the *vali*.

Finally, it should be mentioned that Turkey possesses a Council of State, which is empowered to submit a wide range of administrative acts to judicial review. In addition, the Council of State advises the Council of Ministers on all ordinances made under authority of delegated legislation, but may only advise on such draft laws as are sent to it by the Council of Ministers.

So much for the framework of Turkish public administration; we shall now turn to an analysis of its problems in preference to detailed description of structure and functions.

The organization reviewed

An important event occurred in the history of Turkish administration in 1962 when the Turkish government set up a commission to enquire into the distribution of functions in the central administration. The Commission took a broad interpretation of functions to include, in addition to departmental responsibilities, central and common functions such as planning, statistics, personnel, inspection, research and co-ordination and even the

Q

administrative functions of the Council of Ministers.[1] On the basis of this report it is possible to highlight some of the major problems in Turkish administration. The comments that follow on various aspects of Turkish administrative organization derive largely from the report.

Structure. Within the central administration the 'annexed budget' organizations constitute the largest exception to the principle of direct financial and administrative control. The principal justification for this special status is that the institutions concerned have an independent income arising from their activities. In most cases, however, the amount of this income is quite small, as in the case of State Water Undertakings, and their support by the state is considerable. Sometimes the independent income used to justify annexed budget status is negligible, as when it consists of little more than proceeds from the sale of publications. On the other hand, some organizations, the 'Petrol Office' for instance, are self-supporting. This last organization is indeed engaged on such a large scale enterprise that it ought perhaps to be classed as a state economic enterprise.

The other main justification for annexed budget status is when it is desirable for institutions to be less restricted by central governmental control on cultural grounds. The universities are the prime examples of this; there is a clear need for some safeguards for the universities in their administrative relationship with the Ministry of Education.

Another reason for giving greater financial and administrative autonomy is the desire to give new functions freedom from parent ministries. The desire is understandable. It is feared that to give a new function to an old ministry not noted for the dynamism and flexibility of its administration will mean the new function will not be efficiently performed. Consequently annexed budget status has been given to some new organizations, as, for example, to the General Directorate of State Highways, whose activities in creating a modern road network for Turkey are said, on the whole, to have been very successful. On the other hand, to set up *ad hoc* organizations of this sort disrupts the functional coherence

[1] Merkezî Hükûmet Teşkilâtı Araştırma Projesi Yönetim Kurulu Raporu, *Merkezî Hükûmet Teşkilâtı Kuruluş ve Görevleri* (Ank. T.O.D.A.I.E., 1963).

of the administration; and this has happened to an important extent in Turkish administration.

As we have seen above, another means of allowing a greater than normal degree of administrative and financial autonomy has been to establish organizations with 'revolving funds'. In the creation of this type of organization the aim has been to provide funds for state industrial and commercial undertakings whose activities are not on a sufficiently large scale to come within the category of state economic enterprise. The monies provided are to meet wages and salaries, costs for purchase of raw materials and other supplies; but at the end of each financial year unexpended balances have to be returned to the Ministry of Finance for re-allocation if necessary. It is this last provision that makes the funds 'revolving'.

That there are some 500 of these revolving fund organizations in existence caused some concern to the Commission, which found that those that satisfied the requirement of 'industrial and commercial' activity were, in fact, in the minority. Whilst this much is clear, a great deal of thinking about the activities of these organizations is very confused and a thorough study of them is needed, even to classify them legally and financially. The wide variety of legal provision and administrative and financial practice can easily be illustrated, however. In certain prisons, for instance, surpluses in revenues are distributed to employees as bonuses! Some organizations do not have a 'sinking fund', whilst in some cases the meeting of expenditure from general budget funds, instead of from revenue, provides wildly unrealistic profit figures. Again, special legislation for some organizations allows them to convert unexpended budget allocations into capital. In other words, they have in fact ceased to be 'revolving funds' organizations at all. It is no wonder that in considering these types of administrative organization the Commission seemed to throw up their hands in despair and call for more research.

If the 'revolving funds' category of organization seems to be much abused, the 'special funds' organizations seem to be barely legal. However, they exist and enjoy an almost complete financial autonomy. It is quite obvious from their description that the majority of them should be brought under the direct control of the appropriate ministries.

This enquiry into the overall pattern of administrative agencies reveals a tendency in Turkish administration (which occurs too in personnel administration) to meet the problems created by administrative development by concentrating on getting round legal restrictions. With ingenuity it is nearly always possible to do this; but at the expense of creating administrative confusion. Within this confusion it then becomes possible to condone unsatisfactory practices, such as the payment of bonuses and fringe benefits to employees. Turkish administration is in its main functions fairly rigorous and honest. It is nowhere blatantly and shamelessly inefficient and corrupt; for it is probably possible to make out a legal defence for all seeming irregularities; yet, in parts of the administration, particularly in the smaller and more independent organizations, the Ottoman flavour can still persist.

Legal direction of the administration. In Turkey, as elsewhere, much of the work of the administration is laid down in laws and subsidiary legislation; and this constitutes one element in the control of the administration. It has frequently been alleged by various observers of Turkish administration that one of its major defects is that it is too legalistic, by which it is in part meant that Turkish administration suffers from an excess of legal direction. This is a subject on which the Commission makes some interesting observations.

First, the Commission notes that there is hardly any uniformity in the extent to which a ministry's organization and functions are laid down in law. In the case of some ministries and other bodies, very little is prescribed by law, either of organization or functions. Some have their functions laid down in detail, others only their organization and vice versa. Even the duties of the permanent secretary to a ministry, in the few cases when they are given, can differ considerably.

The Commission notes, secondly, the normal effect of including excessive detail in legislation, namely that of amendment when unforeseen circumstances arise. To obtain amendments in the law is difficult and time-consuming. There is therefore at best much delay in administration, and at worst immobility. Moreover, when amendments are made to the law it seems that they are often badly drafted (and thus admit loopholes) and their possible effects on the administration of other parts of the law are not always fully considered. The result is to create considerable confusion.

This confusion, the Commission sees, would be very much reduced if Turkish civil servants could be guided by a greater amount of subsidiary legislation. A very interesting feature of Turkish administration is that the excess of legal provision is matched by a dearth of subordinate rules and regulations; and this lack is all the more serious when it is remembered that, detailed though legal provision may be, it tends to be detailed in respect only of some features of a ministry's work or organization, and that for some areas of activity there is hardly any guidance at all. The effect of this situation is to give an unusually wide range of discretion to Turkish civil servants and thus to open the door to decisions influenced by traditional attitudes towards the conduct of administration.

At first blush it might seem completely wrong to urge the creation of more rules for Turkish public servants when in administration the encouragement of individual initiative is so generally required. Yet the Commission is probably right. The successful exercise of administrative discretion by an official depends, after all, on his making decisions which are consistent with the policy of his ministry and which reflect the spirit underlying that policy. More detailed regulation would in the first instance act as a means of education in these respects for many Turkish officials and would in the long run probably reduce the extent to which matters are referred up for decision.

The Commission does not explain how it has come about that there is excessive, if uneven, legal provision for the functions and organization of administrative bodies and why nothing has hitherto been done about it. To explain the lack of reform it is probably enough to attribute it to the force of accepted practice. The fact that until very recently most of the higher civil servants in Turkey have been trained in the rather narrow fields of constitutional and administrative law may also be some part of the explanation. The answer to the wider question of why in the first instance such an important place should have been given to detailed prescription of administrative organization and duties by the legislature lies in Turkish history. The problem for the early framers of constitutions in Turkey was to control the arbitrary behaviour of the Sultan's administration. This led to the acceptance of the doctrine of the concentration of all legislative and executive power in the elected assembly; and detailed legal prescription of the duties of the executive arm of government followed naturally from this doctrine.

So, too, does the idea that the elected assembly should directly control the personnel employed by the administration without the use of an intermediary organization like, say, the Ministry of Finance. We consequently find in Turkey that laws establishing ministries and other administrative organizations often include not only details of organization and functions, but also the numbers, titles, grades and salaries of the civil servants to be employed. The legal basis of these arrangements has prevented a wide measure of central administrative control by the Ministry of Finance, whilst the rigidity of the personnel provisions has encouraged in the ministries the development of barely legal devices in the employment of personnel that have seriously disrupted the general personnel system. The Commission is very much aware of these problems and envisages a much greater degree of central administrative control over personnel arrangements by the State Personnel Office and the Ministry of Finance.

The Council of Ministers and inter-ministerial co-ordination. Within the broad framework of organization the Commission discusses the functions, but chiefly the modes of functioning, of the Council of Ministers. The Commission finds, first, that the Council of Ministers has to authorize very many matters of minor importance, such as establishing the amounts of the salaries, or even additions to salaries of rather unusual and very tiny classes of civil servants. Secondly, the Council is overloaded by the tendency of ministers to co-ordinate their activities solely through the Council of Ministers. Given excessive centralization in the ministries, this follows naturally. Thirdly, the Council's methods of working are seen to be inadequate for the pressure of business.

In this last connection we find that the preparation and organization of the work of the Council of Ministers falls largely to the Office for the Examination of Laws and Decrees, which forms part of the Prime Minister's Office. The functions of this Office do not extend, however, to preparing papers other than laws, ordinances or decrees, nor to attending the meetings of the Council and taking minutes of meetings of the Council or any committees it might set up. Only ministers may attend the Council or sit on any committees of the Council. Civil servants and others may attend the Council, or one of its committees, only by specific invitation for the meeting in question and then only in order to give information. The notification of decisions taken in the Council to those who have to take action or need to be informed is haphazard. The minister primarily concerned, or the Prime Minister, notifies the Office for the Examination of Laws and Decrees verbally, or in writing, of decisions which have to be prepared in the form of decrees.

To remove these vagaries the Commission recommends the appointment of a cabinet secretariat and—a revealing point—is at some pains to point out that the sorts of qualities required are not those usually associated with the use of the word 'secretary' in Turkish. The Godolphin tradition of 'never in the way and never out of the way' is not native to Turkey.

Finally, the Commission observes that the Ministers of State in the Turkish Council of Ministers are too involved in looking after the affairs of the organizations attached to the Prime Minister's Office to be able to play a real part in co-ordination between the ministries. In so far as this is due to the excessive number of organizations attached to the Prime Minister's Office, the situation will be improved if the recommendation is accepted to transfer four of these nine organizations to certain ministries.

The major problem of the overloading of the Council of Ministers needs to be solved, as the Commission sees, by a greater degree of co-ordination lower down, which would include the development of advisory cabinet committees, properly serviced by a cabinet secretariat. Bearing in mind the problems of ministerial responsibility, the Commission would like to see the reversal of the trend of giving inter-ministerial committees or commissions powers of decision. For the same reason the Commission thinks it is not wise to have both ministers and civil servants as members of such bodies.

On the need for co-ordination between administrative organizations at levels below that of committees of the Council of Ministers, the Commission is very definite and is on the whole optimistic that effective means of co-ordination will be found. This optimism does not stem from the experience of inter-ministerial co-ordinating committees so far. They have suffered from inadequate servicing; and they have often not been accorded sufficient importance by the ministries, with the result that they have not been attended by officials with adequate authority to enable them to state confidently the policies of their ministries. Inter-ministerial co-ordination is a difficult business in Turkey, bedevilled by traditions of ministerial independence. Yet the Commission is hopeful that the newly created central organs like the State Planning Organization and the State Personnel Office will be able to achieve a great deal.

Planning. In the new Constitution (Article 29) it was stated that economic, social and cultural development would be planned. The State Planning Organization was in fact established by the N.U.C. in 1960 before the Constitution was drawn up.

The law establishing the State Planning Organization attaches it to the 'Prime Ministry'. The Organization is divided into the High Control Council and the State Planning Bureau. In addition to the Prime Minister (or a Deputy Prime Minister) the Council is composed of three ministers chosen by the Council of Ministers, the Head of the Planning Bureau and the three Heads of the Departments into which the Bureau is principally divided. These departments are of Economic Planning, Social Planning and Co-ordination.

The functions of the State Planning Organization are advisory, both in respect of the economic and social plans and the administrative machinery in the ministries and other governmental organizations connected with their implementation. This last sphere of activity brings the Planning Organization full square into the field of administrative reform. The ministries may be advised on the subject of the co-ordination of their activities in connection with economic and social policy. The High Planning Council acts largely as a filter. It studies the plans in order, it is laid down, to check that they are politically consistent with governmental objectives and that technically they are satisfactory. In the absence of any technical experts on the Council other than the Planning Organization's officials—who prepare the plan—technical review by the High Planning Council is hardly feasible.

Turkey is now (1969) in the second year of her second five-year plan (1968–1972 inclusive), but politically and administratively the transition to a planned economy has not been completely smooth and uneventful.

As we have seen above, the Planning Organization has run into political difficulties of two sorts.[1] The planners first appointed after the revolution came to resent measures inspired by political considerations that would in their view upset the financing of the plan. Secondly, the exercise of influence over the Planning Organization came to be a matter for dispute between the parties forming coalition governments, the New Turkey Party being concerned in particular to influence the Planning Organization to adopt positive attitudes towards private enterprise. In practice this competition resulted in bargaining for the post of Deputy Prime Minister deputed to the Planning Organization, and led in turn to the Prime Minister himself becoming less concerned with the Planning Organization. Thus, the Planning Organization, it was felt, was pushed further down the hierarchical organization than had been originally intended, and in this way was moved from the centre of the stage. In this connection it is interesting to note that the Minister of Finance does not have a place *ex officio* on the Council.

A fundamental organizational consideration is whether the High Planning Council should continue to be composed half of technicians and half of politicians. Although this mode or organization does help to make the politicians concerned fully aware of the problems of planning, it does create or foster a tendency for the technicians to enter into political decision—and this had happened in Turkey. In this respect the Commission on Functions recommends that the High Planning Council should be transformed into a wholly professional body of non-political representatives of all ministries concerned with the plan. The inclusion of officials from all ministries concerned would overcome another defect in the constitution of the High Planning Council, namely that only three ministries at most are directly represented.

On the administrative side certain trends are seen to have occurred. A rather excessive degree of centralization seems to have come about in the collection of basic data; for example, on economic and other resources the Planning Organization is said to have done too much itself, instead of relying on, and merely consolidating information that can be provided by ministries. The answer is that it is often quicker and produces more reliable

[1] See above, pp. 75–6.

results for the Planning Organization to do such work itself; but it is clearly better in the long run to ensure that ministries are satisfactorily equipped to collect reliable basic data themselves.

So, too, in the preparation of objectives and the plans to achieve them it is often urged that the Planning Organization should concentrate more on getting the ministries to take the initiative. There are in existence in fact co-ordinating committees to bridge the gap between the ministries and the Planning Organization, but how far positive co-ordination has been achieved is difficult to say. The Report of the Commission on Functions is critical, if rather vaguely so, though improvement seems to have taken place since then.[1] Certainly the need for encouraging initiative in planning in the ministries is of first importance, and not least for the implementation of planning. The whole problem is really to fire with enthusiasm for planned development as many officials as possible. This means that the planning Boards set up in ministries (for it is generally more agreeable to carry out one's own ideas than to make the plans and watch over their implementation) should always contain the principal executives in addition to planning experts and should be firmly under the chairmanship of the permanent secretary. Otherwise in the Turkish experience, planning tends to wither away. To prevent withering away at provincial and lower levels provincial co-ordination boards have now been set up under provincial governors who, if exceptionally difficult problems arise, may report directly to the State Planning Organization.[2]

Statistics. Turkish statistical services are chiefly performed by the Statistical Institute which is attached to the Prime Ministry. To have a central statistics office does not imply however that all statistics are collected centrally. A survey by the Planning Organization in 1962 showed that of 105 central administrative organizations in Turkey, seventy-two collected statistics, and that

---

[1] Planning Boards in ministries and other organizations make quarterly reports to the State Planning Organization on implementation of plans. For these reports the State Planning Organization now uses printed forms in order to obtain exactly the information required.

[2] Turkish State Planning Organization, *1964 Annual Programme* (Ankara, 1964), p. 245.

in fifty-eight of these seventy-two organizations there were statistics sections for this work. Half of the organizations which collected statistics published the results.

Should all statistics be compiled centrally? The Turkish Commission wisely concluded not, on the impeccable grounds that all parts of the administration should be encouraged to be as statistics conscious as possible. The Turkish situation is by no means perfect, however, chiefly because at the time of the Commission's enquiry there was no overall plan governing the collection of statistics. Ministries collect statistics as they think fit, without the benefit of advice and control from the State Statistics Institute. Then again, ideally statistics are collected for some purpose; and there is obviously a need for the State Statistics Institute and for ministries to follow the lead of the planning authorities in deciding which statistics it is necessary to collect.

The relations between the State Statistics Institute and the Planning Organization have not been kept out of politics. During the period of the second coalition government, these relations provided a subject for dispute between the coalition parties. In its Annual Programme for 1965, the State Planning Organization showed that its dissatisfaction with the central statistical service had not diminished.

With the State Statistics Institute's present system of collecting data, it is not possible to present accurately yearly developments in agriculture, industry or other sectors, or to make a real evaluation of the implementation of the Plan. In most fields it is necessary, either to collect directly, or to obtain from other sources, the information which the State Statistics Institute cannot collect itself. It should be noted that statistical information for planning activities cannot be obtained in time and is not reliable because of the lack of experienced technical personnel in the State Statistics Institute.[1]

This is a damning indictment.

Administrative research: improvement and advice. The Turkish Commission on Administrative Functions in its survey of central administrative organizations found that most of them had organizations attached to them for functions variously described

[1] Turkish State Planning Organization, *1965 Annual Programme* (Ankara, 1965), p. 391.

as 'research', 'survey', 'study' and 'advice'.[1] About one-fifth also had small organizations specifically devoted to administrative improvement, whilst in a further 30 per cent this function was given to one of their other research, advisory or survey boards.

To find administrative improvement (organization and methods work, as it is often more normally known) allocated to bodies set up for other purposes, is by no means unusual. With the exception perhaps of legal advice sections, there seems to be little concordance between title and function in these variously styled boards. For instance, organizations which go under the title of survey boards, or some similar name, have been variously found to give advice on draft laws and regulations; to engage in research on administrative and technical matters; to advise on the collection of statistics, on planning and on administrative improvement. In the matter of research it is probable that much too little administrative and statistical enquiry is undertaken; and scientific research would no doubt benefit from centralization in a scientific research agency, as the Commission on Administrative Functions has recommended.[2] The whole subject of the work and composition of these various advisory bodies and administrative organizations awaits thorough study. It is commonly held that such survey and advisory bodies often provide places of refuge for officials of high rank who for some reason or other have been moved out of the general administrative hierarchy.

Whilst the position with regard to research, survey and advice is very confused, a clearer picture of some of the efforts in the direction of administrative research and improvement is discernible. These matters are being tackled in some of the ministries and other central organizations, often under the impetus of the Institute of Public Administration for Turkey and the Middle East, one of the organizations attached to the Prime Ministry. The Institute contributes more directly to administrative im-

---

[1] There is little information available on the numbers of staff employed on such boards, whether they are full-time or part-time, whether they represent outside organizations to any extent, how many subordinate staff they control, etc.

[2] Some 2,400 scientists and technicians are shown as working in research organizations in the forty-five central organizations surveyed by the Commission.

provement by providing courses for civil servants and by a vigorous programme of research.

Inspection and audit. The need for internal inspection in public administration arises when in the normal course of supervision it is not possible to know whether the administration is performing as it should. An official in a supervisory position usually knows when an official under his supervision is working well and correctly, but only if he is really able to examine his work. Often he can, but if the work is highly technical he may not be able to do so, because he may not himself be expert in the work. Or it may be decided not to allow supervisors to examine their subordinates' work because the examination can be arranged more officially, or more impartially, by using a corps of specialist inspectors. Or again, the total organization may need to be examined from time to time. So the need for internal inspection arises. It is also necessary for the administration to inspect citizens in actions they are by law obliged to carry out; it is necessary, for example, for officials to inspect factories to ensure they conform to safety laws. This is usually known as 'external' inspection.

Turkish inspectoral services are organized by each ministry and by some other organizations (e.g. general directorates). The chief employers of the 2,200 inspectoral staff are the Ministries of Finance, Education, Interior and Labour. Inspectors are employed by seventeen different organizations, including thirteen ministries, and chiefly at the centre. By and large, inspectoral staff either have undergone courses in inspection (as in the Inspection Organization of the Ministry of Finance and the Ministry of Labour), or they are recruited from among a fairly wide range of serving officials as the need arises (as in the Ministry of Justice and the Ministry of the Interior). For the most part inspectors engaged on the more technical inspectoral functions are organized into inspectorates in which they are able to make their careers.

Turkish inspectoral services do not generally distinguish between internal and external inspection in their organizational arrangements. In the few cases where there is a conscious distinction, internal inspectors are sometimes authorized to carry out external inspections also when necessary. The principal argument for this is that inspection of an external sort often requires inspection of the internal administrative unit connected with the external function.

As we have seen, inspection can be more or less technical in character. Chief among the more technical factors is that of financial audit, so that it becomes sensible to talk of financial inspection on the one hand and administrative inspection on the other. Nevertheless, in the Turkish system, there is some fusing of these functions in the same personnel—to an extent that verges on the dangerous. Dangers arise when the ministries or other organizations are left to inspect the work of subordinate organizations, as the Ministry of Education is left to examine the boarding-house accounts of schools with boarders, or when a ministry is authorized to inspect organizations related to, but not falling within, the category of public organization, and not therefore the responsibility of the Inspection Board of the Ministry of Finance. In these cases it is essential to ensure that the inspectoral staff is properly qualified to audit accounts, or will restrict itself to a general inspection of activities whilst ensuring that proper financial control is provided by qualified personnel. The question of inspection by inspectors of the appropriate qualifications has also arisen in the Ministry of Justice where administrative inspectors have examined, among other things, the personal conduct of judges and how well they maintain discipline in court.

These examples of overlapping illustrate the need for inspection to be carried out by the personnel with the appropriate qualifications. Another form of overlapping would seem to occur when more than one Inspection Board is seen to be inspecting the same or, more often, very closely related functions, or at least to be empowered to do so. For example, the inspection of provincial health centres is the responsibility both of the Ministry of the Interior and the Ministry of Health. Or again, we find that health inspection in the schools involves both the Ministries of Health and Education. Such overlappings are not, however, necessarily undesirable, since the inspection by each department may be from a different angle. There are, however, cases of serious overlapping as when the Ministries of Agriculture and the Interior both inspect the enforcement of laws affecting the protection of peasant holdings.

A basic trouble with Turkish inspectorates is really that they are regarded by the ordinary officials as a sort of ministerial police force; and this is said to discourage initiative for fear of mistakes, to the point of inducing inertia. This image of the inspector as a policeman is sharpened when, as so often, he is used to investigate personal disputes between officials, or between officials and members of the public. Moreover, administrative inspection is probably used in some cases when straightforward administrative supervision is needed. Inspection needs to become more positive —to become, that is, a means of assistance and even of education for officials.

Legal control—the Council of State

We have seen that the Turkish Council of State has enjoyed a history of nearly one hundred years. After an early blooming it withered away until it was powerfully revived under the Atatürk regime. In the 1950's its prestige suffered a blow when it was prevented from challenging dismissals of public officials and when, through the mode of election of some of its members, it was brought too closely into politics. One of the aims of the 1960 revolution was to ensure its political independence and also its authority against any administrative act whatsoever.

It was also becoming clear during the post-war decade that the secondary problems of the Council of State were not being solved. Complaints of the malfunctioning of the Council have been numerous and still persist. One writer (in 1963) revives an old complaint and adds some new ones.[1] There is criticism of the quality of the personnel in the Council of State, particularly in the subordinate administrative courts, many of whose decisions are overturned by the Council on appeal. More attention needs to be given to education and training, including study visits to European countries with administrative courts. Greater interchange of personnel between the Council and the administration is urged (every Council of State seems to be accused of not understanding the administrators sufficiently).

The delays caused by the initial analysis of cases by legal 'spokesmen' who examine for points of law could be better done

---

[1] The following and other criticisms are made in an interesting article by a member of the Council of State, İhsan Olgun, 'Danıştay ve İhtiyaçları', *Türk İdare Dergisi*, no. 284 (1963), pp. 44–54. They repeat criticism made in an earlier more systematic study, Türkiye ve Orta Doğu Âmme İdaresi Enstitüsü, *Devlet Şurası Üzerinde Bir İnceleme*, 3 vols., Ankara, 1960.

after the précis work of the 'rapporteurs'. Decisions should be more regularly published, and arranged by subject, not by alphabet; they should also be fully reported in order to show the principles on which the decisions rest. There are more mundane —but important—criticisms. The Council needs a new building; a private place in which to work is almost impossible to find. Nor is there a satisfactory library.

The chief cause underlying this administrative confusion— immediately a product of too heavy a work load—is the growth in popularity of complaints by members of the public against administrative acts. They are now better educated. They know they may obtain redress through the Council and they are less and less intimidated by the bureaucracy. It is not only the public, however, which increases the burdens of the Council of State. The administration itself can be difficult by often according formal acknowledgement to an unwelcome decision whilst expending time and energy to avoid having, in fact, to honour it. Or again, the administration will refuse to apply an obviously applicable Council ruling to a new case similar to one in which an unwelcome decision was given.[1] They will take it to the Council instead. Delay by useless and time-wasting questions is another tactic. Other criticisms of the Council of State emerge from a valuable statistical analysis made in the 1950's of a sample of 2,131 cases of complaint against administrative acts handled by the Council between 1947 and 1954.[2] This study shows that over half of the cases dealt with by the Council were taxation cases—and dealt with by just one department within the Council. Many of these cases, moreover, which came on appeal from decisions of lower taxation commissions, were brought by the Ministry of Finance anxious not to lose any revenue. Another interesting discovery was that a high proportion of decisions made by provincial and sub-provincial administrative councils, acting as subordinate administrative courts, were rejected on appeal by the Council

---

[1] There is an illuminating example of administrative obstructiveness in *Devlet Şurası Üzerinde Bir İnceleme*, vol. III, p. 78. The Ministry of Finance is reported as having obliged each village school teacher to make separate application to the Council of State for payment of special assignment allowances supplementary to salary. The Ministry did not accept that they should apply to all similar cases what had been won in one case.

[2] R. V. Presthus and Sevda Erem, *Statistical Analysis in Comparative Administration: The Turkish Council of State* (Cornell, 1958).

(between 45 per cent and 50 per cent). These cases were principally concerned with boundary disputes between villages, con-
demnation of property and compulsory purchase. Yet another
interesting discovery was that civil servants did not fare very well
in disputes with the state. Whilst they came out well in disputes
over pay and eligibility for pensions, they fared badly in the matter
of dismissal (not subject to review under the Democrat regime
from 1956), promotions, disagreement on amounts of pensions
and compulsory retirement. It was also found that procedural
errors accounted for a large proportion (19 per cent) of rejected
cases—an indication that more attention to popular education
about the means of legal redress is needed. The chief reason for
such rejections on procedural grounds was failure to comply
with the ninety-day time limit for submission of claims to the
court. It is not, however, the case in Turkey that would-be liti-
gants are put off by thought of expense. Litigation before administrative courts is cheap—neither legal aid nor personal
appearance is necessary.

The Constitution of 1961 seeks to solve the two major problems
connected with the work of the Council of State which had
emerged during the era of Democrat Party government. The first
was how to prevent a government from simply declaring in any
law that it was not subject to administrative control by the Council of State. The second problem was to prevent the government
from influencing the Council through its control of the Grand
National Assembly, which appointed the members of the Council
of State under the 1924 Constitution.

The answer to the first problem is contained in Article 114
of the Constitution, which lays down that no act of the administration may be excluded from the control of the judicial authorities. It is interesting in this regard that the Turkish Council of
State has not developed at any time the doctrine of *acte de gouverne-
ment*. This would have admitted the exclusion of certain administrative acts from its consideration, and would have been urged no
doubt by the Government during the 1950–60 era.

The second problem is taken care of in Article 140. The election of members of the Council of State is now made by a commission formed from the members of the Constitutional Court,
the candidates being named separately by the Council of Ministers
and by the General Council of the Council of State itself.

R

A solution for the less critical problems faced by the Council of State has been sought largely in a new comprehensive Council of State law; but two shortcomings seem to have been judged serious enough to warrant their inclusion in the Constitution. The first concerns the time limit (of ninety days) within which an appeal against an administrative act must be lodged. This is now counted from the date when the administrative act was notified in writing, thus avoiding disputes about when the administrative act in question took place. The second addition to the Constitution lays down the important principle that the administration is henceforth responsible for paying damages. Previously the unsatisfactory situation obtained that officials were personally subject to actions for tort.

The new Council of State law, which was required by the Constitution, came into effect from the beginning of 1965.[1] Although the aim of the law is the comprehensive ordering of all important aspects of the Council's organization and functioning, no change in the basic principles which govern the Council's work has been undertaken—as is stated in the Preamble to the new law. The Council's principal functions are still to advise the government on draft laws and ordinances and to hear and decide administrative disputes and complaints by members of the public against the administration. The Council is a court of first and last instance, in the latter case hearing cases appealed from subordinate administrative courts. As we have seen above, the decisions of subordinate administrative courts in the provinces and sub-provinces are all too often successfully appealed to the Council of State, and appeals from the taxation courts are also often unnecessarily, if not successfully, appealed. The problem of the proper staffing and organization of the work of these courts is therefore important. The new law leaves this aspect of the working of administrative justice for subsequent legislation on the grounds that the complexities of the situation would have delayed the emergence of the new law, which is restricted in consequence to the Council of State itself.

Under the new law considerable attention is given to the conditions of employment of the Council's personnel. The principal aim of these arrangements is to prevent the government from exerting influence over discipline, promotions and dismissals.

[1] *Danıştay Kanunu*, no. 521, 31 December 1964.

A valuable innovation is the provision of opportunities for members of the Council of State to study the work of Councils of State abroad.

There is also some reorganization of the Council, which for its judicial functions now has nine departments (previously five) in addition to a General Council of the Judicial Departments. The remedies that are available are actions for annulment against illegal acts and actions for damages, which extend to cases of administrative contracts (i.e. principally contracts between private persons and the administration). In the field of administrative acts, which comprise general acts (rules) as well as acts relating to individuals, there is as yet little codification, except in the field of taxation. As regards administrative contracts, the Council has recently tended to broaden its definition to include, for example, the lease of an oil depot owned by the municipality.[1]

On the other hand, unlike the French Conseil d'Etat, the Turkish Council still leaves many areas in the field of governmental contract to private law. Finally, it may be mentioned that whilst the bulk of Turkish public officials are subject to administrative law, a large number, chiefly those employed in the public enterprises, are still subject to private law.

How far these new measures have improved the functioning of the Council of State it is not yet possible to say. Some recent decisions of the Council have been much criticized, particularly the use of its power to suspend an administrative act until the principle at stake is discussed. This has been criticized as too great an interference with the administration. There have also been accusations of ineptitude in the Council's handling of cases concerning refund of taxation on imported motor cars. In this case, the Eighth Department was at serious odds with the General Council of the Judicial Departments. It was alleged that the Eighth Department made unnecessary haste to reach decisions on certain claims for refund (and that the Ministry of Customs and Monopolies helped in this) *after* a final decision had been taken by the Council of State's General Council, which solved the dispute between the Eighth Department and the Judicial Depart-

---

[1] The example is taken from T. B. Balta, 'Administrative Law' in T. Ansay and D. Wallace (Eds), *Introduction to Turkish Law* (Ankara, 1966), p. 79. Professor Balta's contribution to this publication gives a very clear account of the present organization and functions of the Council of State.

ment's General Council, but *before* that final decision was published in the Official Gazette, when it would become operative. It looked like sharp practice.[1] The Turkish Council of State has had its ups and downs and has been subject to much criticism. In so far as its cases are occasions for dispute between markedly different social and economic attitudes (as in the case of taxation on imported motor cars) that underlie political differences in Turkish society, its future may well be somewhat troubled. If these sorts of differences are settled elsewhere within the political machinery, there seems no reason why under the new dispensation it should not prosper.

[1] See Yaşar Karayalçın, 'Danıştay'da Skandal mı', *Forum*, 1 April 1965.

CHAPTER XV

Departmental Functions

It is still difficult to envisage the Turkish administrative machine as a whole despite the attempts made to co-ordinate it and give it unity by such bodies as the State Personnel Agency or the Institute of Public Administration. The emphasis is still on the individual ministries or general directorates. This is partly due to the French tradition, partly to the fact that administrative modernization preceded the achievement of popular political control. The Commission on Organization and Functions devoted considerable time to departmental functions and the following discussion of the problems that arise again derives largely from the Commission's investigations.

Financial functions

Economic policy, revenue and expenditure. With the establishment of the State Planning Organization in 1960, the Ministry of Finance lost its functions as the chief co-ordinator, at official level, of national economic policy. Just how co-ordination now takes place in every respect is not altogether clear, although the High Planning Council is now the supreme advisory organ to the government in matters of economic and social policy. That co-ordination difficulties exist is apparent. The Commission sees the role of the Ministry of Finance as the supplier of information to the State Planning Organization. The Ministry of Finance should also be responsible for the carrying out of certain aspects of economic policy, as for instance monetary credit and interest rate policies; but in the *making* of monetary and financial policies the State Planning Organization must participate if economic plans are not to be endangered. Indeed, the State Planning Organization enters into the co-ordination of monetary and financial policy with the Ministry of Finance and the Central Bank on the basis of three-monthly reports from the Ministry.

The classic functions of any ministry of finance are the raising of revenue and the control of its disbursement in accordance with governmental policy and, of course, under conditions of probity.

As a society develops, governmental policy tends to be differentiated into economic and political aspects, although the two are often interwoven. The Ministry of Finance then, as in Turkey, advises on the effects of economic policies, as for instance on whether a new tobacco will increase revenue or lead to a decline in revenue through decreased smoking. However, when overall planning is undertaken, taxation policies must fall within the purview of the planning authorities. (Tobacco growing, for instance, might need encouraging, not taxing.) So in Turkey the State Planning Organization must participate in the economic aspects of revenue-raising policies. That co-ordination has not in this respect been perfect has been one of the complaints of the planners.

There are, moreover, other undesirable features of revenue raising, when, for instance, the proceeds of certain taxes are allocated beforehand to some particular service. However desirable in some ways, state revenue derived from football pools should not necessarily go into the promotion of sports activities, but to where most needed. Nor, in the same vein, is it necessarily right to levy special taxes for, say, the Turkish Standards Institute from public enterprises, banks and industrial concerns.

The participation of the State Planning Organization in the preparation of estimates expenditure is also of course essential if investment is to proceed as planned. The procedure is for spending organizations to submit their estimates to the State Planning Organization on forms provided for the purpose.[1] As from 1964 a start has been made with the system of programme budgeting in which expenditures are grouped into programmes of objectives to be achieved instead of being shown as separate amounts to be spent, for example, on salaries, transport, investment or maintenance. In this way, and with the help of stricter costing, it is hoped to be able to see whether the derived results have been achieved as efficiently as possible. In sum, in its revenue and expenditure functions, the Ministry of Finance now works—even if imperfectly—under the advice of the Planning Organization.

---

[1] A new classification of public expenditures defines investment more closely, eliminating from this category, for instance, transfers of funds to state economic enterprises and expenditures on minor items of maintenance.

Financial control

Programme budgeting leads us into the question of financial control. As the Commission on Organization and Functions sees, the classification of budgetary allocations by 'project' is the only way to ensure that the money is spent on what was originally intended. To include provision for building a laboratory in a sub-division of a budget classified as 'construction' is logical enough, but makes it difficult to stop the allocation being used for, say, a garage. It is not the control of the expenditure, but the control of functions that is really at stake, and the Commission sees that the Ministry of Finance is not in a position to cope with this sort of control. The main evaluation of projects it sees as the concern of the ministries concerned, in accordance with the general standards determined by the State Planning Organization.

The Ministry of Finance is, however, responsible for the control of expenditure in a technical sense—for the preparation of accounts, which are audited by the Court of Accounts—and for the collection of revenue.[1] Within these fields a number of technical problems arise for which the Commission suggests solutions. For example, the powers of the ministries and other spending departments might be increased to include actual payment, the keeping of accounts, and some degree of financial audit; and this would leave the Ministry of Finance to concentrate on general matters, like prescribing the principles of accounting and carrying out research in these matters. Then again, much of the time of the General Directorate of the Budget and Financial Control in the Ministry is taken up with giving individual rulings relating to expenditure in response to numerous requests from spending departments. There is seen to be a greater need for uniformity here and greater use of general regulations. The present practice also encourages finance officials of spending departments to ask for opinions when the law or regulation is already clear enough. In the collection of revenue, the Commission sees it is necessary to curtail the administration's right to appeal to the Council of State when tax appeals commissions give decisions favourable to citizens. The Commission is fully aware in this and other matters of the pressure to have every administrative decision vetted by

[1] The Ministry of Finance has of course other important functions of a purely *financial* sort, like the supply of money. These are not examined here.

the highest authority. Part of the reason for this in taxation matters it ascribes to the lack of properly trained personnel in the provinces. It notes, too, the lack of 'certified public accountants' in Turkey, a specialized professional body that could be responsible to some extent for the soundness of the taxpayer's declarations and the accuracy of his calculations. What emerges most strikingly from the Commission's detailed analysis is a respect for the probity and capacity of the senior personnel in the Ministry of Finance, coupled with doubts about the initiative and training of officials in the lower reaches of the financial administration. The lack in Turkish society of a professional body of certified accountants shows how much easier generally is the task of public administration in more developed societies where professional organizations with their own ethical standards ease the relations between official and citizen.

Industrial, commercial and agricultural functions

It needs no more than stating that a country bent on rapid industrialization requires an efficient Ministry of Industry. To staff a Ministry of Industry efficiently requires above all, however, the availability of technically qualified expert personnel. Turkey's Ministry of Industry finds them difficult to obtain—to the extent that numbers of technical personnel have to be borrowed from the state economic enterprises, who are short of personnel, too.[1] The Ministry of Industry borrows personnel from the economic enterprises the more easily since nearly all these enterprises come under its control. One of the problems faced by the Ministry is in fact the control of the state economic enterprises, though the immense problems involved cannot be discussed here.

Quite apart from the difficulties involved in these functions, the Ministry has other problems. In order to guide private enterprise, the Ministry should be in a position to provide expert technical and economic advice. In order to see the position of Turkish industry as a whole, it is necessary to compile records on private industrial enterprises. The maintenance of standards of quality in Turkish industry is also another function of the Ministry vital to the prestige of Turkish manufacturers. Then again, the Ministry has to regulate the prices of the products of monopolies, and to register and negotiate patents. In the performance of all these very

[1] They are generally able to pay higher salaries than ministries.

basic functions there appear to be quite serious defects, though it must be admitted that the compilation of information from members of the public is extremely difficult. Questionnaires to enterprises, for instance, largely go unanswered. There is not generally in evidence much sense of responsibility to help the state; but more than this, there seems to be a general slackness in Turkish society about completing minor administrative chores unless a heavy and effective penalty is attached. One area of the Ministry of Industry's activities where there is a deal of delay and bureaucracy is in application of laws relating to mining. The difficulty of making surveys at distances from the capital (there is no provincial organization), the disputes that naturally arise and in this connection, the absence of a register of mines to record exploitation rights—all these so burden the administrative organization as to hold up the development of mineral resources.

In the critically important field of energy for industrial development, the Commission on Organization and Functions discovered that electrical power was the concern of a number of different organizations, including parts of three different ministries. This not unnaturally resulted in bad co-ordination and overlapping, particularly in survey and research activities. The matter has since been taken in hand with the creation of a new Ministry of Energy and Natural Resources.

In the field of commerce, the Ministry of Commerce is charged with regulating and developing foreign and domestic trade. In this field the Commission encountered a number of problems of location of functions and co-ordination. Should the Ministry of Commerce continue to concern itself with maintaining standards in Turkish agricultural products (which it does, for example, by opening and testing consignments for export on the docks)? Or should this function not really belong to the Ministry of Agriculture? Again, should the Ministry of Commerce continue to be responsible for policies on bread and cereals? (The price of bread in Turkey, where so much is eaten, is a major political issue.) Or should this function be given to the Ministry of Agriculture, which is responsible for the production of wheat? It is tempting to say that the management of the food industry should be given to the Ministry of Agriculture, and the Commission recommends this—on the grounds of better co-ordination. Yet it is not always desirable that one ministerial organization should be concerned with both the production of food and with checking on sanitary conditions in food production, and with quality and price. Such an omnibus organization can too easily come under the influence of those who produce and market food.

The performance of some of its other principal functions by the Ministry of Commerce is less open to debate. The promotion of exports is of crucial importance to Turkey; it is therefore unsatisfactory to find its officials (in the Directorate of Foreign Trade) numbering no more than 17. A special fund organization set up to promote exports is badly organized, relying as it does for direction on the efforts that can be spared for it by a full-time senior official of the Ministry of Commerce. Then again, the important task of developing fisheries for domestic and foreign trade has not been given proper attention over a number of years, the directorate concerned having been moved about from one ministry to another several times. It is described by the Commission as in a state of lethargy and not much concerned with anything but regulating fishing through fishing wardens.

In agriculture[1] there are similarly many matters that could be improved. The Ministry fully recognizes that there is inefficient use of natural resources, that production is still too low, that agricultural processes still lack technical knowledge, that farm equipment is bad and investment erratic, that marketing of products needs to be further developed, and, above all, that the proportion of the population employed in agriculture is higher than for many underdeveloped countries. First, it is necessary to re-fashion the Ministry, so that it may concentrate its activities around the basic problems of increasing the amount and quality of food. If current views are accepted, this will mean that certain organizations, like the General Directorate of Forestry and Meteorology, would be detached from the Ministry. As to the functions of irrigation and land development, land survey and the like,[2] they seem to be appropriate to whichever organization is given the responsibility for land reform. Other organizations, like

[1] For information on the organization of the Ministry of Agriculture see *A Reorganization of Turkish Agriculture*, translation of Report prepared by Project Management Board of the Organization Project Group in the Ministry of Agriculture, USAID (Ankara, 1965).

[2] The functions of the General Directorate of Soil and Water (*Topraksu*).

the Soil Products Office and the fisheries organization of the Ministry of Commerce, should be attached to agriculture.

Perhaps the chief needs for development in agriculture are extension services to farmers that really will bring the benefits of modern technology to every farmer; and in this there are considerable problems in the training of a sufficient number of extension workers. It is also seen to be necessary for the Ministry to develop a regional organization to reduce problems of coordination between directorates of the Ministry.

Tourism

Another function productive of national wealth in Turkey is tourism. The Commission on Organization and Functions found that the personnel employed in tourism numbered no more than thirty-four, and that plans did not allow for more than a complement of sixty-four persons. Tourism is combined in Turkish administration with information and press functions; and until recently tourism has been the junior partner. The emphasis in the past has been to publicize the achievements of Turkish democracy inside and outside Turkey. Now the emphasis is changing to that of making known to potential tourist exporting countries Turkey's undoubted attractions. Responsibilities for disseminating abroad information about Turkey not touristic in character, and for collecting foreign radio and press opinion of Turkish affairs, could therefore be transferred to the Ministry of Foreign Affairs. As to the government's relations with the Turkish public through press and wireless, it is coming to be seen that this would be best managed through an office attached to the Prime Ministry. In the field of tourism itself a deal of development is envisaged that will include use of a broadly selected consultative council and a regional organization.

Public works and communications

Development programmes entail vast expenditures on bricks and mortar, not to mention concrete and steel. When, as in Turkey, a large share of development is directly undertaken by the state, the demand on the Ministry of Public Works is considerable. The Ministry of Public Works in Turkey has the task of erecting most of the buildings required by other ministries; but housing construction is undertaken by the Ministry of Reconstruction and

Resettlement, military construction by the Ministry of National Defence and miscellaneous building by some other agencies. The result of this division is some overlapping of functions, and indeed duplication, as, for instance, when the Ministries of Public Works and Reconstruction and Resettlement both carry out research on construction materials and planning.

A more complex problem than this, however, is the construction and maintenance of national transport systems. The Ministry of Communications seems the rightful home for these functions, but in fact it shares them with the Ministry of Public Works in respect of national motor roads—or more precisely with the General Directorate for State Highways attached to the Ministry of Public Works. In fact the Ministry of Communications is very little concerned with national motor roads. It is more closely concerned with Turkish National Railways, which is a state economic enterprise; but without overall responsibility for all communications it cannot develop a national transport policy.

Social services

In any developed country the problems to be faced in the administration of the social services are considerable. In a country like Turkey they are immense. In the field of health, for example, centres established for the purposes of *preventive* medicine have gradually developed into medical *treatment* centres. In order to fill a gap in the provision of preventive medicine in schools, the Ministry of Education has established a General Directorate of Health, which does not, however, really function at small town and village level. The preventive medical services that exist seem to rely excessively on doctors when much less extensively trained personnel would suffice. In the area of sanitation there is a very big problem in the growth of shack suburbs around large towns where live so many of the excess population that has drifted to the towns. In the field of medical treatment there is little co-ordination between hospitals, largely because they are not all administered by the Ministry of Health and Social Assistance, but by the other ministries, or by municipalities to which they belong. The problem of financing and administering a national health service seem insuperable, but a start has been made in a pilot region.

The social welfare services in Turkey are, not unnaturally, in an underdeveloped state. There is no unemployment insurance.

Employees generally are entitled to a range of benefits, including health, but in fact the vast majority of the workers, namely the farmers, agricultural workers and tradesmen, do not qualify for anything. The huge gaps in provision of social assistance are to some extent provided for by municipalities, ministries (the Ministry of Reconstruction and Resettlement, for example), by voluntary bodies on a more or less *ad hoc* basis. There is practically no co-ordination, however. Given the country's financial resources there is no easy solution; it is one long uphill struggle.

A large part of the burden for social amelioration is borne by the Ministry of Reconstruction and Resettlement. It has the function of resettling persons from over-populated areas by providing them with the wherewithal to begin a new life. Immigrants enter into its field of activity and so do the victims of natural disasters. The preparation of the principles of a housing policy is also among the functions of this ministry, but little has been done, partly because there is no history of state provision of houses in Turkey. Clearly there are now urgent problems in this field with the growth of slums on the outskirts of the towns. The effects of economic and social development are pointing out with new urgency the need for physical planning, and it is the Ministry of Reconstruction that must undertake this task.

In education the problems are no less serious. There is a wide-open field for development of education and training of all sorts, but for sheer financial reasons only a limited amount can be undertaken. Even so, there are administrative problems where solution would lead to more efficiency in what is done.

In the first place, the Ministry of National Education comprises both cultural and educational functions. The suggestion made by the Commission on Organization and Functions that cultural functions, such as care of monuments, should be hived off into a new Ministry has so far not borne fruit. Within the purely educational field itself there is an unfortunate rigid division between general and technical education, with a consequent duplication of inspection and planning departments. Then again, the Ministry of Education's Advisory Council is composed more of educational specialists than of representatives of consumers of the service. In this connection the organization of parent–teacher associations on a national basis might be beneficial, as local parent–teacher associations are not effective. A serious administrative problem is the provision and effective supervision of hostels for university and other students. Of course there are other serious problems of establishing satisfactory curricula for the schools, of building and of staffing more grammar or high schools (*lises*), of producing satisfactory textbooks; but a discussion of these problems will take us out of administration into the problems of Turkish education. One problem of administration that most persons seem, rather uncharitably, to agree upon is that the ex-school-teachers who largely staff the middle and upper ranks of the Ministry of National Education are not born administrators. Ministries of Education in many countries seem to rank low in administrative efficiency in the eyes of civil servants in other ministries.

Traditional functions

Finance, Justice and Law and Order, and Foreign Affairs are the oldest functions of government. Finance has been dealt with above and foreign affairs fall outside the scope of this study. The administration of justice in Turkey falls primarily to the Ministry of Justice, though the Ministry of National Defence provides for the administration of judicial functions in the military sphere.

The administration of justice covers a wide range of functions from enforcing the decisions of the courts to the appointment of public notaries and the maintenance of various legal records. One function that needs to be kept under review is the systematic publication of decisions taken by supreme judicial organs. Nor is statistical information as complete as it might be. One of the large problems is the volume of work in the courts and the need to streamline administrative and financial procedures. There is some need, too, in the absence of a jury system perhaps, to devise means of giving weight to social factors. The attachment to courts of social workers is envisaged as one way to help achieve this.

The preservation of law and order—as well as the chief responsibility for managing the system of provincial government—falls to the Ministry of the Interior. Within law and order falls the task of maintaining security on the frontiers and also traffic control.

For the performance of the police functions necessary for law and order the Ministry principally employs both police and gendarmerie, although there are various classes of guards, watchmen and constables. The first problem that arises is whether it is necessary to have both gendarmerie and police—and this especially because the headquarters and training organizations of these two police forces largely duplicate each other, even although their spheres of operation are different, the police being confined to municipalities whilst the gendarmerie works normally in the countryside. The reasons why the gendarmerie remains are partly traditional. The gendarmerie, which is in character a military organization, has always been attached to the Ministry of the Interior as a security force. As its non-commissioned ranks are made up of soldiers, it is also more fitted to the hectic work of bandit and smuggler elimination that seems endemic to the wilder eastern provinces. Above all, perhaps, being composed of soldiers, it is relatively cheap. The chief criticism, however, of the gendarmerie is the important one that it is much too heavy-handed when dealing with the peasantry. It is fairly well agreed that a better trained, better educated civil police force would be a great boon in the countryside.

General conclusions

Distribution of functions. The Commission proposed after its survey a number of changes in the distribution of functions. Those which are of a major order were the recommended redistribution among the ministries of twenty-three major administrative units, for the most part general directorates or directorates. Six of these re-allocations are from one ministry or other administrative body to another, whilst the remainder would constitute two new ministries. In this transfer of functions one ministry, the Ministry of Customs and Monopolies, would disappear. The two new ministries whose establishment the Commission recommends are a Ministry of Energy and National Resources and a Ministry of Culture. In creating the former, the Commission would provide for unified control of a number of organizations concerned with water resources, electricity, atomic energy, refined oil products and coal mining and other mineral resources. The new ministry would remove the serious problems of overlapping and co-ordination in the fields of research and planning between the General Directorate of State Water Works and the Electrical

Works Research Office. The government acted quickly on the recommendations of the Commission in this respect by setting up a Ministry of Energy and Natural Resources in 1963.

The chief reason for the recommendation for a Ministry of Culture was to prevent the overloading of the Ministry of Education which is now becoming apparent and can be expected to increase substantially in the future as plans for the expansion of education begin to materialize. The work of the present ministry would also be increased by the recommendations of the Commission for it to absorb the General Directorates of Physical Education and Pious Foundations from the Prime Minister's Office. The new Ministry of Culture would lighten the load of the Ministry of Education by assuming its functions in the fields of the fine arts, the National Theatre, museums, libraries and ancient monuments. The new ministry would also administer pious foundations and would receive press and broadcasting; functions from the present Ministry of Press, Broadcasting and Tourism, which would then be responsible for tourism. A Ministry of Culture has not, however, been set up, and one new ministry has been established contrary to the advice of the Commission on Organization and Functions, namely the Ministry of Village Affairs. The management of administrative reform has been given to a small Commission for the Reorganization of Administration and Administrative Methods.[1] The new commission has sponsored two studies, one on Central Administration in the Provinces[2] and the other on Local Administration. It has also recommended to the Council of Ministers the general principles that should underlie administrative reorganization.

Performance of functions. It is one of the merits of the work of the Commission on Organization and Functions that it did not believe in the redistribution of functions alone as the golden key to administrative reform. In one section of its report an attempt is made to judge how well functions are performed.

The Commission notes, first of all, although aware that it is treading on political ground, that some functions which it thinks ought to be performed are not being undertaken at all. For example, no official studies of movements of population are

[1] Set up by decree of the Council of Ministers, 5 June 1964.
[2] See below, p. 259n.

made; such studies would obviously be invaluable to guide policies in many spheres.

Secondly, there are those duties which are said to be performed, being included in laws or subsidiary legislation, which are not in fact being performed, either for lack of organizational arrangements, or for lack of effort. For example, plans have not been made for the geographic distribution of industry in accordance with the broad plan for industry. Again, plans to provide other means of livelihood for the inhabitants of villages in, or on the edge of, forests with a view to protecting the forests from their depredations have not been put into effect.

Thirdly, there are very obvious differences in the extent and quality of administrative services as between regions, between town and country and even between parts of towns. This is particularly true, for example, of the organization for the prevention of disease, whose ranks it is difficult to fill.

Fourthly, the Commission distinguishes functions which, although provided in most ways with an adequate organization, are not treated with as much importance by the administration itself as is their due. They may originally have been located lower down in the hierarchy than was warranted by their importance, or they may have declined in influence. For example, the fishing industry remains underdeveloped and there is insufficient encouragement of co-operatives and inadequate stimulus of exports by the Minister of Commerce in spite of the fact that adequate organization for all these functions exists in most respects. Whilst this category of faults may be perceived in every field, it is apparently most observable in the spheres of agriculture, industry, commerce, tourism, education and health.

Why have these shortcomings in execution arisen? The first reason which the Commission adduces is that of sheer financial shortage. The second is the inequality in the freedom to use their financial resources which can exist between organizations which perform the same types of functions; and this can mean *inter alia* that officials in 'annexed budget' and other types of organizations are paid better than officials in ministries. The most important reasons are indeed seen to lie in personnel difficulties, which are widely recognized as being very serious. The quality of administrative leadership is also criticized; the inspectorates, for instance, being said to be more concerned with detecting faults than with

s

helping to prevent them. Again, the maldistribution of functions is a factor in their being badly performed; and so are excessive formalism and ill-conceived measures of centralization. Yet finally, the Commission recognized that the surest way to improvement is that there should develop among all civil servants high and low, a spirit of self-reform. The Commission rightly deplored the prevalence of the notion that there is a talisman outside the administration in the shape of a neat formula whose adoption will lead to immediate improvement.

CHAPTER XVI

The Central Administration in the Provinces

Apart from the Ministry of Foreign Affairs, all the ministries and a number of other central government organs possess provincial organizations, though not all are represented in every province. The system by which central authority is reconciled with local democracy owes much to French example. Elected councils are related in various ways to the centrally appointed officials of the Ministry of the Interior, of whom it will be recalled the governors of the *il* (the *vali* and of the *ilce* (the *kaymakam*) are the most important. Provinces and municipalities have elected councils. It will be noticed that the system provides for a distinction between town and village, whereas the French system does not distinguish between the two, making the Commune serve for both. Over half of the *valis* and 80 per cent of the *kaymakams* are graduates of the Faculty of Political Science of Ankara University, almost all the remainder being graduates in law. The officials of all the ministries which are represented in the provinces are responsible to the *vali*, or *kaymakam* in the first instance, again after the French pattern.

The problems facing Turkish central administration in the provinces are generally acknowledged to be serious; and they have now been studied in more depth than was possible for the Commission on Organization and Functions.[1]

Regionalism

What is to the fore in the present discussion of the problems of Turkish provincial administration is a groping towards a new regionalism. The present division of the country into provinces does not, firstly, provide areas ideal for the administration of every service and, secondly, needs to be modified in the interests of regional planning, for which units greater than those of each of the sixty-seven provinces are required.

---

[1] By a group under the direction of A. T. Payaslıoğlu, *Merkezî İdarenin Taşra Teşkilâtı Üzerinde Bir İnceleme* (Ankara, 1965). Statistical information in this chapter derives from this report unless otherwise stated.

The need for areas of administration larger than provinces is recognized in the 1961 Constitution[1] and with more emphasis on development and planning nearly two-thirds of the seventeen ministries and about one-third of the remaining twenty-five central organizations, have developed regional organizations. Of all central organizations, including ministries, that have developed regional organizations only about one-third participate in the normal system of provincial organization under the direction of the *vali*. The traditional pattern of central administration in the provinces has been considerably distorted.

Matters have been made worse in this respect by the lack of uniformity in the regions selected by these organs of the central administration and in the choice of towns as regional centres; and when the regional organization has been set up there has been little if any attempt to take measures to secure co-ordination between the regional officials and the governors and sub-governors of provinces.

It is now generally accepted that there should be regions, but that they should be regions relevant to planned development and which take into account the needs of all services. So far ten suitable planning regions have been identified and studies are being undertaken on the division of the remainder of the country into a further five regions.[2] Yet a certain amount of disquiet is evident. There is the fear that regions may develop ambitions for some degree of political autonomy, and this might be troublesome in Eastern Turkey where there are many Kurds. Again, there is the fear that regional governors of very great power might arise against whom the organs of democracy would be but puny opponents. Over-mighty *provincial* governors are not a problem, but an over-mighty *regional* governor could become one.

[1] Article 115 states that for certain functions authorities may be set up on a wider than provincial basis.

[2] So far economic development has occurred most in the regions around Istanbul, Izmir, Adana and Ankara. This seems to be reflected in civil service statistics. In the provinces of Istanbul, Izmir and Ankara there are 1·5 civil servants in the provincial administration to every 100 citizens. In other provinces the ratio is 1 to 100. Nearly one-fifth of all civil servants of the central administration in the provinces are employed in Istanbul, Izmir and Ankara provinces. Some 22 per cent of all civil servants in the central administration (including the provincial organization) work in these three provinces, either in the central administrative offices or in the provincial organization.

To avoid this sort of danger, one suggestion is that there should be not a regional governor, but a committee of provincial governors in each region to act as a co-ordinating authority for the provinces in the region. Such collegiate responsibility does not really accord with Turkish administrative traditions. The natural tendency is to give power to individuals, but not on too permanent a basis. A more acceptable solution might be to adopt from France the idea of a regional governor to take the initiative and have power of decision in economic matters but who would otherwise merely co-ordinate all administrative activities of the provincial governors within the regions. The chief opposition to this development comes from those who remember the inspectors-general of regions set up shortly after the war of independence whose heavy-handedness was renowned.[1]

In whatever way regional developments take place the present system of provincial administration will no doubt remain. There is no suggestion yet that the present provincial system should be abolished. Rather it should be reformed to remove its worst and generally admitted defects.

Problems of areas

Quite apart from the need for more rational regional arrangements the system stands in need of reform in other ways.

In the first place, there are considerable differences in area and population among the sixty-seven provinces.[2] The largest has fourteen times the area of the smallest; and the most populous has twenty-eight times as many people as the least. There is, however, a deal of misgiving about changing boundaries. For the most part the present provinces have a long history, being the sub-provinces (*livas*) of Ottoman times. It seems inadvisable,

[1] These Inspectors-General (*Umumî Müfettişler*) were concerned with security, in which field they had considerable powers. A co-ordinating governor concerned principally with economic and social development would be very different.

[2] A useful description of Turkey's administrative divisions is contained in *Türkiyenin İdarî Taksimatı*, Ankara, 1961, (Türkiye ve Orta Doğu İdare Enstitüsü). Half the provinces have populations between just over 200,000 and just under 400,000. One-sixth fall below this group and the remainder, one-third, above it. Another disparity among provinces lies in the number of sub-provinces. Three-quarters of the provinces have between five and nine sub-provinces. One has four; the remainder have between ten and eighteen.

therefore, to break apart long-established administrative units to which the population is accustomed. The opinion of just over half of the provincial governors when asked about provincial boundaries in 1956 was that they did conform to the facts of geography and economics; and over three-quarters of the governors thought the capital cities of provinces were suitably sited.[1]

Boundary problems in provincial administration are an endless source of disagreement everywhere, and Turkey is no exception. From the discussions held in administrative congresses and the reports of commissions set up by the Ministry of the Interior and from other enquiries it is difficult to find agreement; but the general trend of opinion is towards an increase in the number of provinces, which would be achieved by the elevation in status of a number of sub-provinces.[2] Yet, it is not intended that changes should be many.[3]

At the sub-province level there are a number of problems, of which the first is again the boundary problem. A commission set up by the Ministry of the Interior in 1960 recommended that a sub-province should be between 600 and 1000 square kilometres in area and should have a population of not less than 13,000 to 24,000. It is interesting to note that recently sub-provinces have been set up only 200 square kilometres in area and with less than 15,000 population in Rize and Trabzon, whilst in Çankırı some recently established sub-provinces have populations of only about 10,000.

Nevertheless in 1956 70 per cent of *kaymakams* declared that they were satisfied with the size of their areas, and 76 per cent found the capitals of the sub-provinces suitably placed on social, economic and historical grounds. However, although the *kaymakams* find the sub-provinces suitably set up, there is a shortage of *kaymakams* for them. In 1965 there were eighty-two short and

---

[1] See *Kaza ve Vilâyet İdaresi Üzerinde Bir Araştırma* (Ankara, Ank. Üniv. S.B.F., 1957).

[2] *Merkezî İdarenin Taşra Teşkilâtı Üzerinde Bir İnceleme*, p. 21. The authors of this study emphasize, however, the need for a thorough-going study of the problem, province by province.

[3] The number of sub-provinces has increased by 46 per cent since 1928 when there were 391; Turkish population, however, has about doubled during the same period. By contrast the number of Turkish provinces has not changed much. There were seventy-four in 1921, fifty-seven in 1933 and there are now (1969) sixty-seven.

it was not expected that the shortage would be made good by normal means before 1968. This is because *kaymakams* have to be graduates of either faculties of Political Science or Law.

The shortage will become more acute if steps are taken to ensure that those sub-provinces in which the *vali* has his head-quarters are also provided with *kaymakams*. At present this is not obligatory, with the result that usually the sub-provinces in which the provincial centre is situated is administered directly by the *vali* without a *kaymakam*. As these provincial centres are usually places of large and rapidly expanding population, the *vali* is much occupied with the affairs of the centre sub-province. It is generally thought that *kaymakams* should now be appointed, starting with those sub-provinces where regional centres will be located. The argument that in small sub-provincial centres the *vali* can easily double-up as *kaymakam*, and ought to be allowed to do so, is attractive for reasons of economy. But the real answer in such situations is so to reorganize the sub-provinces that the centre (and other) *kaymakams* have enough responsibility to occupy them full-time.

A particularly difficult problem occurs at the next lower administrative division, the *bucak* or 'district'.[1] It is no less than whether the *bucak* should continue to exist.

The district is a legacy from the nineteenth century. With the increasing effectiveness of communication it has declined in importance as an administrative and representative organ between village and sub-province. In 1929 the district council was abolished and all administration was given to a district official.[2] Yet in 1949 an attempt was made to reinvigorate the district. It now became necessary for the district official to have a secondary school (*lise*) education. An establishment of doctors, midwives, veterinary surgeons, agricultural officials and so on was to be set up, but only according to need as determined by the ministries concerned. Moreover, district councils and commissions for advisory and administrative purposes were to be set up, part elected by village councils and municipalities and part appointed from among local officials. In fact, very few of these administratively equipped districts have been set up and amount to no more at present than some 190 out of the 923 districts. Furthermore, it seems that reasons of economy have of recent years obliged ministries to

[1] Its older name is *nahiye*.   [2] Known then as *nahiye müdürü*.

withdraw staff from the district level, so that the number of fully equipped districts is probably now less than 190. Consequently, most districts will have no more at best than a few gendarmerie, a census clerk and a general clerk, in addition to the district official. In practice, some of this modest complement of personnel may not be present. Indeed, nearly 140 districts are without their officials. Of those who do exist, 32 per cent have not had the *lycée* education laid down as necessary. The figures confirm this observer's inexpert impression that district office buildings mostly need rebuilding. This level of governmental structure is visibly decaying.

There is a boundary problem here, too. One-third of the sub-provinces have no districts; 12 per cent have more than three. The question is whether the system should be reorganized and refurbished, or whether it is worth the expense.

The arguments against retention are formidable. The very decay of the system, it is said, shows it is not necessary. To re-move steps in administrative hierarchy is always good for con-tact with citizens. Above all, the crucial co-ordinating agency for local administration, including community development, is seen to be the sub-province. On the other side, the district official is de-picted as the go-between for the common people and officialdom. Of only moderate education, he can understand both peasant and educated official. One promising solution put forward is for the larger viable districts to be converted into sub-provinces, leaving other districts gradually to disappear, as communications de-velop to make it possible for the peasant to deal direct with the sub-province. Districts within municipalities seem to serve no purpose at all.

The next significant problem is that of the administration of the village (*köy*). The position is that the elected village headman (*muhtar*) is overworked and is likely to be more so as schemes of community development get under way. For once elected, the headman of the village also becomes a government official. In this capacity not only does he have to notify infectious diseases, help tax collections, return statistics of births, marriages and deaths and the like; he may also be called upon to assist the ad-ministration in almost any way. Moreover, he can be prosecuted under civil service laws, like any other officials, for alleged irregularities. The tendency is for the headman to be given more and more to do. If there is no school teacher or *imam* (religious functionary), there are no other official persons in the village. The school teacher or *imam*, when either exists, may assist the headman clerically on a part-time basis; but the weight of duties is such that it is generally held that the headman really needs a full-time clerk. The Turkish Commission on Organization and Functions recommended appointment of a full-time clerk out of village funds; but that a clerk should be paid by the state seems more appropriate, bearing in mind the meagre resources of many villages. It is sometimes claimed that the normal administrative burden of the headman is unnecessarily increased by officials who get him to do work they should do themselves, or who call him for consultations too frequently to district or sub-province centres. Perhaps the effectiveness of the headman would also be enhanced if he were better educated. In 1962 only 43 per cent were shown by an enquiry to have attended school, while 32 per cent could neither read nor write.

The management of provincial administration

As we have seen, the *vali* is the head of the central administration in the province and is an official of the Ministry of the Interior. It is laid down that in principle provincial organizations set up by other ministries are under his control, although the immediate heads of such organizations belong to the ministry concerned. The exceptions to this general rule are the provincial organizations of the Ministry of Justice and the Ministry of National Defence. However, as we have seen, it has proved possible for central organizations to set up provincial units outside the *vali's* control. Unless these are simply units of a truly regional organization to which provincial areas are not relevant, or unless they are out-stations of the centre—like agricultural research institutions—only administrative confusion results if they remain outside the co-ordinating influence of the *valis* or *kaymakams*.

The essential problem between the *valis* and the *kaymakams* on the one hand, and the provincial organizations of other ministries on the other, does not stem from co-ordination but from the authority accorded to the *vali* to control the officials of other ministries who work in the province. For in the first place, the *vali* does not have much say in the appointment of heads of other ministries' provincial organizations, nor is it possible for the *vali* to transfer more junior personnel of other ministries from his province or even within it, save on the recommendation of the provincial 'head' of the ministry concerned. Despite these limitations on his hierarchical power, the *vali* is responsible for carrying out the duties imposed by laws, ordinances and regulations. From the evidence available it is not yet really possible to say how far a *vali* can and does control the work of the organizations under his charge. That he does have a difficult time is fairly clear and, indeed, it is said that in the Council of Ministers there is a tendency for ministers to present a united front against the Ministry of the Interior on these matters of provincial organization.

Community development

The village community, or the citizen himself, can all too easily come to be regarded as the lowest level in administrative organization, not as the reason for it. There is, however, something of a new spirit abroad in Turkey in this respect. After a long period of discussion of the approaches and techniques of the new notion of community development, the government set up in 1963 a Ministry of Village Affairs.

To set up a ministry was evidence both of Turkey's earnestness in the cause of community development and of her welcome readiness to adopt without undue delay administrative devices that seemed successful elsewhere. There is also a strong current of feeling in Turkish society that the administration often treats the peasant harshly and unsympathetically and too paternalistically. Certainly it is difficult for the peasant to think of government as a helpmate, but as a master more inclined to place limits on his initiative than to encourage it. Also at village level the complaint is heard that despite centralized provincial administration, one ministry does not seem to dovetail its plans much into those of another. So a Ministry of Village Affairs should help co-ordinate as well as promote self-help in the villages.

It is as yet too early to judge the success of the new ministry.[1]

---

[1] A good introduction to the subject is F. Yavuz, *Memleketimizde Toplum Kalkınması (Köy Kalkınması)* (Ankara: Türkiye ve Orta Doğu Âmme İdaresi Enstitüsü, 1964). See also Köy İşleri Bakanlığı, *Köy İşleri Bakanlığı Kuruluş Çalısmaları* (Ankara, 1964).

It has of necessity started slowly by experimenting with community development in six sub-provinces in six different provinces in 1963, and again in six more sub-provinces in 1964. Voices have been raised in criticism of the decision to found a new ministry so soon and without waiting for these experiments to be evaluated. The Commission on Organization and Functions was of the view that community development would best be managed under an inter-ministerial board, with corresponding co-ordinating boards at lower levels, down to and including the village. This would be to use, and improve, for the purpose of community development the existing administrative machinery, to which the villages are accustomed. New bodies running in parallel with the existing organization, it was thought, would cause rivalry and duplication.

CHAPTER XVII

The Civil Service

The Turkish civil service is in the process of what promises to be fundamental reform. In June 1965 an Officials' Associations' Law[1] was passed which regulated for civil servants the right given in the Constitution to employees to establish organizations to represent their interests. Although, unlike other workers, civil servants are not allowed to strike, their freedom to form associations is a development that may well turn out to be of the first significance.

During 1961–5 other laws aimed at a general reform of the whole personnel system were taken in hand. Four separate laws were to deal with civil servants in (i) municipalities, (ii) special administrations (chiefly the universities), (iii) the state economic enterprises, and (iv) the central administration. Another law, a new Retirement Law, was also put in train.

The first of these laws to appear was that for officials in the central administration.[2] It was a substantial reform; but it is necessary first to discuss the personnel system as it operated during the period of this study in order to appreciate the need and significance of the reform.

Statistics. A survey made by the State Personnel Office shows that in 1961 there was an establishment for nearly half a million public servants in all, in Turkey, in various types of public and semi-public organizations.[3] Table 11 opposite shows the distribution of public servants actually employed on 1 November 1961. (The numbers of posts are shown in brackets.)

It has been explained above[4] how from 1926 a system of classification of civil servants developed. In so far as the central administration is concerned, the classes shown in Table 12 opposite

[1] Memurlar Sendika Kanunu, no. 624, 17 June 1965.
[2] Devlet Memurları Kanunu, no. 657, 23 July 1965.
[3] Türkiye Cumhuriyeti Başbakanlık Devlet Personel Dairesi, *Devlet Personeli Rejimi Hakkında Ön Rapor* (Ankara, 1962), pp. 118–19.
[4] See above, pp. 47–51.

TABLE 11

Numbers of Civil Servants, 1 November 1961

Central Administration	State Economic Enterprises	Municipalities	Other	Total
290,740	97,682	35,069	28,999	452,490
(313,391)	(115,582)	(35,069)	(31,332)	(495,374)

Source: Devlet Personeli Rejimi Hakkında Ön Rapor.

were in existence in 1961. The proportions of the total number of *established posts* in the central administration in 1961 was as follows:

TABLE 12

Proportions of Civil Servants by Class of Employment, 1961

Salaried Officials	Permanent Auxiliaries	Temporary Auxiliaries	Daily Wage Workers	Contract Personnel	Total
%	%	%	%	%	%
65·25	27·93	2·47	4·15	0·20	100
					(313,391 posts)

Source: Devlet Personeli Rejimi Hakkında Ön Rapor.

This is a rough indication of the structure of the central administration. It is not possible to know to what extent it presents a realistic picture. It is said, for instance, that many officials have been transferred to auxiliaries' categories (intended for porters, messengers and the like) because means have been found of paying them more as auxiliaries than if they had stayed as officials. Again, many persons employed in fact as officials have been paid on a daily wage basis, a category of employment originally intended for casual manual workers. Or, again, many temporary auxiliaries have been temporary for so long that they are indistinguishable from permanent auxiliaries.

The distribution of civil servants of the central administration among the larger ministries is as in Table 13 overleaf.

(The figures for Education include teachers; judges are included in the figures for the Ministry of Justice; and religious functionaries in those of the Ministry of Religious Affairs.)

TABLE 13

Distribution of Civil Servants by Major Ministries

Ministry	Percentage of Total
Education	33·87
Health	12·45
Interior	8·51
Justice	5·68
Finance	5·50
Agriculture	4·83
Religious Affairs	4·51

Source: Devlet Personeli Rejimi Hakkında Ön Rapor.

Structure. The basic structure of the personnel system until 1965 is apparent from the figures given above showing divisions into salaried officials, permanent auxiliaries, temporary auxiliaries and daily wage workers. It has been shown above[1] how, particularly during 1950–60, the auxiliary and daily wage categories of employment came to be used as a means of employing civil servants at higher rates than were possible under the officials' *barême*. It seems that these developments continued unabated during the period 1961–5.

These developments occurred outside the basic officials' *barême* set up in 1929 and to some extent undermined it. However, the officials' *barême* system developed diseases of its own, with the result that it came to be realized that the only remedy was to replace it with a new scheme.

External injury

Some of the basic ills that have affected the officials' *barême* system are as follows.

First, provision was made for the appointment to positions within the *barême* system that were described as 'exceptional' and 'specialist'. 'Exceptional' positions are intended for appointments to offices in the Presidency, in the private offices of ministers, to posts of ambassador, provincial governor, legal adviser and translator. The necessity for politically and personally acceptable persons in most of these posts can be taken as sufficient to justify their existence. The device has been somewhat over

[1] Chapter III, pp. 48–9.

employed, however; 'exceptional' posts appear in organizations where they seem hardly justifiable, such as in the State Planning Organization and the Petrol Office.

More important and more harmful has been the use of 'specialist' posts as a means of recruitment at higher than normal salaries. There should certainly be flexibility enough to recruit specialists from outside the service on the basis of attainment in their speciality, if there are none suitable already in the service; but the system is one clearly liable to abuse. For example, should a training in sociology or political science qualify an entrant for a specialist appointment?

Specialist appointments have chiefly occurred in the Ministries of Reconstruction and Settlement, Press, Broadcasting and Tourism, and Industry, followed by the Petrol Office and State Water Undertakings. 'Exceptional' and 'specialist' categories of appointment amount to just over 1 per cent of all those employed in the central administration. This is not overall a large proportion, but it must seem a larger problem to the *barême* officials in the middle and upper reaches, where 'specialist' and 'exceptional' appointments are of course normally made.

Another development within the system is the extravagant use of part-time employment. In principle, a civil servant is not allowed an additional occupation. An exception was first made, however, for certain civil servants (principally school teachers) to allow them to undertake part-time teaching posts. This helped meet the need for teachers. The principle came soon to be extended to other professions so that if, say, a municipality had a vacancy for a doctor which could not be filled, then a doctor already in government employ could be appointed to the post as an additional duty. The system has come to be much abused, by all accounts, to the extent it has become a means of paying additional salary without significant increase in responsibilities. The lack of detailed control over established posts by the Ministry of Finance has resulted in the creation and perpetuation of many posts filled on an 'additional duty' basis for which there is no real need. Again, the condition that 'additional duty' is only to be permitted when there are no suitable persons from outside to fill the post does not seem to have been everywhere satisfied. Another rather similar device has been to appoint deputies to posts whose holders are absent or for which a suitable person cannot at the moment be found. This basically sensible device has been extended in scope, it is said, far beyond the original intention underlying it.

Other devices have also been used as a means principally, it is claimed, of supplementing salaries. Allowances for rather unusual duties are sometimes paid, a device again fairly easily open to abuse. Again, it is said that transfer has sometimes been used as a means of appointing an official to a higher grade than possible in his own office; but by use of another loophole he might be allowed to come and work where he was before.[1]

Internal injury

Recruitment. We have seen that appointment by examination, qualifying or competitive, was one of the reforms of the Atatürk period. The law required that a qualifying examination was to be replaced by competitive examination when there was more than one applicant for a post. The law was not so tightly drawn, however, that it could not be interpreted differently by the ministries and there was no central body responsible for recruitment. Sometimes there have been too few posts vacant to justify the expense of advertising and holding a competitive examination. For some parts of the administration it has been difficult to attract any candidates at all; to subject them to the burden of qualifying, or, worse, competitive examination would have frightened them away altogether. The latitude allowed to ministries by the law meant that when examinations were held they could vary in stringency. Employment in some parts of the administration is nevertheless eagerly sought after, notably in the Ministry of Foreign Affairs and the Court of Accounts; and the competitive examinations for posts in these departments are of a high standard. For the most part, however, it would be fair to say that the examination system has not worked satisfactorily.

This is also partly because, as we have seen, the system of examination has not been the exclusive means of recruitment. Other methods of recruitment have drawn off candidates who would otherwise be forced to go through the examination system, and this means that fewer candidates for entrance by examination present themselves; and this in turn justifies dispensing with the

[1] These comments on the working of the system derive chiefly from discussions with civil servants.

examination system on grounds of paucity of the numbers of applicants.

It might be mentioned in parenthesis that the basic idea of admitting the professionally trained without examination stems from a long practice of permitting graduates of certain institutions to enter the public service without examination. This is by no means as lax as it may sound. The basic system of recruitment the Turks adopted at the end of the nineteenth century was French, and it was a method that was close to their own tradition of training specially selected persons for the administration. The Faculty of Political Science, Ankara University, as it is now known, was until 1946 primarily a school for training civil servants, particularly for the Ministry of the Interior. The object of certain commercial schools was similarly to train persons for service in the Ministry of Commerce. As these educational institutions have moved away from the administration by catering for a wider range of educational needs, the system needs now perhaps to be completely dismantled. There is no doubt that adherence to this older view of training and recruitment to the public service is partly responsible for the failure of the open examination system to take deep root.

Another manifestation of older ideas is apparent in another method of recruitment still in use. Some ministries offer bursaries to persons who are prepared on completion of their studies to enter the ministry as an official, at least for a period of obligatory service. There is often competition for these bursaries, but entry to the public administration is automatic on satisfactory completion of the course of education. The principle of open competition is thus avoided.

It is difficult to estimate how many civil servants have in fact been recruited on a truly competitive basis. There are statistics; but it is impossible to judge how competitive any so-called competitive examination is in fact and what sort of standard is called for. But clearly the incompatibility between the older and newer methods of recruitment needs to be realized more fully. A centrally administered competitive system—with recruitment by no other means—would go some way to improving the standard of recruits. It would also remove much complaint about favouritism in appointments.

T

Promotion. The Turkish system of promotion has been a nightmare of complexity. It became so complex because the system adopted under the Atatürk Republic was too simple to allow for development.

Basically an official could be promoted by appointment to the next grade in a schedule of available salary grades, after serving at least three years in his grade, but only provided there was a post carrying a higher grade. Selection for promotion was then ostensibly on merit; but it is generally recognized that seniority counted for more in practice. The defect with the system was that it was not possible for an official's salary to be increased unless he was appointed to a higher post. There were no salary steps within grades. Therefore the pressure for more senior posts was considerable and establishments of senior posts have to some extent become inflated. This inflation incidentally weakened still further the relationship, never very strong in the Turkish system, between salary and level of duties.

To escape from these difficulties, other devices have been used to provide salary increases. For instance, it is possible for officials to be promoted for a maximum of two salary grades without actually being appointed to a higher post, the salary difference being paid as a special allowance.

Again, the pressure to use higher posts as they become available in order to promote, and thus obtain higher salaries for those waiting for salary increases for a long time, has emphasized seniority and has made promotion by merit very difficult by normal means. Yet able people have somehow to be moved up the hierarchy if they are to be retained. This has resulted in the emergence of a device which breaks the hold of seniority by allowing in certain cases competition for posts from those in two grades below the post to be filled. More interesting, accelerated promotion has been made possible to posts with higher salary grades but without payment of the salary that would normally attach to the higher grade posts. In other words, officials have accepted higher status, more influence and better prospects without a higher salary.[1] Thus it has often occurred that an official in charge of an organization is less well paid, or is at a lower salary grade, than his subordinates. By 1960, it was coming to

[1] Appointments in other categories as 'daily wage worker', 'specialists' and so on can also create this situation.

be realized that the system had become not just confused, but chaotic.

Reform

During the period covered by this study the personnel system has functioned as described above, yet the period has also seen vigorous efforts to put things right, for which the first step was the setting up of the State Personnel Office in December 1960, to be directed by a State Personnel Board. That something serious was intended was clear from the composition of the Board. It was small enough for efficiency, having only seven members. These members were appointed by the Council of Ministers, but with the exceptions of the Chairman and Secretary-General, on the recommendation of the Ministries of Finance, National Education and National Defence and the High Control Board for the State Economic Enterprises. Finally, there was one member representing the civil servants themselves. There was no special representation of the State Planning Organization and the Institute of Public Administration for Turkey and the Middle East. There are difficulties about giving small organizations as important a place as the large especially on a small committee, but something has probably been lost.

The functions of the new organization were very many. They included the classification of officials, partly for the sake of the principle of equal pay for equal work and the determination of the general principles that should govern recruitment and promotion and training. Indeed, the Board was given authority to review practically every aspect of the personnel system and to make recommendations. The scope of its activities is very wide, embracing not only all civil servants in the central administration but those too in the state economic enterprises.

In setting about its first task of review and recommendation for reform the State Personnel Office's procedure has been straightforward and effective. Its first problem was to recruit for itself a staff sufficiently able and experienced in personnel matters to be able to tackle the problem. The difficulties inevitably encountered in this respect in a developing country were met to some extent by sending some of its staff abroad to study personnel systems, and by the popular device of inviting experts to come and advise.

The principal result of advice and discussion was a determination to discover what the major problems really were. The first task was then to set down clearly the facts of the present position, both statistically and descriptively. It was appreciated that it was not possible to recommend reform unless the existing situation was fully known and understood. This spirit of enquiry led to the report on the personnel system to which reference has been made.[1]

The next stage was to decide how to organize the recommendations for reform. It was decided that the task should be handled as follows. A new Retirement Law and an Officials' Trade Union Law were seen to be essential, the latter in fact being required by the Constitution. All other personnel reforms were then to be included in four separate laws for (i) municipalities, (ii) special administrations (chiefly the universities), (iii) the state economic enterprises, and (iv) the central administration.

The first measure to be passed was the Trade Union Law for Officials which came into effect in June 1965.[2] This gave officials the right to form associations but not the right to strike. The law had been eagerly awaited. By 26 July forty associations had been recognized. The other remaining law with which we are concerned is that for the personnel in the central administration which came into effect on 23 July 1965.

The procedure adopted by the State Personnel Office in promoting the law is of interest. A number of basic proposals were submitted to the Council of Ministers as a possible basis for a new personnel law. With some minor modifications these proposals were approved by the Council of Ministers. They were then published in the Official Gazette as 'The Principles of the New Personnel System'.[3]

A draft law, however, was not prepared before the ministries, the universities and other bodies and persons had an opportunity to make their comments upon it. In consequence many discussions took place between the State Personnel Office and those who would be affected by the proposed Personnel Law. The

---

[1] *Devlet Personeli Rejimi Hakkında Ön Rapor.* The descriptions of present personnel practices in the report are not always as full as is desirable for a complete understanding of the working of the system, however.

[2] *Memurlar Sendika Kanunu,* no. 624, 17 June 1965. It should be mentioned that civil servants with professional qualifications had been free to join professional associations since 1953. School teachers have had a Federation since 1948.

[3] *Resmi Gazete,* 21 May 1963.

proposals received from these sources were published; reports by foreign experts on the Turkish personnel system had also been published by this time, by no means the usual fate for experts' reports in developing countries.

After this admirable process of public discussion the new draft law was discussed by the Council of Ministers in August 1964 and sent to the National Assembly. It was passed by parliament nearly twelve months later in July 1965.[1]

The new law introduces very far reaching changes into the personnel system; of which the most important are as follows.

First, the law seeks to bring order into the jungle of Turkish personnel administration by introducing a system of classification of personnel. Although a great deal is left to be spelt out in regulations to be prepared by the State Personnel Office, the general classification system is clear enough. Classes are envisaged for the many scientific, technical and professional occupations found in the public service, including, for instance, doctors, teachers, judges, police officials, architects, typists and so on. The classes specifically mentioned in the law, however, are an 'administrative', an 'executive' and a 'clerical' class. Particular importance is laid on the value of the 'administrative' or managerial class as 'the class which carries the chief responsibility for taking important decisions and for carrying out administrative duties at the highest level'.[2] This highest administrative class is envisaged as comprising the permanent secretaries (to a ministry), the assistant permanent secretaries, the general directors and assistant general directors, provincial governors and sub-provincial governors. This classification system, which is as yet by no means clear in detail from the outline in the Personnel Law, is much inspired by the British and other European models. The American type of classification was considered, but despite its advantages in some important respects, was rejected. Its rigorous classification of every post, resulting in the creation of many thousands of pay-grades, was thought to be too complex, too expensive, too inelastic and not conducive to the creation of a career service.[3]

[1] *Devlet Memurları Kanunu*, no. 142. July 1965. There is now an official English translation, published in 1965 by the State Personnel Office.

[2] *Devlet Memurları Kanunu Gerekçesi.*

[3] See Devlet Personeli Dairesi, *Devlet Personel Heyetince Hükümete Sunulan*

It is intended that there shall be movement between classes, although the qualifications for entry into each class would have to be fulfilled. It is, therefore, feasible that specialists in other classes would be able to move into the general administrative classes where there is a need and provided they satisfied the requirements for the classes of general administrators. The difficulties that will arise when schemes for such transfers are drawn up will probably be very great, much more so than for movements from say the 'executive class' to the 'administrative class'. In these respects the Personnel Law is only a prelude to a lot of hard thinking and bargaining. Much reformulation of basic principles may indeed take place.

One drastic reform which the classification system does make possible is the abolition of the categories of permanent and temporary auxiliaries and the restriction to purely manual workers of the daily wage categories. Civil servants in those classes will presumably now be transferred to their appropriate classes.

As in the British civil service, the classification system to be used makes it possible to describe the nature of the work of groups of civil servants (though not of each post, as in the American system). Recruitment can now be arranged on the basis of the qualifications necessary for each class; and as the classes will presumably be fairly large, and spread over a number of ministries, central recruitment becomes an obvious development. It is indeed provided for in the Personnel Law; every half-year all departments are required to notify the State Personnel Office of all vacancies, which then have to be advertised centrally. Whenever there are more candidates than posts competitive examination becomes the rule; and the examinations are directly supervised by the State Personnel Office. The system holds promise of considerable improvement over the present casual arrangements.

A third important innovation concerns salary increases and promotion, with neither of which, as we have seen above, can the present system cope. In between salary grades there will now be salary steps; and promotion to the salary of a higher grade can only be made if the responsibilities of the higher grade are

---

Teklifler (Ankara, 1963), pp. 21–2 for a rigorous discussion of the suitability of the American system to the Turkish civil service.

assumed. Promotion, as distinct from salary increase, can be made to a post one salary grade above the present after at least one year's service in the present grade—but on the basis of merit and only if there is a post vacant. As to additional duties or acting posts (in the absence of the real holder) which have been liberally used to provide more salary, these are now to be stringently controlled. Other smaller loopholes have also been closed.

Indeed, these measures designed to prevent the system from breaking up have a good chance of success because a fourth and very fundamental change has been introduced by the new Personnel Law. This is the introduction of a system to vary officials' salaries in accordance with changes in the cost of living. If economically it works (the system is itself inflationary), then the new personnel arrangements will start off with some possibility of success.

The Personnel Law also contains other important innovations. For instance, the distance between the lowest and highest salaries has been considerably widened in order to provide greater incentives. Training is henceforth to be planned under the direction of the State Personnel Office with the co-operation of the Institute for Public Administration for Turkey and the Middle East. It is now obligatory for departments to establish training units and to establish and carry out their programmes under the guidance of the State Personnel Office. Increased social benefits are provided for officials, including considerably increased allowances for serving in the less developed parts of the country. Disciplinary measures have been somewhat increased in the name of efficiency, but the civil servants continue to be protected from arbitrary dismissal, a real danger before 1960.

The civil servant's political rights do not enter into the new law since they are guaranteed in the Constitution. A civil servant may vote and be a candidate in national elections, but to join a political party or engage in political activities is forbidden. Unless he wishes to resign, it seems he can only in fact, present himself as an independent candidate.

The new law makes improvements in the civil servants' working conditions, although conditions were already quite good. The work week is now reduced to forty hours from a previous possible maximum of forty-four excluding overtime. There will probably be a five-day week instead of the present five and a half.

Holidays will now vary from twenty to forty days a year, in accordance with length of service, which will mean rather more leave for most civil servants. Taking into account public holidays the Turkish civil servant on maximum leave works for 159 days out of 365! This is about the same as his counterparts in Western countries.

One of the most interesting innovations in the new law arises from the recognition of the right of civil servants to establish associations to represent their professional interests. The Personnel Law makes provision for discussion and advisory joint councils to be formed of representatives of both civil servants and the administration. To supervise these Whitley-type bodies the Personnel Law establishes a Public Personnel High Council and a State Officials' High Council. Perhaps the most important feature of all this extensive programme of reform is that its application will be watched over by the civil service associations now brought into being by the Officials' Associations Law.

This point is sometimes overlooked by those critics of the new Personnel Law who see dangers in it for the freedom of the civil servant. They point to the large powers of regulation which the law gives to the State Personnel Office. This can lead to arbitrary decisions which the Constitution, it is claimed, seeks to prevent by requiring (Article 117) that officials' qualifications, appointments, duties, authority, rights and obligations, salaries and other payments and other personal affairs should be decided by law. If parliament is not to watch these matters the new associations will perhaps do so.

A second criticism of the new arrangements is of the new 'administrative class'. The professional associations see this as a means of undermining their status within the civil service; and are not much convinced by official assurances that transfer to the 'administrative class' will be easy if possible. Their eventual attitude will depend on the qualifications for entry into the various classes and of course on the salary scales attaching to the professional classes. There is also a certain amount of genuine feeling that to establish a superior 'administrative class' runs counter to the alleged, socially democratic nature of Turkish bureaucracy. Again, there is a basis in the Constitution for this view in Article 12 that 'no privilege is recognized to any person, family or group or class'.

Only the next five years will fully reveal whether the new system introduced by the Personnel Law is really going to reform Turkish administration. Yet it is apparent that during the five years since 1960 Turkey has really made up its mind to grasp this nettle. If the same seriousness of purpose continues to be shown, there seems now little reason why the personnel system should not be put on a firm footing.

CHAPTER XVIII

Civil Servants

From the statistics available it is possible now to construct a profile of Turkish officials.[1] In this chapter we shall attempt this for all civil servants and then examine the social and educational background and the career patterns of selected groups of officials, chiefly those in the highest positions.

Profile

Nearly one-third of Turkish civil servants[2] work in Ankara, Istanbul and Izmir, (Ankara 16 per cent). The service is predominantly male. About 19 per cent of all civil servants are women; they are twice as numerous in the 'general' as in the 'annexed' budget organizations. In every age group men exceed women. Women are mostly found in the 20–29 age group (37·1 per cent of their total), then in the 30–39 age group (27·1 per cent). This suggests, although the evidence is not conclusive, that the trend is towards greater employment of women. It is rather surprising in a relatively underdeveloped country—and one where women are still generally secluded—to find that there are so many women in the civil service. In Britain only about one-third of the non-industrial civil service is made up of women.

The largest single employer of civil servants is the Ministry of National Education (42 per cent of the general budget organizations' total), followed by the Ministry of Health and Social Assistance and then by the Ministry of Justice. (Teachers, doctors and judges are included in these totals.) The largest employer among the annexed budget organizations is the General Directorate of Forestry.

How well educated are Turkish civil servants? Only about 8 per cent had no schooling, 26 per cent finished their formal educa-

---

[1] The statistical information is contained in a survey made in 1963 by the State Personnel Office. The survey is now published in English by the State Institute of Statistics, *The Government Personnel Census I, Organizations in General and Supplementary Budgets, December 1963* (Ankara, 1965).

[2] Civil servants in the central administration.

tion at primary school, 11 per cent at middle school, 5 per cent at *lycée*. Some 33 per cent attended technical or commercial schools. Those with higher education formed about 17 per cent of the total.

Of these 17 per cent with higher education (some 47,000) 13,000 attended teacher training colleges. Lawyers form the next largest group (7,000), followed by social scientists (5,000) and doctors and veterinary surgeons (4,500).[1] The order then is: Arts (3,500), Sciences and Technology (3,000), Agriculture (2,000), Military Academy (1,000). Those trained as teachers are found almost all in the Ministry of National Education, as might be expected. Half of the law graduates are in the Ministry of Justice, and 18 per cent in the Ministries of Finance and National Education. Of the 566 graduates in economics nearly 200 are employed by the Ministries of Finance and National Education. Students of politics are chiefly found in the Ministry of the Interior and the Finance Ministry. Most of the arts graduates are also in the Ministry of National Education, and so are half the science and technology graduates, mostly probably as teachers. The overall pattern is fairly clear and it would be tedious to go on through the list. Apart from the Ministry of National Education, which recruits from many disciplines for its teacher force, ministries recruit those whose subject of higher education is appropriate to the ministry's work. How far this applies to those in the highest directing or administrative posts we shall see later. From the statistical summary it is not possible to know whether the employment is actually in specialist posts or in general administration. One rather interesting discovery is that of the 1,200 with Military Academy background only 100 are employed by the Ministry of Defence. The largest single employer is the Ministry of the Interior, presumably in the gendarmerie. The largest number with higher education in the Ministry of Religious Affairs are those whose subject of higher education is unclassifiable!

The next question to which we can find a statistical answer is the mode of entry into the civil service. Those who entered the civil service by competitive examination account for only 19 per cent of the total. This is a very low figure, but all sorts of employees are included, for many of whom (e.g. porters) a

[1] Figures are to nearest 500. The subjects of higher education of some 8,000 are not known.

competitive examination would be inappropriate. Those who entered without examination amounted to 31 per cent; those who were obliged to join the civil service because they had received state assistance with their education form another, surprisingly large, proportion at 30 per cent. Entrants by qualifying examination, non-competitive, formed the remaining 7 per cent. Of the large ministries National Education, Agriculture and Health and Social Assistance recruit by the obligatory service method to a large extent. Competitive examination entrants are prominent in the Ministry of Finance, the Ministry of the Interior and oddly enough the Ministry of Religious Affairs. Just how competitive the various competitions were, is of course, important but not possible to learn.

Another indication of the attention that has been given to the Ministry of Religious Affairs is the fact that 35 per cent of its employees have received 'In-Service Training' as compared with an average for the Civil Service as a whole of 15 per cent of its personnel. These will, of course, represent courses of training for religious men, as too the higher-than-average figure of 22 per cent for the Ministry of National Education will reflect teacher training, refresher and other courses for school teachers. In fact, apart from these two ministries, organizations with personnel performing technical tasks show most training. The Ministry of the Interior and the Ministry of Finance, on the other hand, show half the average figure for training. This it seems is a field in which Turkish public administration could usefully develop its training activities.

In previous discussions mention has been made of the evils of devices of second jobs and deputyships. According to the figures the abuses are more imagined than real. Only 8·4 per cent of those employed in the civil service have additional duties, and the great majority of these only have one extra post. They are to be found principally in organizations where the opportunity to exercise professional skills is most available—notably in the Ministries of National Education, Health and Social Assistance, Agriculture and in the General Directorate of Forestry. It may not be—assuming the figures really do reflect the true situation—that these devices are much used, but internal jealousies and rancour are certainly aroused. The overall numbers of persons in 'specialist' or 'exceptional' positions is also very small (at 1 per cent of the total), but high in certain, usually new, or very central, organizations, like the State Planning Organization, nearly 19 per cent of whose personnel were employed in these untypical categories.[1] Among the ministries the number of these usually better-paid posts is highest in the Ministry of National Defence. Another contention that has been discussed earlier is that many civil servants perform duties different from those associated with their posts. Such would be the case if, say, a teacher in a teaching post were employed on general administration in the ministry. The feeling is that this sort of disease has gone a long way in the Turkish body administrative. The figures state, however, that 91·5 per cent of all civil servants are employed in duties appropriate to their posts. Those organizations that show the greatest discrepancies in this respect are the General Directorate of Highways (27 per cent), Ministry of Religious Affairs (25 per cent), Agriculture (25 per cent), Land Deeds and Survey General Directorate (21 per cent) and the Ministry of Public Works (18 per cent).

Not all the detailed statistical information available has been exploited in drawing the general picture given above. If we were to do so we should obtain the following profile of the typical Turkish civil servant. If there is indeed such a person he is thirty-five years old (in 1963), had attended a middle school and probably had some professional or technical education. He entered government service by means of obligatory service in return for education, or he entered without taking any examination. He would have been in government employ for ten years and will retire on government pension. His salary is 600 lira a month (£24), out of which he pays £6 rent. He is married and has two children.[2]

Social and educational background

Provincial Governors and Sub-Governors. From the information above we obtain some idea of the characteristics of Turkish civil servants, particularly those relating to his place in the administrative system. We lack, however, so far, any knowledge of the civil

---

[1] Considerable differences exist between ministries in numbers of civil servants at different levels of remuneration. The older ministries generally pay least, but this may reflect differences in functions.

[2] This description of a typical Turkish civil servant is based on an analysis of the survey contained in *The Government Personnel Census I.*

servants' relationship to society and also of how careers develop. We look first at the representatives of the government in the provinces, those two important personages the *vali* and the *kaymakam*.

Enquiries into the social and educational origins of *valis* and *kaymakams* is made possible by a very useful pioneer study of provincial and sub-provincial administration made in 1957.[1] From it we can learn something of the social and educational background of *valis* and *kaymakams*, who would certainly be regarded as among any category of higher civil servants. They are particularly important because they are directly in contact with provincial life and very influential in their areas. The following table shows the social background of *valis* and *kaymakams* in terms of their fathers' occupations.

TABLE 14

Occupations of Fathers of Valis and Kaymakams

Profession	Valis	Kaymakams
	%	%
Civil Servant (and military officer)	40·0	16·0
Retired persons (profession not given)	8·9	16·0
Professional (doctors, lawyers, engineers)	8·9	5·7
Traders and Manufacturers (of some standing)	15·6	4·9
Small traders, artisans	6·7	13·1
Farmers and peasants	13·3	21·6
Office employment (not in public service)	—	1·3
Unskilled workers	—	1·6
Private means, no profession, and no reply	6·6	19·6

Source: Kaza ve Vilâyet Üzerinde Bir Araştırma, 1957. In that study there appear to be arithmetical errors in the total (344) of *kaymakams* in the sample (Table 5). The figures add up to 306. This affects the percentages given, which in the study only add up to 88·6 per cent. It is assumed that the numbers given for each professional category are correct and new percentages have been worked out on that basis.

---

[1] Ankara S.B. Fakültesi/New York University Graduate School of Public Administration and Social Service, *Kaza ve Vilâyet İdaresi Üzerinde Bir Araştırma* (Ankara, 1957). This now somewhat outdated study derives largely from information obtained by questionnaires. It is quite informative on many aspects of administration in the provinces and studies attitudes of

It is clear from this study that *valis* come from a rather higher social background than the *kaymakams*; and we shall see later how they compare in this respect with the higher civil servants working in the ministries in Ankara. A point of interest that the authors of the study make is that two-thirds of the fathers of *kaymakams* of civil service background were lesser officials. To most *kaymakams*, therefore, their appointments have brought them social advancement.

On the educational background of these important officials there is some interesting information. Of the *valis* 60 per cent attended the Faculty of Political Science, Ankara, and nearly all the remainder the law faculties of either Ankara or Istanbul. By comparison, over 80 per cent of the *kaymakams* were graduates of the Political Science Faculty, Ankara, 14 per cent from the two law faculties mentioned and the remainder from elsewhere. It may be that the *kaymakams*, being younger, show where the trend lies. If there is increased recruitment from the School of Political Science, where education is necessarily broader than in the law faculties, senior provincial officials will be increasingly better equipped to cope with modern problems. Yet it is very interesting to see that the subjects of academic study that *kaymakams* and *valis* find most useful are public law and administrative law, followed then for *kaymakams* by private law and technical knowledge. Economics and finance come at the bottom of their list. The *valis* find public administration the second most useful subject and put private law in fourth place after technical knowledge. Economics again comes low down. Perhaps they are too narrow in their outlook as yet, too much affected by their largely legalistic training, but they are not blind to their lack of technical knowledge. This is an area where some educational preparation might be undertaken.

When it was said above that the trend in the education of provincial administrators may be more to the Faculty of Political Science than to the law faculties it was assumed that the route to the *vali's* post was from or via the *kaymakam* level. In fact it is the case that all but about 40 per cent of *valis* have been *kaymakams*. Quite a number of them have had other posts besides, though all

---

valis and *kaymakams* to various administrative problems. There is room now for another study refined in certain particulars.

within the central administrative service in the provinces or in the Ministry of the Interior in Ankara. Over half, for instance, have served as officials within a *vali's* office; nearly 40 per cent have been assistant *valis*.[1] About a third have worked really low down, as district officials for which *lise* (*lycée*) qualifications are normally sufficient. A third have been on the Ministry's Inspectorate, and one-fifth have worked in other posts in the Ministry. It is all rather narrow perhaps, but *valis* clearly have a great deal of experience of the provinces. Turkish governors are not expatriates from the large cities fretting all the time to get back. They have had to adjust themselves to provincial life. They seem quite to enjoy it.

One aspect of their careers they clearly do not enjoy, however, is what seems to be an excessively high transfer rate. The British tradition is that a civil servant should be moved to new work every four or five years. This seems to satisfy a balance between never being in a job long enough to do it really well and becoming stale. Most *kaymakams* think they should stay in one place for at least two or three years—and at most three to five years. In fact, over 92 per cent of them are moved before $2\frac{1}{2}$ years, mostly after between ten to twelve months' service in one place. This seems incredibly short and one wonders what real knowledge of local problems a *kaymakam* can obtain in so short a time. There has to be a balance between the need for impartial administration and too close an identification with local interests; the situation as it was ten years ago is a sort of general post which if it still persists surely needs rectifying. More studies are clearly indicated.

Valis too, think they should be changed within three- to five-year periods. Yet over four-fifths of them, it seems, are transferred in less than three years, and mostly within from six to eighteen months.[2]

Finally it might be noted that the birth places of *valis* and *kaymakams* do not relate to their places of work. Given such a

[1] One-third of promotions to *vali* are in fact from this rank, rather more than a quarter from *kaymakam* posts and about one-fifth from the Inspectorate. Promotion can in fact be direct from a *kaymakam's* post but is often from a range of posts superior to that of *kaymakam* to which *kaymakams* are often appointed.

[2] There were only 41 *valis* in the sample, as compared with 316 *kaymakams*.

transfer rate it would be surprising—though not altogether impossible—for them to do so. One curious fact is that the Aegean and Black Sea areas do not produce many *valis* and *kaymakams*. Perhaps it is because, as is suggested in the study, these areas are traditionally noted for their commercial activity and private enterprise. This sort of enterprising mind is just the sort that needs to be recruited for participating in the task of economic and social development, in which provincial governors must play a large part.

Civil servants in the ministries. Another study of the social and educational background of Turkish officials is of those who work chiefly in the capital.[1] The first group is that of officials working for the most part in the three highest administrative grades in Turkish ministries, but also includes inspectional and advisory personnel in the highest ranks.[2] The second group is that of officials in the middle ranks of the public service.

The material for this study was obtained from two surveys. That for civil servants in the highest ranks was obtained in the summer of 1964 from questionnaires personally distributed to, and collected from, all civil servants in this category employed in the central administration in Ankara, but excluding the Ministries of Foreign Affairs and National Defence. The 150 who were found to be in the highest grades mentioned above cannot be said to constitute the whole of the Turkish higher civil service. Such an entity has never been defined. If it were, it would undoubtedly include many civil servants not in these top grades, but those who were made the subject of this enquiry would certainly form part of it.[3]

The material for the study of civil servants in the middle ranks was similarly obtained by means of questionnaires, but during the late summer of 1962. As there is also no official definition of a

[1] C. H. Dodd, 'The Social and Educational Background of Turkish Officials', *Middle Eastern Studies*, i, no. 3 (1965) pp. 268–76. The substance of this article is reproduced here.

[2] The ranks in question are those of permanent secretary (*müsteşar*), assistant permanent secretary (*müsteşar yardımcısı*), general director (*genel müdür*), the chairmen of ministerial boards of inspection, and other officials in similar advisory and controlling positions.

[3] Of the 150 officials to whom questionnaires were distributed 136 were collected.

middle class of officials in Turkey, the methodological difficulties of deciding who could be considered as being in the middle ranks were considerable and cannot be fully described here. Briefly, a rough and arbitrary definition of which officials could be considered as working in middle grades was made in two ways. First, the title of each post or range of posts in each ministry was discussed with those familiar with the ministry or ministries in question in order to establish which posts were of middle standing. Secondly, further enquiry was undertaken in the ministries to discover which officials with technical titles (such as 'engineer') were in fact engaged on administrative duties which could be described as of middle grade importance. Eventually a sample of 914 officials was obtained, representing as accurately as proved to be possible 10 per cent of those employed on administrative types of work in the middle reaches of the Turkish central administration.[1]

(i) Social origins

The social origins of civil servants in the highest and middle grades, by reference to their fathers' and paternal grandfathers' occupations, are shown in Table 15.

On the above figures it may be said, first, that whilst there are considerable similarities in the social origins of officials in the middle groups and those in the highest ranks, the latter do have a much more professional background—and this is particularly the case if the military officer background is regarded as professional. It should, however, also be mentioned that about half of those in professional occupations were closely connected with the public service. This is obviously so in the case of judges, who, like school teachers, are defined as public servants. It could, therefore, be said without much distortion that about 60 per cent of the highest

---

[1] Of the 914 officials only 42 per cent returned their questionnaires, but the returns for some ministries were higher than for others. Of the ministries (eleven out of sixteen) which returned more than 60 per cent of their questionnaires 202 questionnaires were collected. It is from the examination of these questionnaires that the tentative conclusions about civil servants in the middle grades of the Turkish civil service are based in this study. However, the conclusions drawn from these 202 questionnaires have been checked with those derived from study of the questionnaires returned from ministries whose officials returned less than 60 per cent of the questionnaires. The differences are not generally large, but are indicated where necessary.

TABLE 15

Occupations of Officials' Fathers and Grandfathers

Occupations	Fathers' Occupations		Grandfathers' Occupations	
	Highest Ranks %[a]	Middle Groups %	Highest Ranks %	Middle Groups %
Civil servant	23·5	30	12	11
Military officer	22	10	8	7·5
Professional (chiefly teachers, lawyers, doctors, holders of religious offices)	29	13	12	11·5
Traders (standing unspecified)	11	8·5	20	9·5
Shopkeepers, artisans, small traders	3·5	9·0	9·5	9·0
Farmers	7·5	16·5	29·0	31·0
Office employment (not in public service)	—	1·5	1·0	1·5
Unskilled workers	1·0	2·5	1·0	4·0
Private means	1·5	1·0	3·5	1·5
No reply or illegible	1·0	7·5	5·0	13·5

[a] Percentages given to nearest ·5 per cent.

officials and about 46 per cent of the middle officials have a public service background so far as their fathers' occupations are concerned.

Secondly, it seems to be generally accepted that the occupations of military officer, judge, doctor, higher civil cervant and other broadly professional positions place their holders in the Turkish upper class or upper-middle class. It is clear, then, that many of the officials studied—and particularly those in the highest ranks—have enjoyed their present social standing long before entering the public service. They have no occasion to feel that they have improved on their positions in society by virtue of their public service careers, nor indeed that they have ever had any need to do so. In this respect they differ somewhat from the *vali*, whose social background does not appear to be quite as elevated as these higher civil servants (Table 14, p. 286). The ten-year gap between these two studies does, however, make comparison risky. The much less elevated social background of the *kaymakams* suggests that the central administration in the provinces is the sector of the administration that provides an avenue of social ascent for the less privileged.

Thirdly, the examination of grandfathers' occupations shows that the public service, professional and largely upper-class occupations of the officials' fathers is not matched by their grandfathers, whose occupations were much more diverse and not so socially elevated. This situation suggested an examination of the immediate social background of the fathers of the present officials who were also high officials, military officers or followed other professional occupations; and this has been done in the case of the present highest officials. As the numbers involved are small, this can be no more than a very rough indication of what the pattern of recruitment was like half a century or more ago. At that time it seems that rather less than 30 per cent of the officials had been drawn from those with a civil service, military officer or other professional background. To look at it in a rather different way we find that only 4 per cent of the present highest officials have a purely civil service background for two generations and that only 19 per cent have a civil service, military officer or any other professional background which extends over the two generations. The main conclusion from this study is that recruitment to the Turkish public service has become much less diversified during the past half century. There may be an established tradition of son following father in the profession of public administration in Turkey, but rapid expansion has diluted its effects.[1]

(ii) *Educational background*

The basic information on the educational achievements and the places of birth and education of the highest officials and the educational attainments of those in the middle group is given in Table 16.

When we come to examine the environment of the officials' education up to and including the *lise* we find some differences between the highest officials and those in the middle group.

---

[1] I am grateful for comment on the figures by N. P. and L. R. Roos, 'Changing Patterns of Turkish Public Administration', *Middle Eastern Studies*, vol. IV, no. 3 (1968) p, 272.

TABLE 16

Educational Attainments of Turkish Officials

Stage at which formal Education ended	Highest Officials %	Middle Group Officials %
Primary (*İlk Okul*)	—	—
Secondary (*Orta Okul*)	—	25
Grammar or High School (*Lise*)	1·5	35
University or other Higher Education	98·5	40[a]

[a] The percentage of graduates from ministries with less than 60 per cent of questionnaires returned is much lower at 17 per cent. The probability is that the more educated official is more likely to return a questionnaire.

Detailed information on the educational environment of the highest officials is given in Table 17.

In contrast with the information given in this table, we find that only 16·5 per cent of the middle-group officials were born in Istanbul, Izmir or Ankara, that only 12 per cent received their education up to and including the *lise* exclusively in these cities and that only 32 per cent (compared with some 60 per cent of the

TABLE 17

Places of Birth and School Education of Officials in Highest Grades

	Istanbul, Izmir and Ankara %	Other Places %
Place of birth	34	66
Primary School (*İlk Okul*)	33	67
Secondary School (*Orta Okul*)	41	59
Grammar or High School (*Lise*)	57	43

highest officials) have had some part of their education in Turkey's three largest cities.

One point of interest to arise from these figures is the extent to which the highest officials have received their *lise* education in Istanbul, Izmir or Ankara. This large-city environment is increased, moreover, when more detailed examination of the information reveals that cities of the second rank like Bursa, Eskişehir, Konya and Kayseri were the places of *lise* education for a further 18 per cent of the highest officials. Altogether, then, some 75 per cent of the highest officials have received their *lise* education in large towns; and this is somewhat surprising when it is seen on further examination that some 55 per cent of the highest officials were born in small towns and villages and received their early education there. Although further study would be necessary to confirm it, the explanation seems to be that many of the villages and small towns in question were in the vicinity of the large towns.

The university education of the officials studied also calls for some comment. Nearly all those who have received a university education have attended the universities of Istanbul or Ankara (until recently the only two large universities). Nine of the 136 highest officials, however, received their university education abroad, whilst a further eighteen studied in foreign universities after graduating in Turkey. This university education abroad was in Western Europe and the United States.

As to the subject of study of the highest officials, we do not find that a very large number of them have studied law and fewer still are graduates in general 'arts' subjects. Scientists and technologists are most numerous (37) and are found chiefly in the Ministries of Agriculture and Public Works. The graduates of the Faculty of Political Science,[1] Ankara University, come next (33) and are employed principally in the Ministries of Finance, the Interior, Commerce and Labour. Graduates in law constitute the next largest group (21) and are chiefly to be found in the Ministries of Justice and Finance and in organizations forming part of, or attached to, the Prime Minister's Office. All but one of the doctors of medicine (15) work in the Ministry of Health and Social Assistance, whilst the eleven officials who have read 'arts' subjects, including education, are in the Ministry of Education. Both for the highest officials and for those in the middle group the pattern is the appointment of graduates to ministries whose work closely relates to their studies. The traditional independence of ministries has helped to bring about this situation; and this development in turn reinforces the independence of each ministry and makes inter-ministerial co-ordination less easy. Nevertheless, the practice of obtaining technical competence in senior officials

---

[1] The subjects studied were, broadly, politics and economics and public administration, but at the time the present officials were students the courses had a more legal bias than is the case today.

is a much respected one which works with success in the administrative systems of many countries.

Perhaps the most interesting of the facts about the social and educational background of the Turkish officials is that the highest officials are recruited very largely from the professional class, including in this sense those with higher civil service and army backgrounds, as well as the normal professional occupations. As we have seen, this situation does not seem to have obtained some fifty years ago. What probably has happened in the Turkish case—and no doubt has its parallels elsewhere—is that in a partly developed school and university system the children of the professional classes are considerably over-represented. This probably occurs because professional parents are naturally the first to appreciate the value of an education and, moreover, live in the large towns where schools are inevitably first opened. Quite extensive educational development is really necessary before the children of the peasants in the villages and the poor workers in the towns begin to appear in all levels in the educational system in large numbers. The heavily professional and upper-class element in the highest posts may be no more than a temporary phenomenon related to the stage of educational development reached.[1]

One way to accelerate the process of recruitment from a wider social background to the highest positions is to make promotion possible within the public service for officials of merit who lack academic qualifications. This clearly does not happen, however, in Turkey, as very nearly all the highest officials studied have received a higher education; and indeed the legal requirement of a higher education for the highest posts makes this situation unavoidable at present.

Can it be said that the facts of the social and educational background of Turkish officials suggest explanations of the major characteristics of Turkish public administration? Some points of connection between social and educational background and the character of the administration seem to be fairly clear.

First, if, as observers of Turkish administration maintain, the senior and middle-grade Turkish official does not know enough

---

[1] Indeed the trend, for which there is now some evidence in the case of *kaymakams*, could be towards greater recruitment from a peasant and provincial background. See N. P. and L. L. Roos, op. cit., pp. 286–7.

about the 65 per cent of the population which is engaged in agriculture and lives in the villages, or if again the official does not take much interest in what is happening at the lower levels of administration, then recruitment from a wider social background might well be part of the solution. Again, if officials in the highest ranks are so narrowly technically qualified that they become immersed in the detail of their own specialism to the detriment of the overall problems of their ministry, a change in educational patterns for the highest civil servants is indicated. Perhaps it might also be suggested without being too fanciful that by being restricted to persons of an upper-class and professional background the highest ranks of the Turkish civil service may be deprived of the energy and seriousness of purpose that is characteristically associated with the upwardly socially mobile. The progress of the present Turkish highest officials to their high positions has no doubt not been achieved without effort, but given their social and educational background it would not be unfair to describe it as smooth and natural. To provide greater opportunities within the service for the energetic and socially ambitious might be no bad thing for the general efficiency of the service, even although in the process something of the naturalness in the exercise of authority and the urbanity of manner characteristic of the present highest officials might be lost.

Career patterns

Satisfactory information on the patterns of careers of Turkish civil servants is available only in respect of those in the highest ranks.[1]

The first question that might be asked is how broad is the administrative experience of Turkish higher civil servants.

An examination has accordingly been made of their administrative experience by reference to the types of organizations in which they have worked. For this purpose types of organizations have been divided into those falling within (i) the central administration (including annexed budget organizations), (ii) the state economic enterprises, (iii) the organs of municipal and provin-

---

[1] The information that follows is derived from the questionnaires completed by the officials in the highest ranks. Of the 136 questionnaires collected the career information in four of them was not sufficiently clear to warrant their inclusion in this analysis.

cial government, and (iv) private enterprises. The upshot of this study, of which it would be tedious to tabulate the details, is that the higher civil servants are overall very little experienced in other than central administrative organizations. Moreover, they have not moved much among the central administrative organizations. On average they have each moved less than twice during their careers; and even this is a somewhat inflated figure, because what has been recorded in computing this average as a change of ministry may sometimes be no more than a transfer of the directorate or general directorate in which the official was working to another ministry. To what precise extent this has occurred is not possible to say from the information available without a detailed knowledge of organizational changes in Turkish administration over the period covered by these officials' careers. As no more than an impression it may be said, however, that about one-third of changes from one administrative organization to another within the sphere of central administration represent transfers of functions, not of persons. Bearing this not precisely calculated factor in mind, we must conclude that the Turkish higher civil servant is very much a specialist in the work of his own ministry, by experience as well as by training. This has considerable advantages in encouraging an expertise in the work of the ministry, but probably does not help in fostering good co-ordination or to go further, a sense of the unity of the administration and a greater ability to comprehend it in its entirety.

The Turkish higher official is not then very broadly experienced administratively. Is he also limited in his experience of administrative problems as they seem in the countryside away from the large cities? It is perhaps to be expected that one concomitant of making a career in a single organization is a wide experience in the organization, including those parts of it situated in the provinces. A civil servant in the British Administrative Class can normally expect to spend his whole career in London; and the practice of transfer from one ministry to another within the Administrative Class makes this the more possible. The higher posts in a Turkish ministry are filled almost always by appointment from within the ministry, a circumstance likely, it seems, to increase the probability of appointment of some officials serving outside the capital to posts at the centre.

In a relatively underdeveloped country like Turkey it is also probably more important that higher civil servants should have experience of administration in the provinces. Not only is the life of town and country very different in terms of amenities, there is also a cultural difference of considerable importance that has often been noted. The (largely western) educated stratum, in which higher officials are a very important element, often finds it difficult to understand, and get on terms with, the peasant or the local businessman or tradesman, often semi-literate and bound by religious as well as by local loyalties. Particularly in a less developed society a feel for the provinces seems to be a necessary part of the equipment of a higher official and the only way to acquire this is for him to work there.

TABLE 18

Average Number of Provinces in which Higher Civil Servants have worked, by Ministry

| | | Average no.[b] of Different Provinces in which each Official has worked | |
Ministry	No. of Officials[a]	(a) including Ankara, Istanbul and Izmir	(b) Outside Ankara, Istanbul and Izmir
Prime Ministry	9	4	2
Agriculture	12	4	3
Commerce	7	2	1
Communications	9	1	0
Customs and Monopolies	3	1	0
Energy and Natural Resources	5	2	0
Health and Social Assistance	14	3	2
Finance	12	1	0
Industry	5	1	0
Interior	9	8	6
Justice	6	3	2
Labour	5	4	3
National Education	15	3	2
Tourism, Press and Information	4	1	0
Public Works	9	3	2
Reconstruction	5	2	0

[a] Satisfactory information is only available for 129 higher officials.
[b] Averages are to nearest integer.

The Turkish higher officials' experience of work in the provinces is not negligible as the following table shows. It is clear from the table below that those with the most experience are, as is to be expected, the senior officials in the Ministry of the Interior. It is also interesting to observe that higher officials of the Ministries of Agriculture and Labour have some breadth of provincial experience.

When we examine the proportions of their careers higher officials have spent in the provinces outside Ankara, Istanbul and Izmir we find as follows:

TABLE 19

Average Proportion of Careers spent by Higher Civil Servants in Different Provinces, by Ministry

Average Proportion of Careers[a] *(in Percentages)*

Ministry	Ankara	Istanbul and Izmir	Other Provinces	Abroad or Military[b] Service
Prime Ministry	65·5	11·5	23·0	—
Agriculture	53·0	17·5	29·5	—
Commerce	82·0	2·0	7·0	9·0
Communications	95·0	1·5	2·5	1·5
Customs and Monopolies	94·5	—	1·5	4·0
Energy and Natural Resources	93·0	—	2·5	4·5
Health and Social Assistance	49·5	8·5	42·0	—
Finance	85·5	—	13·0	2·0
Industry	97·0	—	1·0	2·0
Interior	38·0	9·0	52·0	—
Justice	66·0	5·0	29·0	—
Labour	67·5	5·5	27·0	—
National Education	43·5	12·5	37·5	6·5
Tourism, Press and Information	56·5	—	18·0	25·5
Public Works	69·5	2·0	28·0	0·5
Reconstruction	90·0	—	10·0	—

[a] Career includes prior service in other administrative organizations where this has occurred.

[b] A military post before commencement of an administrative career is not taken into account, the length of service being counted from the first administrative appointment.

It may be observed from Table 19, p. 299, that although in some ministries the higher officials have seen service almost exclusively in the capital, most ministries have a sizeable proportion of senior officials with provincial experience. On the whole senior officials in Turkey give the impression that they do have an understanding about what is happening in the provinces; and that some of them have provincial experience may well account for this. By and large too, it is those ministries with extensive responsibilities in the provinces where the provincial experience of the higher officials is most marked.

Finally, we may look at these higher officials' careers in order to discover what have been the normal routes to promotion. This has been done by listing the three previous posts occupied by (i) *müsteşars* (permanent secretaries), (ii) *müsteşar yardımcıları* (assistants to permanent secretaries), (iii) *teftiş kurulu başkanları* (heads of inspectorates), and the two previous posts held by *genel müdürs* (general directors).[1]

To take first the permanent secretaries, we find that only three of the thirteen have moved to their posts direct from being heads of divisions with executive functions. Only two were previously assistants to permanent secretaries, whilst of the remainder three were heads of inspectorates, one was an adviser, one the head of a research board, one a teacher in an institution of higher education, one a delegate for his ministry abroad and one a member of the Court of Appeal. In their three previous posts only five out of the thirteen were heads of general directorates, or directorates or their equivalents. The recent experience of the permanent secretaries is in short quite mixed, but there is a preponderance of posts that are more 'staff' than 'line' in character. The recent experience of all but one of them has been in his own ministry, where nearly all of them have also in fact spent all their careers.

This institutional longevity is also apparent in the case of all but three of the thirteen assistants to permanent secretaries. Only two of these officials have moved to their posts from that of

---

[1] Some high-ranking officials, such as advisers, heads of research boards, have been omitted from this study as they are relatively few and only found in a small number of ministries. For this study the information in the questionnaires is sufficiently clear in the case of thirteen permanent secretaries, thirteen assistants to permanent secretaries, eleven heads of inspectorates and sixty-one general directors.

general director, or its equivalent, but seven of them have had responsibility for general directorates or directorates in their previous three posts. Assistantships to general directors have been the immediately previous posts for three, whilst as many as six have moved to their posts from inspectoral research and advisory positions. One had been a doctor and another a training college teacher. In their previous three posts four had experience at some stage as assistant to general directors, whilst four held inspectoral or advisory positions.[1] Their experience is again varied.

The heads of inspectorates, who show rather more movement as between ministries than those so far considered, also have a mixed background. In their immediately previous posts they divide equally (five each) into (i) those with administrative responsibility as heads of 'line' organizations and (ii) those in inspectoral research and advisory posts. The one remaining had been a cultural attaché abroad. Of the eleven heads of inspectorates, as many as nine were employed in inspectorates at some stage in their three previous posts, but seven held posts of direct administrative responsibility, there being an overlap in five cases. In their careers heads of inspectorates have by no means escaped the responsibilities of administrative command.

The general directors in the Turkish administrative system enjoy high status—and justly so—for they are placed at important apexes of administrative responsibility. They are on the whole of lower status than the permanent secretary, but the gap is a narrow one.

For the most part the general directors have been brought up in the ministries in which they serve. Only about one-sixth have transferred from other ministries. Two-thirds of them show experience in posts of administrative responsibility (as directors and the like) in their two immediately previous posts. About one-third were so employed in their immediately previous posts. About one-sixth were inspectors or advisers before being appointed as general directors and a similar proportion were employed as assistants to general directors. The general impression is one of a fair amount of diversity of work. This broadly conforms to the pattern for the other grades we have

[1] Some, of course, fall into more than one of these categories and accordingly are counted twice.

considered, but the 'line' experience of the general directors is rather more marked.

In conclusion, it may be said that the higher officials in Turkish administration perform tasks for which they have been trained and in which they must develop a great deal of experience. They do not move about between ministries very much, nor do they seem much called upon to perform tasks for which their education has not broadly fitted them. There is great merit in this practice. Civil servants who have a real expertise in the functions of their ministries, including some technical knowledge, are surely the best sorts of higher civil servants for developing countries. It is not the impartial amateur, but the expert vitally interested in the technical problems and achievements of his ministry, who perhaps serves a developing society best. From this point of view Turkey is served well, especially as its leading administrators have a very long experience in their ministries and must be well acquainted with sheer administrative problems. The defect, if there is one, may lie in a lack of overall civil service experience, which is bad for co-ordination and a sense of overall purpose. Perhaps devices might be developed of transfer and promotion, that would help make the administration as a whole cohere more and broaden and enliven the discussion in some of the ministries. Better education, more training and above all greater prospects of advancement might also make a deal of difference.

General characteristics

Against this factual background what may be said of the character and style of Turkish public administration? Here reliance must be on impressions derived from a few years of working in a Turkish institution and from the contacts this involved with various parts of the administration.

On the whole Turkish administration is reasonably efficient, but the competence varies according to various factors. The first factor is the simple one of the organization concerned. Some ministries are much better than others. The older ministries are reliable, stocked with people of good sense, but rather slow. The new ministries and organizations bustle with activity, rather burst their seams with the energy they contain, but tend to be unreliable. They get the immediately important task done with considerable

efficiency, but the longer term—in the long run equally important
—task gets rather neglected.

This leads to a second factor. Turkish administrators work well
in a crisis. All administrators tend to give of their best when up
against it; but the effect of urgency upon Turkish officials seems
particularly electric. In such situations the energy and time that
will be thrown in is quite remarkable. The way to get the best out
of Turkish colleagues is to let administrative affairs degenerate to
the somewhat critical and then tackle them.

This is perhaps another way of saying that the normal day-to-
day process of administration is not too impressive. Foreign
experts' reports and gossip are full of criticisms of the lack of
application to mundane administrative matters. There is some
truth in this; but the situation is more complex than it seems.
Turkish administrators in the middle and lower reaches usually
perform the necessary routine tasks of administration very well,
especially in the longer established organizations. This is because
such organizations have had time to lay down procedures in
routine matters. In newer, often more flexible, organizations,
however, routine matters can easily be neglected. This really
suggests that in a new situation (the organization of routine can
be a new problem in a new or expanding organization) the power
of initiative is not very great. This is a valid criticism; it ties up
with the legalistic attitude and the inadequacy of the middle
reaches which has been discussed above. Decisions about quite
minor innovations are then made by top administrators. The
dangers that then arise from excessive reference to higher levels
do not need elaboration.

Beyond all this, however, it is probably fair to say that there is
something of a shortage of Turkish civil servants with an en-
quiring but practical interest in what might be called the mech-
anics of administration. It may well come back again to the problem of personnel in the middle levels. What one misses in
Turkish administration is the man or woman, not perhaps of
marked intellectual capacity, who takes a pride in perfecting his
particular piece of administrative machinery. It is a lack of
administrative craftsmanship. Its roots no doubt lie deep in
Turkish society; its explanation lies in the nature of Turkish
economic and social development. It is not a craft that can be
taught in a crash course—as perhaps the rudiments of carpentry

might be. It is a question of the generation of a range of careful and thoughtful attitudes towards minor, but cumulatively important administrative problems—attitudes that are perhaps changing (for the worse) in highly developed Western societies.

This lack of personal interest and involvement in minor administrative tasks perhaps explains the confusion that arises when new administrative organizations are set up. This is certainly a crisis situation which generates energy, enthusiasm and excitement. In such a situation everyone gets deeply involved in the discussion of the major aims and objectives of the new organization; immense energy goes into getting the new organization to the stage of performing its major functions without delay. Yet the effort rarely goes into creating a sub-structure to underpin the institution. Matters like filing, salary and expense payments, and proper servicing of committees go by the board. The result is that the administration of the new organization itself becomes so impossibly flexible that it loses coherence. The end result is normally the imposition in sheer desperation of the time-worn Turkish administrative procedures. This imposition can be something of a dead hand, so inflexible that the new institution is crippled. In such cases the inherent dislocation between policy making and execution in Turkish administration becomes abundantly manifest.

The administrative capabilities of higher civil servants are very difficult to judge anywhere. (The selection of first-rate top administrators is also a most difficult task.) Higher civil servants in Turkey are almost invariably courteous and helpful; even when they are sometimes rather proud, as they have a right to be. They are not particularly vain about their achievements; administrative vanity, according to one distinguished Turkish civil servant, is a particularly British characteristic. Among themselves their manner ranges between the paternalistic and brotherly, depending on the age and status of their clients or colleagues. There is not as much hierarchical stiffness in evidence as might be expected, but respect for rank in a way goes very deep. On the, I suspect rare, occasions when a civil servant flays his subordinates they are quickly reduced to mutes. Yet it is not inconsistent with this that they might well endeavour by words in appropriate ears to unseat their chief. The traditional fluidity in top posts encourages such efforts. If properly used this tradition of fluidity provides an opportunity for the rapid promotion of talent. If administrative excellence is constantly re-fortified as *the* administrative ideal, there is no reason why this Turkish administrative characteristic should not lead to excellent results. To date the achievements of Turkish administration have been considerable; and in this respect alone Turkey stands out from among many countries of equivalent and superior levels of economic development.

CHAPTER XIX

Postscript and Conclusion

Postscript

Since the 1965 elections nothing exciting enough has happened in Turkish politics to engage anything but a passing notice in the world press. It could look like an ominous calm; but closer inspection reveals a fairly ruffled surface.

The first matter of interest was the character of the new government and its programme. It emerged that Demirel was so powerful within the party that his principal rival, Saadettin Bilgiç, could be excluded from government. Although there have been rumours from time to time of governmental changes that would include him and his supporters, they have come to nothing very much. Demirel still seems secure as leader of the Justice Party, but has had to change course from time to time in response to pressures within the party.

When in 1965 the Justice Party came to power after so convincing a victory the first question was whether this would mean a Restoration. Would the Justice Party follow in the footsteps of the Democrats? Would there also be a campaign of revenge? The Justice Party has certainly adopted some policies that have raised fears, or hopes. They pressed on with legislation for a general amnesty with the aim of wiping the slate clean for those committed for political offences at Yassıada (all of whom had by now been released by one dispensation or another). All civil rights were now restored to them, except the right to join or form political parties or to be members of parliament. The whitewashing was opposed principally by the People's Party and was fiercely resented by the life senators. The inclusion in the amnesty of persons of substance who had tried to evade customs' dues was also made out by its opponents to be in harmony with the general tone of Democrat Party administration.

A real parliamentary crisis occurred in the spring of 1966 when the government tried to obtain amendments to the Electoral Law that would replace by a simple majority system the proportional representation system that had been adopted for the Senate. It was no doubt with the partial Senate elections in mind (July 1966) that this move was made. The attempt was met by a filibuster, which disrupted the work of the National Assembly. The government had to admit defeat, but was nevertheless very successful in the Senate elections in June, when the party increased its share of the poll to 56·9 per cent (as compared with 52·7 per cent in 1965), whilst the People's Party share of the vote remained much the same at 29·6 per cent.[1] After the elections the government did not press further with its amendment to the electoral law, but as we shall see, the problem of electoral reform has arisen again in a rather different form.

The Justice Party's success in the elections was ascribed by many, including İsmet İnönü, to that party's exploitation of religion. In fact since the Justice Party came to power the influence of religion is widely held to have increased. How far it has increased it is difficult to say. Certainly no direct attack had been made on the institutions of the secular state; but it seems to be the case that religious influences have increased generally—for instance among the student body and within the Ministry of Education—and that religious propaganda has been more copiously disseminated by the followers of Said Nursi (the *Nurcular*) who came to prominence in the 1950's. The dangers of the religious movement to the Turkish secular state have been authoritatively indicated by a number of important personages, including the President of the Supreme Court of Appeal. However, the new President of the Republic, Cevdet Sunay,[2] formerly Commander in Chief, has made the necessary point that religion and reaction are not the same thing. The crux of the matter seems to be that in a country where the alarm against communism is now always being sounded off, religion can be seen to have its prophylactic uses. Nevertheless, in October 1966, the government bowed to criticism sufficiently to replace the Head of the Presidency of

[1] Only 52·6 per cent of the electorate went to the polls. The comparison is with the results from the same twenty-three constituencies in the 1965 general elections. The Justice Party gained at the expense of the minor parties, excepting the Workers' Party, whose vote remained about the same. (Source, *Cumhuriyet*, 7 June 1966.)

[2] Cevdet Sunay was elected President (unopposed) in March 1966, in place of Cemal Gürsel, whose health was by then beyond repair and who died in September 1966.

Religious Affairs, a vigorous participant in the religious movement. Nothing of explicit danger to the Turkish state has arisen
as yet, but there are deep fears that the religious movement is
being allowed to develop an organization that could be dangerous.

The attitude of the military to the religious revival must of
course be important. It might be expected that the military, the
self-professed guardians of Atatürkism would be firm against
religious reaction. In June 1966 the new Commander-in-Chief,
Cemal Tural, certainly warned the armed forces against the
Nurcu movement, but did not omit to stress the dangers of the
extreme left at the same time. A few days later three cadets of the
War School in Ankara, the centre of the attempted coups of 1962
and 1963, were cashiered for spreading now rather outmoded
racialist propaganda—but not without religious overtones—the
Turanism that seeks *inter-alia* unity with Turks in Central Asia.
More recently, in 1967, the military command has concentrated
its cleansing energies on the alleged danger from communists
within the armed forces. On the whole, the military seems to have
accommodated itself very well to the new political situation; and
a very telling demonstration of this occurred in December 1965,
when Tural, then Commander of the Land Forces, apparently
wrote a letter to the Ministry of National Defence, urging that
a pardon should not be extended to the authors of the February
1962 and May 1963 abortive coups. The acid test is whether
the senior commanders enjoy the loyalty of the more junior
officers. At present they probably do.

As to the loyalty to the Justice Party government of the other
historic institution—the civil service—by now it should by right
have been forfeited, but probably has not. There are two substantial reasons why officialdom should be disturbed by the new
government. First, the new government has been responsible for
a quite large displacement of top officials. It seems that a new group
of officials has been placed in many important posts. When there
is no accepted tradition of absolute civil service impartiality, or if
new masters require different personalities with whom to work,
change in the highest bureaucratic positions is perhaps inevitable
sooner or later. The Justice Party government might have
avoided much criticism if it had proceeded more slowly.

The other reason for civil service dissatisfaction has been the
failure of government to put into effect the new Civil Service

Law. Although the changes have been accepted in principle, new regulations relating to the classification of all officials and other important aspects of reform have not yet appeared. This is perhaps because the work of classification has been given to each ministry by the State Personnel Office. Quite apart from the considerable technical difficulties involved in classification—and the shortage of trained personnel in the ministries to undertake it —it has proved difficult to obtain agreement among ministries. Unable to resolve all their differences, they have simply referred the matter back to the Council of Ministers.

Perceiving that regulations relating to the classification of positions were not going to be easily achieved, the government decided to make an interim increase of 15 per cent in all civil servants' salaries. This was criticized on the grounds that it was a palliative—which it was. Yet given the administrative difficulties, it is difficult to see what else could have been done. One significant feature of these troubles with the civil service has been that the civil service unions have not made their voice heard very much.[1] They have satisfied themselves with a few protests. It would be interesting to know why they are so passive. It may be that the restrictions in the State Personnel and Trade Unions Law are in part responsible. Civil servants are neither allowed to strike nor to demonstrate in meetings or processions; and there is no recognized negotiating machinery. Even more important, perhaps, is the absence of 'career' guarantees for trade-union leaders. The still very authoritarian character of Turkish administration will not permit trade unionism to develop overnight.

One of the principal features of Turkish politics since 1965 has continued to be the discussion inside and outside the People's Party of its new slogan 'left of centre'. Rightists in the party have demanded its abolition, others have been prepared to keep the policy, but drop the slogan. A third group under the leadership of Bülent Ecevit, a much respected and successful former Minister of Labour in the period 1961–5, has come out strongly for both the doctrine and the slogan as well as for more vigour in matters of propaganda and organization.[2] This group, which İnönü supports, emerged victorious in the party's annual

[1] See Cahit Talas, 'Hükûmet, Personel Kanunu ve Memur Sendikaları', *Forum*, 1 September 1966.

[2] His book *Ortanın Solu* (Ankara, 1966) is full of interest.

conference in October 1966, when Bülent Ecevit was elected the party's general secretary.

Opposition to the influence of Ecevit crystallized around Turhan Feyzioğlu. In May 1967 matters took a dramatic turn when Feyzioğlu led fifty-two senators and deputies out of the People's Party's ranks to form a new Reliance Party (*Güven Partisi*). The resignations occurred on the occasion of an Extraordinary Party Congress, which the threatening split in the party demanded. The exodus of the Feyzioğlu group left the People's Party with 130 members of parliament out of an original 182, a substantial loss. Ecevit's supporters claim that without its conservative, authoritarian politicians, more wedded to politics than to policies, the party can now wholeheartedly advocate reforms and can overcome the party's alleged inability to get through to the ordinary people.

The departure of the Feyzioğlu group certainly seemed to shock the party into greater activity. Bülent Ecevit undertook a very extensive tour of the provinces to explain the 'left of centre' slogan and to listen to the humble. Emphasis on the need to change the existing order also made an impact, but threw the party open to charges of inciting revolution. A relapse into more moderate attitudes and civilized relations with the government (especially over the Cyprus crisis in late 1967) then led to accusations of indecisiveness. The principal difficulty is that a left-of-centre party cannot easily find major issues to contest with a party just right of centre, as the Justice Party has mostly been. Only one really substantial issue has arisen—the proclaimed intention of the Justice Party to change the national remainder voting system. Considering the outstanding electoral success of the Justice Party in 1965 despite the system, why the projected change? The People's Party's view is that the government aims to obtain a greater than two-thirds parliamentary majority in order to be able to change the Constitution.

This sinister motive is denied by the Justice Party. Yet the government has been irritated by a number of decisions that have gone against them in the Council of State and the Constitutional Court. They have had to accept them, but with ill grace. Part of the trouble is that the institutions of state, even the civil service, are identified with the People's Party.

Whether in or out of office the People's Party will always rush to the defence of state institutions; by contrast Justice Party Ministers will complain of the civil service even when in office and it is theirs to direct. This situation is probably bad for the People's Party. Their image is always that of the state-party. What dynamic reform, it is asked, can be expected of a party intent on defence of the *status quo*?

In the Justice Party Demirel has maintained his position. In the party's third 'Great Congress' he was re-elected leader for two years, overwhelming his only rival. The Congress was a victory for the moderates and Demirel seems able for the present to shake himself clear of the influence of the religious extremists to whom he had yielded ground during 1966, when the partial Senate elections took place. Increasingly, however, it is being said that the religious movement is being over-encouraged. The question being asked by Atatürkists is whether the Justice Party can control the force it is releasing.

In the normal course of events, the next crucial point in Turkish politics will be the National Assembly elections to be held in 1969. From the June 1968 local and part-Senate elections there may be some straws in the wind. The People's Party's decline seems to have been halted, while the Reliance Party has not been unsuccessful either. On the point furthest left the Workers' Party seems to be making steady progress in contrast with the parties furthest right, whose fortunes appear to be in steady decline. The Justice Party itself may also have lost some ground, but a small turn-out and the importance of personalities in local elections make assessment of trends risky.

Conclusion

This study of Turkish politics and administration has attempted to concentrate on the problems in Turkish government as they appear primarily to those who study Turkish government in Turkey. This has entailed description of the basic facts of Turkish political experience and emphasis of the institutions through which decisions are made. There is some danger in a concentration on the institutions of government. In many political systems they may not be the significant areas of political discussion and decision; they may only appear to be performing vital political functions. Yet in Turkey the political institutions are not a sham; they take crucial decisions. Turkey is not Iraq of the

1930's. Still less is it Ethiopia or Libya. The democratic institutions are not merely social clubs for traditionalist groups.

Yet Turkish politics is not in quite the same category as British, German, French or American. This is because Turkey's problems are not those of a 'developed' society. Many basic economic and social needs still remain to be met. Consequently, much of Turkey's political experience resembles that of the 'developing' or 'emergent' countries. Indeed, in order to throw into relief some of the salient characteristics of Turkish politics, we might briefly compare Turkish political development with that of emergent nations generally.

We may begin this enterprise by observing that the chief feature of political systems that have not been modernized is the political control of society by traditionalist groups. Of these there are often two, which normally work in unison—namely, the official, feudal-based class and the class of religious notables, including the scholars. The Ottoman Empire fits into this category of pre-modern societies well enough, but the early professionalization of both army and civil service introduces an unusual and important feature. In its classical heyday the Ottoman Empire recruited to its political elite by achievement rather than by ascription. There was no hereditary aristocracy with political significance. It is true that there were landholders who wielded political power locally, but save for short periods, they did not dominate the centre. It is no doubt due to this more flexible and less conservative traditionalism that in Turkey the traditional governing elite was prepared to lead the process of modernization and provided an education for its members to equip them to do so.

This heritage of modernization by autocratic leadership is one notable characteristic of Ottoman development. Another important feature that marks off Turkey from many of the nations of the Third World is that Turkey has never been a colony. Although often under the influence of foreign powers, Turkey has never experienced the displacement or demotion of its traditional rulers by a colonial power. As we know, in a colonial situation traditional authority is either abolished by the colonial power or, if it is permitted to function in a subordinate capacity its legitimacy is seriously undermined. In either case the hold of the political tradition is drastically weakened. Short of outright acceptance of foreign rule, a society in this situation has no option but to give its mind to constructing new political solutions. If the colonial power accelerates the pace of economic and social change, and offers Western education to its new subjects, the search for new political forms becomes urgent and clamorous. In Turkey until the Atatürk revolution traditional authority was able to maintain its legitimacy more or less intact. Even the Atatürk revolution was led by members of the 'establishment' and in some respects therefore was a *coup d'état* rather than a revolution.

In the light of these considerations it is possible to appreciate why Turkish revolutionaries have always had very responsible attitudes towards the institutions of government. They have sought to reform rather than abolish them. That Turkey has neither been an outright traditional state, nor a colony, must go some way to explain her history of relative political stability.

We can see, then, how what we may regard as the first stage in the process of modernization in Third World countries—the emergence of a Westernized intelligentsia—has occurred in the Turkish situation.[1] The second stage in the process is the need for the intelligentsia to broaden their support in society—their need to 'mobilize the masses'.

The mobilization of the masses means, first, that traditional allegiances to tribal, racial or religious groups, or to an overall traditional structure, have to be broken. As we have noted, this process is partly or wholly achieved in colonies by the colonial power itself when it takes over control. Consequently, in colonial situations the mobilization of the masses is chiefly directed against the colonial power, but it is also aimed at the traditional rulers if they have collaborated with the colonial regime.

The ways in which the new leaders normally seek to influence the masses in a colonial situation are two. One way is to create a nationalist political movement or party—the latter is possible if the colonial power permits a measure of democratic politics. The second method is to find an outstanding leader, a personage who combines an appeal to traditional elements in society with leadership of the Western educated intelligentsia—a Ghandi, for example. The advantage of charismatic leadership is that, unlike a party or movement, a single leader cannot be divided against himself. Often these two methods are used in combination.

---

[1] For an illuminating account of the process of political change in former colonies see F. Mansur, *Process of Independence* (London, 1962).

After the first world war a near colonial situation obtained in Turkey. The Allied Powers occupied the most important parts of the country, including Istanbul, with the Sultan a pliant tool in their hands. It is not therefore surprising to find that at this juncture Turkey followed the more or less normal pattern of development found in colonies. First, Mustafa Kemal put himself at the head of a popular nationalist resistance movement. Secondly he emerged as a charismatic leader. There was just one element, however, that was missing from Kemal's charisma. He was unable to make any lasting appeal to religious sentiments. Although he was at first able to obtain a measure of religious support with the call of 'caliphate in danger', he could not really undermine the influence of the Sultan/Caliph in Istanbul. Unable to mobilize support on any permanent basis, he was in consequence obliged to destroy the religious institution. This was perhaps a more important reason for the demise of Islam in Turkey than the often alleged hostility of Islam to modernization. It might indeed be argued that in the normal course of events there would probably never have been any need for the Kemalist revolutionaries to attack religion to the extent of disestablishing Islam.

We now come to the third stage in the normal political process encountered in colonial states. Having won independence the revolutionary government finds it has to govern. At this point the range of possible development is wide.

One possibility is for the new leaders simply to occupy the top posts in the governmental structure and to rest on what remains of the older traditionalist and newer colonialist legitimacy. Subjects obey because they are used to obeying. This is, of course, especially possible if society has not been awakened and then divided politically as a result of protracted political struggle against the colonial power. It is a mode of governing that may easily, but not necessarily, lead to a sham democracy, to a panoply of democratic institutions manipulated by the new rulers in conjunction with traditional forces. In the process, the modernizing force is diluted, as in Iraq between the two wars. Persia after the first world war is another example of this process, although Reza's revolution was not directly anti-colonial.

A second possibility is to attempt to set up a viable democratic regime. This occurs in a situation in which some sections of society at least will have been made politically conscious by the revolutionary struggle. The trouble with this solution is that if the society is deeply divided by ethnic, religious and other differences there will be no consensus; and in any case it will provide an opportunity for the re-emergence of traditionalist forces. They will now have a forum; they may well learn to use modern political techniques of persuasion and will try to put the clock back. The modern intelligentsia will not tolerate this. Atatürk and his supporters were not prepared to do so when they briefly experimented on two occasions with liberal democracy.

Another possibility is for the new leaders to run the country with the support of the military, or, if the modernizing elite is found in the crucial sections of the military, to have a straight military regime. In the Middle East military/bureaucratic rule itself has a natural historic legitimacy, but the basic trouble with this solution is that the purpose of having a military is to have a fighting service. It therefore breeds attitudes not conducive to civil government. The military is used to ordering, not to persuading. Moreover, even if it is engaged in civil government the military always keeps arms in the cupboard and a proclivity to use them in the back of its mind. Counter coups by disaffected groups are always a real danger.

A fourth possibility is to govern through a single-party regime as Atatürk did. The institutions of democratic government may also be used, but power lies in the single party, and its relationship to the leader and to the masses. If it exists, parliament is a rubber stamp. Such regimes may be predominantly authoritarian or totalitarian in character.

This sort of regime may operate with greater or lesser efficiency. It may really try to reach the people by local village and ward organizations. Atatürk's party did this principally through the specially instituted People's Houses. The contact thus established may be of two sorts. First it may be primarily concerned to inculcate into the people the official doctrine or ideology and in this way a regime augments its legitimacy. Or its main function may be to collect and feed up into the political machine the people's desires or demands. Obviously if these can be met they will be all the happier. In the Turkey of Atatürk the first function overshadowed the second. This was unavoidable in a society whose peasant and town populations clearly wanted a greater place in social and political life for religion, the prime traditionalist enemy for the Atatürk modernizers. The People's Party really did try to indoctrinate the masses, but it was not completely successful. Energy there was, but energy has to be present in proportion to the weight of the obstacle to be removed. Turkish society was penetrated, but not deeply permeated, by Atatürkism.

If the People's Party was not completely successful, its effort was very different in character from that of many other single-party regimes. Many regimes rely much more exclusively than the People's Party on such things as their (naturally diminishing) stock of revolutionary prestige, or on patronage, or on the military, or on traditionalist elements. As we have noted, this last support is particularly valuable in the short run because it brings with it and attaches to the new regime the deference of the populace to their traditional leaders, but the long-term dangers to the purity of the revolution are very great.

Atatürk's People's Party did not rely to an excessive degree on these sorts of support, but rested on them in part. There was no truck with religion, but there were other traditionalist elements in the landowning classes who were still basically Ottoman in their outlook. The Party also included the businessmen and indus-trialists who were beginning to arise in greater numbers in the 1930's and 1940's. They were not unnaturally interested in trying to ensure that the party's étatist doctrines were not rigorously developed.

Whether a single-party regime develops into a multi-party regime must depend on a number of factors. Two that may be postulated as necessary are (i) a degree of individual economic freedom that will enable relatively autonomous groups to develop within society and (ii) a marked homogeneity in society—a lack, that is to say, of deep ethnic, religious, regional cleavages. In socially homogeneous societies whose governments prevent private ownership there seem initially to be few internal issues around which a multi-party system might be erected. Only when the economy develops will socio-economic class issues arise to provide a basis for a multi-party system. In societies deeply rent by racial, religious and other divisions a multi-party system would probably destroy government itself.

Turkey has not been much troubled by lack of homogeneity—save for religion and the Kurds, both of which forces have been contained. Moreover, in Atatürk times private economic enterprise was not suppressed, even if it was not much encouraged. In fact, what appear to be two prime conditions for the early emergence of a multi-party system have existed in Turkey.

From this consideration of the general problem we can see that the long-term dangers to the Turkish multi-party system are principally two—and they are interwoven. The first is that the religious traditionalists will use the system in order to overthrow it and return to a more traditional order. The second danger is that as the economy develops political and social strife will become so embittered as to disrupt society. In this connection it must be remembered that Marxism is a lively force in developing societies because it seems to fit the facts of their socio-economic situation, as it did European societies in the nineteenth century. We have seen the effect of this 'new' view of politics in the left-wing struggle envisaged by the People's Party, now 'left of centre'. To the Marxists all the political parties are, of course, bourgeois.

There seems little danger that traditionalism is now strong enough to lead to the overthrow of the political system. The party most reactionary is certainly the Nation Party, but even if that party captured the government it is extremely doubtful if it would overthrow the system. If there were many real religious traditionalists in Turkey they would presumably vote or organize the vote for the Nation Party as the one closest to their aims. That the Nation Party is a minority party is significant. As to the second danger—that of cleavage from socio-economic class divisions—it must as yet be a question for the future.

The present, short-term danger to multi-party politics seems to derive from a desire very pronounced in the former Democrat Party—and not absent from the Justice Party—to maintain its political opponents in a completely subordinate position. Why they should do so derives from a congeries of attitudes in these parties that augment the natural desire for money and power—a position in government still gives very great prestige in Turkish society.

It should first be recalled that the Democrat Party was a splinter group of the People's Party. Its founders were as nationalist as their peers in the People's Party and they inherited typical nationalist desire for social solidarity. They were used to authoritarianism and fundamentally believed in it, despite their expressed desires for economic freedom. Secondly, this nationalist desire for social solidarity is also reinforced by a longer political tradition. The Ottoman Turks never had to bargain with minority groups; they simply excluded them from the political process. There has been little experience of political opposition and consequently an over-readiness to assume that it will quickly lead to the destruction of all political and social stability.[1] Thirdly, the political parties have not excluded the traditionalist elements; they have incorporated them and this seems to be particularly the case in the former Democrat Party and its heirs. Traditionalist, authoritarian attitudes persist within the parties. Then, finally, in the Justice Party are to be found many of the modern right-wing elements that are arising as Turkey develops under a system that includes private economic enterprise. They fear 'communism' and all too readily attach the label to any leftist movement. In a country as relatively poor as Turkey the new industrial and commercial classes see a menace in every sign of leftist activity. They will not readily allow leftist parties to develop without hindrance. The lengths to which the Justice Party went before the 1965 general election to try to obtain the disqualification of the Workers' Party is evidence of their attitude.

The disquiet about a possible return to a dominant party situation in which the lesser parties will be more or less proscribed has of late broken out afresh because attempts to consolidate the liberal democratic system by introducing proportional representation have not prevented the re-emergence of the two-party system. A society as homogeneous as Turkey cannot support a number of significant political parties. The basic political division has been between a more nationalist, more étatist, more populist, more secular, more disciplinarian, more Atatürkist People's Party on the one hand and the less étatist more religious, less austere Democrat or Justice Parties on the other. The differences have been of emphasis rather than of policy. For all its reliance on religious support the Justice Party will not reinstate religion. By the 1960's the two main parties' policies were looking very little different. The old points of difference are now wearing thin and, as we have seen, a new one is beginning to supplant them—the

[1] This and related ideas are discussed in a very stimulating article by Şerif Mardin, 'Opposition and Control in Turkey', *Government and Opposition*, 1, no. 3 (1966), pp. 375–87.

difference between left and right. Even so, their differences are still not great. They may not be great enough to satisfy new aspirations of the under-privileged. If so, and if the Workers' Party is in one way or another proscribed, whilst still respecting the political system, then the liberal democratic system can become a sham. One means by which suppressed social forces would then seek an outlet might be the military, which has not as yet gone further in its upper ranks at least, than adopting an Atatürkist philosophy. It may well resent get-rich-quick entrepreneurs with no sense of the national interest, but as yet it fears socialism. It may well support a democratic system which disciplines a struggle between left and right of centre; and because of its greater trust in the People's Party might watch a sharp move left by that party without too much concern. But if the argument between left and right centre develops into a fight which breaks the bounds of the democratic system, the military might well intervene for the sake of national solidarity and to clear up the mess.

A lot of the mess might well be administrative and not political. The military would be impressed by clean and fair administration. The Democrat Party government was not very efficient administratively. Whilst providing for flexibility—a very necessary administrative virtue—they tended to worsen rather than remedy the chaotic conditions in the administration which began to appear in the 1950's. Less firm administrative control in a country where traditionalist administration attitudes are not yet eradicated cannot help but lead to irregularities of various sorts. The Justice Party has not yet shown the zeal for administrative reform that was one of the characteristics of the N.U.C. during its brief rule. There is also some justification for believing that the Justice Party is less careful about bureaucracy than its rivals. The number of transfers of important officials on the Party's accession to power in 1965 was not very reassuring to the bureaucracy. Rumours of governmental interference, in response to political pressures, with those stalwarts of the Atatürk revolution, the *kaymakams*, seem more frequent than under People's Party rule. The Justice Party has not yet quite got over the Democrat Party's predilection for assuming that the bureaucracy was a branch of the People's Party.

Given that the forces supporting the Justice Party have learned their lesson from the military in 1960 and will not now neglect the state apparatus or proscribe their legitimate opponents, in the short term will all be well? The question in this event is whether the party or parties in opposition will be prepared to accept the legitimacy of a Justice Party government if that party, as seems likely, continues to be successful at the polls. The cry will soon be raised that the Justice Party gets its vote by using the influence of the secular traditionalist classes in the countryside; or that it gets out the vote by exploiting religious prejudice. If, right or wrong, this sort of belief becomes widespread among the intelligentsia, and if it is laced too with accusations of 'capitalist' exploitation, then a fire could be re-kindled. In a liberal democratic system in an underdeveloped society like that of Turkey the agreed means of changing governors must be shown to be real, which means that it must happen. Paradoxically, too much stability can be a dangerous thing.

Select Bibliography

This is a selected list of official and other documents and publications that were most useful for this study. Other bibliographical references, some of which are not included here, occur in footnotes to the text. References to articles in Turkish journals are given only in footnotes.

PRIMARY SOURCES

(i) *Newspapers etc.*

Cumhuriyet The most serious Turkish daily.
Forum A liberal fortnightly review.
Yön A socialist weekly review.
Other newspapers and reviews consulted from time to time; principally, *Milliyet*, *Yeni Istanbul* and *Akis*.

(ii) *Political Parties' Publications*

In addition to the election manifestos, programmes and standing orders of the political parties the following party publications have been found useful.

Adalet Partisi. *Millî Hâkimiyet Mücadelesinde Adalet Partisi.* (Adalet Partisi Genel Merkez Neşriyatı no. 1.) Ank. 1963.

—— Mahallî Seçimlerde Adalet Partisi. (A.P. Genel Merkez Neşriyatı no. 3.) Ank. [1964].

—— *Hükûmet Buhranı, Hükûmet Teşkili, Hükûmet Programı, Kıbrıs Olaylar Karşısında Adalet Partisi.* (A.P. Genel Merkez Neşriyatı no. 4.) Ank. [1963].

—— *Adalet Partisinin İktisadî Görüşleri I* (A.P. Genel Merkez Neşriyatı no. 5.) Ank.: 1964.

—— *Adalet Partisinin İktisadî Görüşleri II.* (A.P. Genel Merkez Neşriyatı, no. 6.) Ank.: 1964.

—— *Radyo'da Adalet Partisi.* (A.P. Genel Merkez Neşriyatı no. 10.) Ank.: 1964.

Cumhuriyet Halk Partisi. *Seçim Neticeleri Üzerinde Bir Araştırma, 1950, 1954, 1957 Milletvekilleri Seçimleri.* (C.H.P. Araştırma Bürosu Yayınları no. 7.) Ank.: 1959.

—— *İnönü Diyor Ki. A. Menderes'e Cevaplar.* Ank.: 1960.

—— *Kalkınma Meselemiz* (C.H.P. Araştırma Bürosu Yayınları no. 22.) Ank. 1961.

—— *C.H.P. 'nin 39 Yıldönümü, 9.9.1962.* Ank.: 1962.

—— *'de C.H.P. 'nin Görüşü. İnönü ve C.H.P.'li Bakanları 20–3 Temmuz*

Y

İl Başkanları Toplantısındaki Konuşmalar. (C.H.P. Araştırma ve Yayın Bürosu Yayınları no. 27.) Ank.: 1962.

——*Amacımız, Yolumuz, Yöntemimiz.* (T.İ.P. Ankara İli Araştırma ve Yayın Bürosu Yayınları no. 1.) Ank.: 1963.

Türkiye İşçi Partisi. *Yurt Sorunları ve Çözüm Yolu (Radyo Konuşmaları).* (T.İ.P. Ankara İli Araştırma ve Yayın Bürosu Yayınları no. 2.) Ank.: 1964.

Türkiye Partisi. *Y.T.P. Kısmî Senato Seçimlerinde Yapılan Radyo Konuşmaları.* (Y.T.P. Genel Merkez Yayınları no. 3.) Ank.: 1964.

(iii) *Official Publications*

(a) *Constitutional and Political:* An English translation of the 1961 Constitution was made for the N.U.C. by A. E. Uysal, S. Balkan and K. H. Karpat, Ank.: 1961. It is reproduced in *Oriente Moderno* XLIII, nos. 1–2 (1963), pp. 1–27. Electoral statistics are published by the State Statistics Institute. Laws and decrees are published in the Official Gazette (*Resmi Gazete*), but the most important laws are often published privately; some of the more important recent laws privately published are listed below. Constitutional and political documents from the *Tanzimat* until 1961 are contained in Feridun Server, *Anayasalar ve Siyasal Belgeler* (İst.: 1962). Other important sources and important privately published laws are:

Türkiye Millet Meclisi. *Millet Meclisi Tutanak Dergisi.* (Proceedings of the National Assembly, 1961–5). Ank.: 1961–5.

—— *Cumhuriyet Senatosu Tutanak Dergisi.* (Proceedings of the Senate, 1961–5.) Ank.: 1961–5.

—— *Türkiye Cumhuriyeti Anayasası ile T.B.M.M. Birleşik Toplantısı İçtüzüğü ve (1 Kasım Tarihli) Dahilî Nizamname.* (The Constitution and the Standing Orders of the Grand National Assembly and the National Assembly.) Ank.: T.B.M.M. Basımevi, 1965.

—— *Türkiye Cumhuriyeti Anayasası ile T.B.M.M. Birleşik Toplantısı İçtüzüğü ve Cumhuriyet Senatosu İctüzüğü.* (The Constitution and the Standing Orders of the Grand National Assembly and the Senate.) Ank.: T.B.M.M. Basımevi, 1966.

—— *T.B.M.M. Albümü.* (Brief biographical details of all Deputies and Senators, 1961–5 Parliament.) Ank.: T.B.M.M. Basımevi, 1962.

—— *T.B.M.M. Millet Meclisi Albümü.* (Brief biographical details of all Deputies in 1965- Parliament.) Ank.: T.B.M.M. Basımevi, 1965.

Personel Kanunu. Ank.: Taylan Yayınevi, 1965. (There is now an English version published by the State Personnel Department of the Prime Ministry. Ank.: 1965.)

Sendikalar Kanunu and Toplu İş Sözleşmesi Grev ve Lokavt Kanunu. Ank.: İnkilâp ve Aka Kitabevleri, 1963.

Erkanil, Mehmet Akif. *İzahlı ve Gerekçeli Danıştay Kanunu. Sistematik Danıştay Kararları* [Ank.: 1965].

Ülker, Reşit. *Gerekçeli, Notlu, Şerhli ve İzahlı Anayasa Mahkemesi Kanunu.* Ist.: Ercan Matbaası, 1962.

Ünver, Hakkı Şinasi (ed.). *Memurin Kanunu ve Memurin Muhakemat Kanunu.* Ank.: Hazine Yayınları, 1965.

—— *Yeni Köy Kanunu ve Muhtar Seçimi Kanunu.* Ank.: Hazine Yayınları, 1963.

Yalçın, Mehmet Ali (ed.). *Siyasî Partiler Kanunu ve Seçim Kanunları.* [Ist.]: 1965.

(b) *Administrative*: The latest civil service statistics are contained in a publication of the State Statistics Institute:

T. C. Başbakanlık Devlet İstatistik Enstitüsü. *Devlet Personel Sayımı Genel ve Katma Bütçeli Kurumlar, Aralık, 1963.* Ank.: 1965. (There is now an English edition. The statistics of personnel in the Public Enterprises are also now published.)

Other selected primary sources are:

İller İdaresi Genel Müdürlüğü. *Mülkî İdare Taksimatı, 1962.* Ank.: İçişleri Bakanlığı, 1962. (Provincial Government Boundaries.)

Köy İşleri Bakanlığı Kuruluş Calışmaları. Ank.: Başbakanlık Devlet Matbaası, 1964. (The Founding of the Ministry of Village Affairs.)

Maliye Bakanlığı. *Devlet Memurları Ücret Rejiminin Hakkında Rapor.* Ank.: 1952. (Ministry of Finance Report on Officials' Salary System.)

Martin, J. W. and Cush, F. C. E. *Final Report on the Administration of the Turkish Ministry of Finance.* Ank.: Ministry of Finance, 1951.

Merkezî Hükûmet Teşkilâtı Araştırma Projesi Yönetim Kurulu. *Merkezî Hükûmet Teskilâtı Kuruluş ve Görevleri.* Ank.: T.O.D. A.I.E., 1963. (The Report of the Commission on Organization and Functions. An English translation is now available.)

Merkezî İdarenin Taşra Teşkilâtı Üzerinde Bir İnceleme.(İdareyi ve İdarî Metodları Yeniden Düzenleme Komisyonuna Sunulmak Üzere Orta Doğu Teknik Üniversitesi İdarî İlimler Fakültesi Dekanı, Dr. Arif T. Payaslıoğlu'nun Yönetimimde Hazırlanmıştır. Ank.: 1965. (Mimeographed. A Study of Central Administration in the Provinces.)

Republic of Turkey, Prime Ministry, State Planning Organization. *First Five Year Development Plan, 1963–7.* Ank.: 1963.

T. C. Başbakanlık Devlet Planlama Teşkilâtı. *İdareyi ve İdarî Metodlart Yeniden Düzenleme Konusunda Hazırlanacak Mevzuatla İlgili Genel İlkeler.* Ank.: 1965. (Report on General Principles by a Commission on the Reform of Administration and Administrative Methods.)

T. C. Başbakanlık Devlet Personel Dairesi. *Devlet Personel Hakkında Ön Rapor.* Ank.: 1962. (Preliminary Report on State Personnel.)

—— *1962 Yılında Devlet Personel Dairesine Verilen Yabancı Uzman Raporları.* Ank.: 1963. (Reports by Foreign Experts on Personnel Matters.)

—— *Devlet Personel Rejimi Hakkında Devlet Personel Heyetince Hükûmete Sunulan Teklifler.* Ank.: 1963. (Personnel Office's Proposals on Personnel.)

—— *Devlet Personel Rejimi Hakkında Ön Rapora Dair Kurumların Görüşleri.* Ank.: 1963. (Views of Various Bodies on the Preliminary Report on Personnel.)

T. C. *Devlet Teşkilâtı Rehberi.* Ank.: Başbakanlık Devlet Matbaası, 1963. (Handbook of Governmental Organization.) An English version is now available published by the Institution of Public Administration for Turkey and the Middle East, *Turkish Government Organization Manual.* Ank.: 1966.

(iv) *Interviews and Surveys*

Personal interviews with Drs. Bülent Ecevit, Turhan Feyzioğlu and Kemal Kurdaş, June–July, 1962, and a number of civil servants.

Survey by questionnaire of 384 civil servants in the middle ranks of Turkish central administration, Summer 1962.

Survey by questionnaire and interview of 136 higher civil servants, Summer 1964.

SECONDARY SOURCES

(i) *Turkish Books*

Abadan, Nermin. *Üniversite Öğrencilerinin Serbest Zaman Faaliyetleri.* (Ank. Üniv. S.B.F. Yayınları no. 135–117.) Ank.: 1961.

—— *Anayasa Hukuku ve Siyasî Bilimler Açısından 1965 Seçimlerinin Tahlili.* Ank.: 1966.

Aksoy, Muammer. *Anayasa Mahkemesi Üyelerinin Seçimi Konusundaki Tartışma.* (Ank. Üniv. S.B.F. Yayınları nos. 147–129) Ank.: 1962.

Ank. Üniv. S.B.F. İdarî İlimler Enstitüsünün Gerekçeli Anayasa Tasarısı ve Seçim Sistemi Hakkındaki Görüşü. (Ank. Üniv. S.B.F. Yayınları nos. 116–198.) Ank.: 1960.

Arsel, İlhan. *Türk Anayasa Hukuku.* Ank.: 1959.

Aybay, Rona. *Karşılaştırmalı 1961 Anayasası.* (İst. Üniv. Yayınları no. 1038.) İst.: 1963.

Balta, Tahsin Bekir, Savcı, Bahri and Abadan, Yavuz. *İncelemeler.* (Ank. Üniv. S.B.F. Yayınları, no. 100–82.) Ank.: 1960.

Balta, Tahsin Bekir. *Türkiyede Yürütme Kudreti.* (Ank. Üniv. S.B.F. Yayınları no. 114–96.) Ank.: 1960.

Beledi yeler El Kitabı (T.O.D.A.I.E., Yayın no. 63.) Ank.: 1963.

Belen, Fahri. *Demokrasiden Diktatörlüğe.* İst.: 1960.

Chailloux-Dantel, Maurice (ed.). *Türkiyede Devlet Personeli Hakkında Bir Araştırma.* 3 vols. Ank.: T.O.D.A.I.E., 1958–9. (Mimeographed.)

Cumhuriyet Senatosu Divanı Seçimleri ile İlgili İhtilâf Hakkında Rapor. (Ank. Üniv. S.B.F. Yayınları, no. 152–134.) Ank.: 1963.

Derbil, Süheyp, *İdare Hukuku.* Ank.: 1956.

Devlet Personeli Meselesi Hakkında Bir İnceleme. (C.H.P. Araştırma ve Dokümentasyon Bürosu Yayınları no. 1.) Ank.: 1958.

Devlet Şurası Üzerinde Bir İnceleme. 3 vols. (T.O.D.A.I.E. Araştırma Serisi no. 7.) Ank.: 1960.

Giritli, İsmet. *Âmme İdaresi Teşkilâti ve Personeli.* İst.: 1963.

Giritlioğlu, Fahir. *Türk Siyasî Tarihinde Cumhuriyet Halk Partisinin Mevkii,* i. vol. 1. Ank.: 1965.

Göreli, İsmail Hakkı. *Devlet Şurası.* (Ank. Üniv. S.B.F. Yayınları no. 36–18.) Ank.: 1953.

Gözübüyük, A. Şeref. *Türkiyede Mahallî İdareler.* (T.O.D.A.I.E., Yayın no. 74). Ank.: 1964.

Karal, Enver Ziya, *Osmanlı Tarihi,* vols. v–vii. Ank.: 1947–56.

Karal, Gülgün. *Teknik Yardım Programları ve Türkiyede Teknik Yardımın İdaresi.* (T.O.D.A.I.E. Araştırma Serisi no. 11.) Ank.: 1962.

Kaza ve Vilâyet İdaresi Üzerinde Bir Araştırma. (Ank. Üniv. S.B.F. Yayınları no. 77–59.) Ank.: 1957.

Keleş, Rüşen. *Türkiyede Şehirleşme Hareketleri (1927–60).* Ank.: S.B.F. Maliye Enstitüsü, 1961. (Mimeographed.)

Mardin, Şeref. *Jön Türklerin Siyasî Fikirleri, 1895–1908.* Ank.: Türkiye İş Bankası Kültur Yayınları, 1964.

Okandan, Recai G. *Âmme Hukukumuzun Ana Hatlari.* (İst Üniv. Yayınları no. 369.) İst.: 1959.

—— *Âmme Hukukumuzda İkinci Meşrutiyet Devri.* (İst. Üniv. Yayınları no. 326.) İst.: 1947.

Onar, Sıddık Sami. *İdare Hukukunun Umumî Esasları.* 2nd ed. rev., 2 vols. Ank: 1960.

Orhun, Hayri. *Türkiyede Devlet Memurlarının Hukukî Rejimi (Umumî Harlarile Tarihî Gelişim ve Bugünkü Durum).* (İçişleri Bakanlığı Yayınları, Seri 3, Sayı 2. İst.: 1946.

Özbudun, Ergun. *Parlâmanter Rejimde Parlâmentonun Hükûmeti Murakabe Vasıtalari.* (Ank. Üniv. Hukuk Fakültesi Yayınları no. 171.) Ank.: 1962.

Özgen, Hilmi. *Türk Sosyalizmi Üzerine Denemeler.* Ank.: 1963.

Savcı Bahri. *Demokrasimiz Üzerine Düşünceler.* (Ank. Üniv. S.B.F. Yayınları no. 155–137.) Ank.: 1963.

Tansel, Selâhettin, *27 Mayıs İnkilâbını Hazırlayan Sebepler.* İst.: Millî Eğitim Basımevı, 1960.

Tönük, Vecihi. *Türkiyede İdare Teşkilâti'nın Tarihî Gelişimimi Bugünkü Durumu*. Ank.: İçişleri Bakanlığı, 1945.

Tunaya, Tarik Z. *Türkiyenin Siyasî Hayatında Batılılaşma Hareketleri*. İst.: 1960.

—— *Türkiyede Siyasî Partiler 1859–1052*. İst.: 1952.

Versan, Vakur. *Âmme İdaresi*. İst.: 1960.

(ii) *Turkish Journals*

Ank. Üniv. S.B.F. Dergisi, 1953–.

İdare Dergisi, 1927– (Ministry of the Interior)

Ank. Üniv. Dil ve Tarih Cografya Fakültesi Dergisi, 1942–.

Annales de la Faculté de Droit d'İstanbul, 1951–. (Mainly in French.)

Ank. Üniv. Hukuk Fakültesi Dergisi, 1943–.

İst. Üniv. Hukuk Fakültesi Dergisi. 1927–.

Belleten, 1953–. (The Turkish Historical Society, Ank.)

İller ve Belediyeler Dergisi, 1945–. (Association of Turkish Municipalities.)

(iii) *Books and Articles: Other Languages*

Abadan, Nermin. 'Four Elections of 1965: Turkey', *Government and Opposition*, I, no. 3 (1966), pp. 335–44.

Ansay, Tugrul and Wallace, Don (eds.). *Introduction to Turkish Law*, Ank., Society of Comp. Law and Middle East Technical Univ., 1966.

Ataöv, Türkkaya. 'The Faculty of Political Sciences of Turkey', *Middle East Journal* XIV, (Spring 1960), pp. 243–5.

Davison, Roderic H. *Reform in the Ottoman Empire 1856–76*, Princeton, 1963.

Devereux, Robert. 'Turkey's Judicial Security Mechanism', *Die Welt des Islams*, N.S., X, nos. 1–2 (1965), pp. 33–40.

—— *The First Ottoman Constitutional Period. A Study of the Midhat Constitution and Parliament*, Baltimore: Johns Hopkins Press, 1963.

Esen, Nuri. *Turkey Today—And Tomorrow*, London, Praeger, 1963.

Fisher, S. N. *The Military in the Middle East*, Columbus, Ohio State Univ. Press, 1963.

Frey, Frederick W. *The Turkish Political Elite*, Cambridge, Mass., M.I.T. Press, 1965.

—— 'Arms and the Man in Turkish Politics', *Land Reborn* (August 1960), pp. 3–14.

Gibb, H. A. R., and Bowen, Harold. *Islamic Society and the West*, vol. I: *Islamic Society in the Eighteenth Century*, part I, London, 1950, part II, London, 1957.

Gökalp, Ziya (translated and edited by Niyazi Berkes). *Turkish Nationa-*

lism and Western Civilization, New York, Columbia Univ. Press, 1959.

Hanson, A. H. (ed.). *Studies in Turkish Local Government*, Ank., Inst. of P.A. for Turkey & the M.E., 1955.

—— 'Democracy Transplanted: Reflections on a Turkish Election', *Parliamentary Affairs*, IX (Winter 1955–6), pp. 65–74.

Harris, George S. 'The Role of the Military in Turkish Politics', *Middle East Journal*, part I, XIX, no. 1 (1965), pp. 54–66, part II, XIX, no. 2 (1965), pp. 169–76.

Heyd, Uriel. *Foundations of Turkish Nationalism*, London, Luzac-Harvill, 1950.

Hyman, Herbert H., Payashoğlu Arif, and Frey, Frederick W. 'The Values of Turkish College Youth', *Public Opinion Quarterly*, XXII (Autumn 1958), pp. 275–91.

Kapani, Munci. 'An Outline of the New Turkish Constitution', *Parliamentary Affairs*, XV, no. 1 (1962), pp. 5–23.

Karpat, Kemal H. *Turkey's Politics, The Transition to a Multi-Party System*, Princeton, 1959.

—— 'Socialism and the Labor Party in Turkey', *Middle East Journal*, XXI, no. 1 (1967), pp. 157–72.

—— 'Society, Economics and Politics in Contemporary Turkey', *World Politics*, XVII (October 1964,) pp. 50–74.

—— 'Recent Political Developments in Turkey and their Social Background', *International Affairs*, XXXVIII (July 1962), pp. 304–23.

Kingsbury, Joseph B., and Aktan, Tahir. *The Public Service in Turkey: Organization, Recruitment and Training*, Brussels, Institute of Administrative Sciences, 1955.

Kinross, Lord. *Atatürk, The Rebirth of a Nation*, London, Weidenfeld & Nicolson, 1964.

Kurnow, Ernest. *The Turkish Budgetary Process* (Ank. Univ. S.B.F. Yayınları, 63–45.) Ank.: 1956.

Lerner, D. *The Passing of Traditional Society, The Modernizing of the Middle East*, Glencoe, Ill., The Free Press, 1958.

Lerner, D. and Robinson R. D. 'Swords and Ploughshares, The Turkish Army as a Modernizing Force', *World Politics*, XV (October 1960), pp. 19–22.

Lewis, Bernard. *The Emergence of Modern Turkey*, London, O.U.P., 1961.

Lewis, G. L. 'Islam in Politics: Turkey', *Muslim World*, LVI, no. 4 (1966), pp. 235–39.

Lewis, Geoffrey. *Turkey*, 3rd ed. rev., London, Benn, 1965.

Mango, Andrew. *Turkey*, London, Thames and Hudson, 1968.

Mardin, Şerif. *The Genesis of Young Ottoman Thought*, Princeton, 1962.

—— 'Opposition and Control in Turkey', *Government and Opposition*, I, no. 3 (1966), pp. 375–87.

Matthews, A. T. J. *Emergent Turkish Administrators* (Institute of Administrative Sciences, Ank. Univ. Faculty of Political Science. Pub. no. 1.), Ank., 1955.

Mears, E. G. (ed.). *Modern Turkey*, New York, Macmillan, 1924.

Mıhçıoğlu, Cemal. 'The Civil Service in Turkey', *Ank. Univ. S.B.F. Dergisi*, XIX, no. 1 (1964), pp. 89–125.

Onar, Saddık Sami. 'Les Transformations de la Structure Administrative et Juridique de la Turquie et Son Etat Actuel', *Revue Internationale des Sciences Administratives*, XXI (1955), pp. 741–86.

Ostrorog, Count Leon. *Angora Reform*, London, Univ. of London Press, 1927.

Özbudun, Ergun. *The Role of the Military in Recent Turkish Politics* (Occasional Papers in International Affairs, No. 14), Harvard, Harvard University Center for International Affairs, 1966.

Presthus, Robert V., with Erem, Sevda. *Statistical Analysis in Comparative Administration: The Turkish Conseil d'Etat*, New York, Cornell Univ. Press, 1958.

Robinson, R. D. *The First Turkish Republic. A Case Study in National Development* (Harvard Middle Eastern Studies, 9), Cambridge, Mass., Harvard Univ. Press, 1963.

Rustow, Dankwart A. 'The Army and the Founding of the Turkish Republic', *World Politics*, XI (July 1959), pp. 543–54.

—— 'The Development of Parties in Turkey', in Palombara, J., & Weiner, M. *Political Parties and Political Development*, Princeton, 1966, pp. 107–33.

Simpson, Dwight J. 'Development as a Process. The Menderes Phase in Turkey', *Middle East Journal*, XIX, no. 2 (1965), pp. 141–52.

Smith, E. C. 'Debates on the Turkish Constitution of 1924', *Ank. Univ. S.B.F. Dergisi*, XIII, no. 3 (1958), pp. 82–105.

Smith, Elaine D. *Turkey: Origins of the Kemalist Movement (1919–23)*, Washington, 1959.

Sturm, Albert L., & Mıhçıoğlu, Cemal *et al. Bibliography on Public Administration in Turkey 1928–57* (Ank. Univ. S.B.F. Pub. no. 88), Ank., 1950. (A Turkish version was also published.)

Szyliowicz, J. S. 'The Political Dynamics of Rural Turkey', *Middle East Journal*, XVI, no. 4 (1962), pp. 430–42.

Tachau, Frank & Ulman A. Halûk. 'Dilemmas of Turkish Politics' (*Turkish Year Book of International Relations*), 1962, pp. 1–34.

Tunaya, Tarik Z., 'Elections in Turkish History', *Middle Eastern Affairs*, V (April 1964), pp. 116–19.

Ulman, A. Halûk & Tachau, Frank. 'Turkish Politics: The Attempt to Reconcile Rapid Modernization with Democracy', *Middle Eastern Journal*, XIX, no. 2 (1965), pp. 153–68.

Ward, Robert E. & Rustow, Dankwart A. (eds.), *Political Modernization in Japan and Turkey*, Princeton, 1964.

Weiker, Walter F. 'The Aydemir Case and Turkey's Political Dilemma'
Middle Eastern Affairs, xiv (November 1963).

—— *The Turkish Revolution, 1960–61. Aspects of Military Politics*,
Washington: Brookings Institution, 1963.

Yavuz, Fehmi. *A Survey of the Financial Administration of Turkish
Municipalities*, Ank. Univ. S.B.F. Pub. no. 142–124.

—— *Problems of Turkish Local Administration* (Inst. of P.A. for Turkey
and the M.E. Pub. no. 82), Ank. 1965.

Index